The
Complete
BORDER COLLIE

BARBARA SWANN

HOWELL
BOOK HOUSE

New York

HOWELL BOOK HOUSE
A Simon & Schuster Macmillan company,
1633 Broadway, New York, NY 10019.

MACMILLAN is a registered trademark of Macmillan, Inc.

Library of Congress Cataloging-in-Publication data

the complete border collie / barbara swann

Library of Congress catalogue card number: 94–73811
ISBN 0–87605–059–3

Manufactured in Singapore

10 9 8 7 6 5 4 3 2

CONTENTS

Chapter One: A PUPPY IN YOUR FAMILY   **6**
The right start; The dog's mind; Sleeping area; Car trips; House-training; Worming; Inoculations; A set of rules for control; Playing with your puppy; Leaving the puppy; Playing fair; Socialisation classes; Living with children; An older dog in the family.

Chapter Two: EARLY EDUCATION   **14**
Learning by experience; Commands; Eye signals; Establishing your position; Recall; The scruff method; Reward; Toys; That'll do/Enough; Timing; Stress; Case Study of Trapper (First lessons; Teething; Retrieve games; Searching; The Stay; The right approach; The extension lead; Car travel; Play; Backyard training).

Chapter Three: PROBLEMS IN TRAINING   **29**
Who is dominant?; Putting yourself back in control; Why do problems develop?; Making the problems worse; Programme for independence; Attention exercises; Behavioural problems; Six steps to problem solving; Planning your correction programme; Voice; Back-up help; Aggression (Possession aggression; Predatory aggression; Aggression with other dogs; Aggression over people; Aggression towards another dog in the house); Livestock chasing; Urination (Submission urination; Other causes); Recall problems; Chewing (Teething; Chewing from habit; Boredom chewing; Attention seeking; Hyper-activity; Over-dependence); Barking (Car barkers; Phone barkers; Attention barkers; Over dependency); Digging; Faeces eating; Jumping up (Jumping up at visitors; Over-excitement on returning home); Mounting; Social sniffing.

Chapter Four: FEEDING   **48**
Principles of feeding; Quantity to feed; The obese dog; Travelling; Older dogs; Working dogs; Fussy eaters.

Chapter Five: HEALTH CARE   **51**
Knowing your dog; General observation; Additional checks; Keeping records; Consulting your vet; Alternative treatment (Herbalist; Homoeopathist; Chiropractor; Acupuncture; Bach and gem remedies; Summary); Common ailments and conditions (Anal glands; Arthritis; Bites and stings; Burns; Colic; Cracked pads; Diarrhoea; Ears; Eyes; Heatstroke; Kennel cough; Mange; Mouth ulcers; Nails; Nervous problems; Nettle rash; Parasites: Roundworms; Tapeworms; Fleas; Ticks; Lyme disease; Poor appetite; Torsion/bloat; Travel sickness; Sprains; Whelping/hormonal problems; Wounds); Hereditary Diseases (Collie eye anomaly; Progressive retinal atrophy; Hip dysplasia; Ceroid Lipofuscinosis); The ageing Border Collie.

Chapter Six: THE BREED STANDARD   **65**
The British Breed Standard; Official Standard of American registries; The American Border Collie Standard; Analysis and interpretation (The head; Eye colour; Nose and nostrils; Facial markings; Ears; Body and substance; Hindquarters; Feet; Tail; Coat; Colour).

Chapter Seven: PRINCIPLES OF GENETICS   **80**
Understanding genetics; Dominants and recessives; Using genetics; Sensitivity to sound and touch; Eye colour; The working eye; Ears; Coat colours (Tricolour; Merle; White; Ticking; Blue); Coat length; Hind dewclaws.

Chapter Eight: BREEDING BORDER COLLIES   **89**
Selecting breeding stock; In-breeding versus line-breeding; When to breed?; Mating the
bitch; The mating; False pregnancy; Managing the stud dog; The gestation period; Ultra-
sound; Preparing for the birth; The birth; Human interaction; Whelping and nursing
problems; Culling.

Chapter Nine: REARING THE PUPPIES   **100**
The first two weeks; Weaning; Antibiotics; Nails; Worming; The big 5; Noise
conditioning; Exploring; The puppy pack; Temperament testing; How to conduct the
tests; Analysing the temperament test; The barrier test; Analysing the barrier test.

Chapter Ten: THE WORKING SHEEPDOG   **113**
Selection; Getting started; The training lead; Avoiding mistakes; Giving commands;
Confidence; Punishment; Finishing work; Coping with non-ideal sheep (Sheep will not
move freely; Flighty sheep; Working a dog into a corner; The flight distance; The
troublemaker); Problems with the dog's work (Breaking the stay; Correcting the out-run;
Down or Stand; The disinterested dog).

Chapter Eleven: TRIALING IN NORTH AMERICA   **130**
Trial history; The National Finals; Judging systems; Class divisions; Trial arenas;
Regional differences; The competition trail; USBCHA National Finals winners.

Chapter Twelve: COMPETITIVE OBEDIENCE TRAINING   **140**
The stay; Heelwork; The Can-do method; Advanced recall; Distance recall; Scent
discrimination; Retrieve (Progressing too fast; Choice of article); Sendaways; Jumps and
jumping.

Chapter Thirteen: THE VERSATILE BORDER COLLIE   **152**
Sheepdog trials; Working trials; Agility; Flyball; Scent hurdle racing; Obedience; Guide
dogs; Therapy dogs; Gundogs; Sniffer dogs; Mountain rescue; Sledding.

Chapter Fourteen: STATUS AND DEVELOPMENT   **168**
Early Records; The first Sheepdog trials; The International Sheepdog Society; Problems
in the breed; The ISDS Stud Book; Registration; Modern Sheepdog trials; Influential
working dogs; The 'pedigree' Border Collie; Champion status is granted; Full
Championship status; Multi-discipline awards; New bloodlines; Breeding programmes;
The Border Collie in North America; Registries; Winning trial dogs; Herding Instinct
test; Controversy over 'pedigree' status.

Chapter Fifteen: THE BORDER COLLIE WORLDWIDE   **184**
Australia and New Zealand (Influential dogs); South Africa; Zimbabwe; Finland;
Sweden and Norway; Belgium; Spain; Holland.

TO MY DOGS
If we listen and watch, they teach us everything. I have
learnt more from my dogs than from any human. It is to
them we owe most – and they truly deserve this dedication.

The Bluealloy Border Collies (pictured left to right): Bluealloy Nell, Gold Award winner, and her daughters, Bluealloy Trim, Platimun Award winner, and Bluealloy Trapper, Gold Award winner.

Acknowledgements

My thanks to the following people who have given me so much help while writing this book:
My husband Eric, and my son, Andrew; Bonnie Barry, Illinois; Barbara Carpenter, Lydney, Gloucestershire, UK; Kathy Conner, Ranch Dog Trainer; Arlene and Jean Haines, Can-Do, Manitoba, Canada; Roy Hunter, Anglo-American Association; Beverley Lambert, Connecticut, USA; Donald McCraig, Virginia, USA; Adrienne McCleavy, UK; Sue McCrilley, UK; Maxine Netherway, Ontario, Canada; Denise Taylor, Redditch, Worcestershire, UK; Anita Vekemans, Belgium (Bouwel); Rolf Franck, Germany (Wulsbuttel); Pam Thrasher, Gibraltar; Magne Akvag, Norway; Pat Kaiser, Merrivale, USA; and Bryan Turner, UK.

Chapter One

A PUPPY IN YOUR FAMILY

THE RIGHT START

Taking a puppy into your household is a major commitment, and it should never be done without a great deal of thought. Once the decision is taken, you must bear in mind that the first two months that your puppy shares with you will dictate ensuing behaviour for the duration of your life together!

The best time to have a puppy is when you have a couple of months with not a great deal going on at home. The ideal times for most people are often September/October or January/February. Many people will tell you that the best time is when the weather gets better in late Spring, but do you really want to be training a young pup when you are going out and about all the time or when holidays are due?

THE DOG'S MIND

Dogs have cohabited with man for many thousands of years and they have a social system not dissimilar to that of our own society. All dogs, even though domesticated for such a vast time, still obey the major laws of the wolf. So if you understand the wolf, you will understand the dog. Nowadays, great efforts are made to understand the different cultures of the many races in our world in order to communicate more easily and beneficially with these people. Exactly the same applies to the dog: if you use their language, you will succeed much faster and more effectively in establishing a good relationship.

I have up to ten dogs and bitches in the household at any time, and I can introduce a young puppy or an older dog at any time, without any problems. The bitches come into season and the normal life of the dogs goes on from day to day, with never a single argument. The young puppies mix in their play periods with the older dogs. I know they will be safe because the dogs run as a wolf pack, with me as Alpha Leader. If you have an orderly household (and if not, you should not contemplate owning a dog), each member knows where they fit into the scheme of things. In the same way, a puppy must learn how to fit in with that society. Gradually, the puppy must be educated to live in a human world, which is very different to a canine world.

Many pet owners start off with the fundamental misconception of thinking that a six to eight week old puppy does not understand what is required in terms of basic behaviour, and is too young to learn. If the puppy starts to show signs of unacceptable behaviour, they simply hope that the pup will grow out of it. Nothing could be further from the truth! The puppy must be taught what is acceptable and what is unacceptable to you, as the 'pack leader'. From the very beginning, the bitch teaches her puppies to respect her, and any other dogs around will reinforce this lesson. It is a very rare puppy who does not obey and toe the line.

Puppies learn surprisingly fast. In a matter of hours, the puppies learn where to suckle milk, and to recognise their mother. In a structured rearing home, the puppies will learn to come when called, and to stop howling when told, and they will begin to realise that they are subservient in status. A puppy would not dare to growl at its mother, except in play, so why let a puppy growl at you? Training starts from the second you take the puppy away from the breeder.

SLEEPING AREA

You should decide on sleeping quarters, long before your puppy arrives home. To start with, a cardboard box, or cheap throwaway vegetable box is ideal, for the pup is sure to chew it. Plastic dog beds are quite resilient, but if you buy one that is the correct size for an adult Border Collie, it will be too big for a puppy. A cardboard box will make a warm and secure bed for your puppy, but it needs to be a strong one. From day one, put the cardboard box in the place you have chosen for the sleeping quarters. A kitchen is usually a good place, for the floor is usually tiled or covered in linoleum, which is easy to clean.

A play-pen type of structure is ideal, as it keeps the puppy in one area, and the puppy learns that there are limits on its freedom to roam – albeit on a temporary basis. However, you must not allow the dog to become possessive about a particular area of the kitchen, such as that used for feeding or sleeping. If you see any sign of this trait developing, be very firm with your puppy, and

Training starts from the first day your new puppy arrives home. Feeding time is the best time to start early lessons in Sit, Wait, and the Recall.

there will be no problem. A dog which knows its rightful place in the family structure is a happy dog. This does not mean that the dog becomes a totally subservient, cringing creature. Every dog deserves to be treated with dignity, and this will evolve naturally as the dog absorbs the all-important early lessons of acceptable behaviour.

CAR TRIPS

Again, the golden rule is to start as you mean to continue. The first time you go out in the car, place your puppy in the area you have designated as the dog's travelling place. If you carry your puppy on your knee because this is the first time, the puppy will think this is where it should always be. I strongly recommend buying a travelling cage, as it can be useful in a vast number of situations. You might feel that it is very expensive, but it will last for the lifetime of the present dog – and subsequent dogs. If you cannot afford the price, then you can make a similar structure from wood and wire-netting. This is an excellent safety measure for the dog. All these little things help to get the puppy off to a good start of trouble-free co-existence, so that you can look forward to having a dog to be proud of.

HOUSE-TRAINING

If your puppy has been reared in a clean, well-organised environment, and has had free access to the garden, then house-training will almost certainly have begun before your puppy leaves the breeder's home. From about two and a half weeks old, my puppies make an effort not to soil their nest area, and by four weeks old the puppies will generally oblige in the yard area, just outside their housing.

Assuming your puppy has been well reared, then the length of time it takes a puppy to be house-trained is proportional to your effort. Most puppies are reared on newspaper. Check with the breeder and see if this is the case. If so, place some newspaper in a convenient spot somewhere near to the door and within easy reach of your puppy's sleeping quarters. Then, gradually move the paper further and further to the back door and finally place it outside. It will be a short time before the puppy can make it through the night without mishap.

In tandem with this, you must allocate a toilet area in the garden. Then each time the puppy wakes up from a sleep and a few minutes after every mealtime, go to the allocated area, and using a suitable command, such as "Hurry up", wait until your puppy obliges. When this happens, give your pup plenty of praise and a tidbit. It is inevitable that your puppy has the odd accident, but remember that a mishap is not the puppy's fault; you have failed in your vigilance.

Whenever you take the puppy out, either on the street or in the park, you are responsible for cleaning up after your dog. Every dog owner must be prepared to take on this responsibility in order to keep the environment clean for everybody's benefit.

WORMING

Adequate worming is vital – both for the puppy's health and that of the family. All puppies carry a roundworm burden, and it is essential to adopt a worming programme to eradicate this parasite. Ask the breeder when the puppy was wormed and make a note of the dates. My puppies are wormed at four weeks, six weeks, eight weeks, twelve weeks, fifteen weeks and then every six months. Up to twelve weeks of age, I prefer to use a liquid wormer, and after that I use a one-dose treatment which is very effective. Ask your vet to recommend a suitable treatment. It is important to give the correct dosage for your puppy's weight; again, your vet will advise.

The liquid wormer should be administered with a syringe, which can be obtained from your vet or from a chemist. Fill up the syringe with the correct amount of liquid, hold the puppy gently, and ease the back corner of the mouth into a spout and steadily squirt the liquid down the throat.

INOCULATIONS

There are a number of major contagious diseases which your puppy must be protected against: hard pad (distemper), parvovirus, hepatitis and leptospirosis, and some also include kennel cough.

The vast majority of vets will advise that your puppy should not be taken outside the house and garden until the inoculation programme has been completed. Injections are usually given at twelve weeks and fourteen weeks, although this may vary according to locality. However, there is no doubt that it is detrimental to a puppy's social development to be isolated from everyday life during this critical period. In Britain, the Guide Dogs for the Blind Association give their puppies an initial inoculation at six weeks, and this gives adequate protection until the pup receives full protection at three to four months of age. Obviously, these puppies are not exposed to undue risks, but it gives the opportunity for all-important socialisation when the puppy's mind is at its most receptive. Guide Dogs have pursued this policy for some twenty-five years with no ill-effect on the thousands of puppies involved. It is therefore recommended that you talk to your vet about when to start your puppy's inoculation programme. You may also wish to discuss whether standard injections are used or whether homeopathic nosodes can be administered. The conventional injection works by using a form of the virus and then making the body produce the antibodies to fight it. The nosode is produced by making a very dilute culture from a particular virus, and then diluting it further to produce the end product, which is a little white tablet. These nosodes can be obtained either separately or as a group to cover all the major contagious diseases.

A SET OF RULES FOR CONTROL

1. Do not let your dog dictate about food – either the type of food or the feeding times. If your puppy refuses a meal, pick up the food-bowl and put it away until the next feed. I have never known a dog who willingly gets to starvation point, and a healthy puppy will certainly come to no harm by missing one meal. If your have this battle for a couple of days, you will cure this type of behaviour for life; if you lose the battle, you will always have a problem. If you emerge as the loser, your puppy will effectively log up a notch in deciding who is to be the boss of the outfit – yes, even at six weeks old. Remember, that from a very early age littermates work out a very strict hierarchy, sorting out who is boss of their little pack – so do not make the mistake of thinking your puppy does not understand what is involved.

2. Always feed your dog after the rest of the household has eaten. Do not give your puppy tidbits while you are eating, unless you wish to do so for the rest of the dog's life.

3. Do not let your six-week-old puppy chew your fingers, and then wonder why you have problems later on. On the first occasion this happens, a deep-throated growl from you, as pack leader, will stop this activity. Do not move your hand away quickly; the puppy will think you are teasing, and the chase instinct is to grab.

4. Do not allow your puppy to run off with an object. If you suspect that this might occur, attach your puppy to a short, light line and then you are back in control. If the puppy does not come back voluntarily, all you have to do is to lightly pull on the line. When the puppy comes towards you, give plenty of praise. It does not matter that the puppy had no option – the important point is that the puppy *did* come back.

5. Toys always belong to you. You allow the puppy to play with them, on your terms. (See the section on 'Playing with your Puppy'.)

6. Make loud noises at feeding time and at any other available opportunity. This will prevent sound-shyness. The reason for making the noise at feeding times is that it is always followed by something pleasurable. Vary the types of noise as frequently as possible.

7. Every day or two, put the food bowl down and let your puppy get started on it. Then, quietly remove the bowl and while praising the dog count for thirty seconds, then replace the bowl and allow your puppy to continue feeding. As pack leader, you have the right to decide when and what will be eaten, and it is your right to remove the food at any time if you so wish. Do it quietly but firmly, and allow each member of the family to do it in turn. This puts the puppy at the bottom of the pack, and rightly so.

8. If you have a very dominant type of puppy, it is essential to practise daily submission for some weeks, and then drop it off a little This is done by rolling the puppy over on to its back, placing your hand gently but firmly on the ribs, and holding the puppy down while you count to thirty. If the puppy wriggles, place firmer pressure and growl very deeply – the puppy must lie still.

Remember the greater the resistance, the greater the need to continue until the puppy will readily submit, i.e. lie quietly without protest.

9. Never allow your puppy (or adult dog) to go through a doorway, entrance or gate in front of you. You must be the first through, and then you invite the puppy/dog to come through. The same applies to the car; the dog must be invited to get in and must wait once in until invited to get out.

10. Tidbits must always be earned, and this applies equally to praise and fuss. Take four tidbits, place one on the floor and tell the puppy to take it. Place the second tidbit on the floor and again ask the puppy to take it; do the same with the third. Then, place the fourth tidbit on the floor and say "No". If the puppy makes an attempt to take it, growl deeply. After a short wait, the puppy may be invited to take it.

Your puppy must learn to earn praise by doing something to please you. Do not allow the puppy/dog to pester for praise; you decide when your puppy deserves the extra fuss.

11. Do not shout at the puppy/dog. In reality, this is a most rewarding and exciting thing for a puppy – it is certainly not viewed as a punishment. Watch a mother with her puppies; you can scarcely hear her rebukes.

12. Give one command – one action – only. (See Chapter Three: Problems in Training).

PLAYING WITH YOUR PUPPY

As already stated, it is important to establish that toys belong to the humans, and the puppy is only allowed to borrow them. Therefore the puppy must not be allowed free access to toys; they should be kept on a high shelf. It is vital to play with your puppy, but it is also vital to let the puppy know that this is at your invitation, and that you always win the toy at the end.

Remember that balls teach the puppy to chase. This is not a bad thing, so long as it is kept under strict control. It is equally important to bear in mind that tug-of-war games teach the puppy to challenge you for supremacy. So just be sure that when you are ready, you take the toy from the puppy. If the puppy is reluctant to give up the toy, place the thumb and second finger of your right hand on either side of the bottom jaw, and with the left hand control and open the mouth. Slip the fingers of the right hand in as the mouth opens and remove the toy, growling deeply at the puppy if there is any show of resistance. It is easy playing tug-of-war with a six-week-old puppy, but try it with the same puppy at six months of age and you will see why this is a game that must be kept under strict control.

LEAVING THE PUPPY

No puppy should be left for long periods, and Border Collies are notorious for their dislike of being left. However, all dogs must be left for short periods, and it pays to build this up gradually over a period of time. Make sure your puppy has been let out to relieve itself, and then settle the pup in the allocated sleeping quarters. Give the puppy a nice bone (marrow bone or a nylabone) and go away for few minutes. Go back, praise the dog, take the bone, and give the puppy a short game with a toy. Right from day one, the pup should be left for brief periods, gradually building these up. The puppy learns that it is not such a terrible thing to be left as it is not long before you come back, and then there is a pleasurable game. In this way, you are building up your puppy's confidence. Obviously there must be a door between you and pup, so your puppy realises you have gone. In order to avoid possessiveness with bones, I use the same routine as I do with the food bowl, taking the bone away from the puppy every so often. I hold the bone in my hand, and occasionally let the puppy chew at the bone in my hand, which has the effect of asserting my control over the puppy.

Children and dogs can form a fruitful relationship, but children must understand that a puppy is a living animal, and not a toy to be played with at will.

PLAYING FAIR

Be fair to your pup; play the game by the rules that can be understood by the canine mentality, and gradually show your puppy what is the correct way. Dog ownership should be a pleasure for both owner and dog. The key word is consistency. Do not tell your puppy off for pulling on the lead in the class, and let the pup pull you all the way home. Be fair; keep to the same set of rules.

SOCIALISATION CLASSES

It is vital that you find a good training club for your puppy. Good clubs have a puppy socialisation class and these are invaluable. Even my 'sheep only' dogs attend these classes. The pup learns to mix with both people and other dogs and they learn to come while distractions are going on around them. Ask your vet, or any local dog people for information about training clubs in your area.

LIVING WITH CHILDREN

Generally, children and dogs can be the finest of friends, each gaining a great deal from the relationship. Both my boys had their own dogs when they were eight to nine years old, and although I supervised matters, they had to attend to the dog's needs in relation to exercise, feeding and grooming. I believe that is an unrivalled way to teach a child responsibility. I also noticed that when they felt the world was against them, as all children do from time to time, they would talk it out with their dog, always a silent and patient listener, and they would soon find that the world was not such a bad place.

However, children have to be taught to respect dogs and to realise they are not toys to be played

Canine law must be respected if you already have a dog in the family. Do not make the mistake of taking the puppy's part in interactions with the older dog.

If you supervise early introductions with cats and other pets, your Border Collie will live in harmony with all members of its new family.

with at will. *Young children, especially, should never be left alone with a dog, for any reason.* They must learn that they must not touch the dog with hands, fingers or feet, except to gently stroke the dog when an adult is present. They may also, under the strictest supervision, be occasionally allowed to hold the dog's lead or to throw an object for the dog to retrieve, but only when permitted by the adult and in the manner shown by the adult.

A child who is taught how to respect a dog in the correct manner gains so much from the relationship, and they also learn how to respect people in the big world. A good child/dog partnership is a pleasure to watch.

AN OLDER DOG IN THE FAMILY

If you already have a dog in the household and you are bringing in a new youngster, then again it is vital that the canine law is strictly carried out. The older dog must always have everything first, e.g. fed first, the lead put on and off first, put into and out of the car first, and so on.

Watch out for a typical scenario of the two dogs playing a game, and the pup annoys the older dog. The older dog puts on a big pretence of snapping at the pup (if you watch carefully the teeth are usually closed) and the puppy squeals as though half-murdered. The danger here is that the owner goes to protect the pup, shouts at the older dog and sympathises with the pup – and now the owner has built in a potential hazard for the future. The older dog is aggrieved, rightly so, and the puppy (which deserved a telling-off) gets bad behaviour not only reinforced but praised by Alpha Leader.

When this situation occurs – and it does with every new addition – either leave them alone, or else growl at the puppy and just ask the older dog quietly to be steady. All fighting problems are owner-instigated, so if they occur you only have yourself to blame – not the dogs.

Chapter Two

EARLY EDUCATION

There are a vast number of books which deal solely with training your dog, and each discipline has its own range of books. I therefore plan to concentrate on the principles of early training and education, and then give a case study of my dog, Trapper, focusing on her foundation work and the areas where problems most commonly arise.

LEARNING BY EXPERIENCE

The majority of Border Collies are slow maturing. This can be seen particularly in the head, which does not really come into its final form until the dog is two and a half to three years old. A sheepdog is rarely of much use until this age, when suddenly everything seems to come together. Think of the child starting off at pre-school. There is no point in giving this child algebra to do. The junior schoolchild cannot sit major exams, and the secondary schoolchild cannot take a university degree. However, the logic of suiting each task to the individual's maturity and capability seems to desert the average dog trainer. So many trainers persist in pushing their dogs into advanced lessons far too quickly. It is important to remember that those early, formative years are not wasted. The child gains a great deal of experience in all manner of skills and activities during this time, and so it should be with a dog.

To prove a point recently I asked my bitch, Nell, to jump the scale. She had never seen such an obstacle in her life as she had only been used for sheep work. However, she had learned to jump in order to get into her sheep when needed. When confronted with the scale, she did 5ft 6ins with no fuss whatsoever. By using her experience and maturity she brought her skills to bear on a new situation. My puppies get a lot of free exercise out in the fields with the adults, who enjoy jumping tree trunks and other obstacles as part of their play. At first the pups have to run under or be helped over the obstacle, but very soon they learn to follow the adults, jumping over the obstacle. I always give the command "Over", and so the lesson is learned without the need for any formal training

Frequently, when all nine of my dogs are running free, I give the recall whistle in order to maintain overall control. The puppy does not realise this is a command, but, not wishing to be left behind, the pup responds with the adults – and so the recall whistle is learnt as a part of everyday life. A great deal can be achieved without the dog ever knowing a lesson is being taught. In this way, commands and obedience become a way of life; response becomes automatic, making for reliability. There is no pressure on the youngster, and there is no opportunity for problems to develop, as in formal training situations. There is the added bonus that the dog learns to obey in any situation – not just in the 'ring' or 'on home ground'.

When I was young, all my brothers and sisters had to learn the piano and sit for exams. My music teacher would take us round to a number of different houses so that we could practise in strange rooms and on different pianos. This helped enormously when it came to going into the examination room and playing before the examiner – and the teacher's success rate went up accordingly. It is the same for the dog: there is no substitute for experience. Training for me and my dogs is a way of life, and because of this, I can go anywhere and know they will never let me down.

There is another point that trainers fail to take into consideration, and that is the problem of variable performance. If your dog is a biddable type, bred for work, a willing learner, and eager to do the tasks allotted, the dog will never give you short of its best *on that day*. However, dogs like humans, do not always feel one hundred per cent. Bitches, in particular, are subject to hormonal changes which may affect their behaviour. Communication between trainer and dog is limited, and so the dog cannot explain why, on that occasion, the performance was below par. However, the trainer's disapproval could well affect the dog's confidence, and the relationship between dog and trainer could suffer. So, if the standard is lower than usual, do your best to think why this is – there is a ninety per cent chance that the fault lies with you.

COMMANDS

The words of command you choose need careful consideration before you start to use any, or introduce a new one. For example, if your dog is called 'Kit', there is no point is using the command "Sit", because the dog will constantly misunderstand what you want. Recently, my husband asked me to trim his beard – all of a sudden my dog, Trim, started to leap up and make a fuss. She had picked up the word 'trim' from our conversation and thought I was calling her. I am sure that this happens more often than we realise: dogs pick up words from our conversation and react – and then wonder why they get grumbled at.

Sometimes, for a reason unknown to us, a dog will dislike a command and will be wary of responding to it. Be on the alert, and if you detect a problem with a command, change it. My dog, Bracken, did not like the command "Find"; it just did not activate any enthusiasm. However, when the command was changed to "Seek", she would put much effort into the job. There was no explanation for this, other than the fact that she was not happy with the original command. There was another instance of this sensitivity to commands when I was asked to help a lady whose dog failed to respond to the "Sit". The dog would not sit fully on the ground and was clearly ill at ease. I advised her to totally change the command and re-train. When I saw her some weeks later, the dog was sitting correctly and with confidence. Obviously the word had started to worry the dog, and the situation had deteriorated accordingly.

It is vital to give *one* command and *one* action. Do not fall into the trap of repeating the command because the dog is not paying attention, and then giving praise. All you are doing is teaching the dog that there is no praise or correction for the first command, but all is well when the command is given twice. Consequently, the dog thinks it is a double-worded command. The trouble is that you rarely understand the complexity of the command that the dog has in its own mind. It is like a husband and wife planning to spend a huge windfall of money. Frequently, their ideas are poles apart. It is the same with the interpretation of a command. The trainer's idea of a command may be very different to the dog's perception.

This is not limited to verbal commands; it also applies to eye signals and hand signals. Sometimes a trainer will give a command, and, unknowingly, sway their body at the same time. Dogs are so observant that they detect the most subtle body language. So, unless you are totally sure that your dog is being wilfully disobedient, do not blame the dog. Sometimes the trainer has muddled the dog so much, the dog is no longer sure what the command means. Try tape-recording a training session from time to time and then listen to it very carefully. You will be really amazed at the number of mistakes you make!

EYE SIGNALS

A dog who has a good relationship and a confident one with the owner, watches both face and eyes. My dog, Trapper, is extremely sensitive and I rarely need to reproach her, but she does get worried if I have to correct Todd, who is the opposite type altogether. Trapper has found her own answer to this problem. While I am reprimanding Todd with my voice, I smile at Trapper who then relaxes completely, knowing she is not in trouble.

I smile as a signal of approval or to boost a dog's confidence. I stare hard, straight into the dog's eyes, if I feel the dog is about to transgress. This can often prevent the mistake occurring; a stern look can frequently be used as correction instead of the spoken word. I can look at one individual in a group of dogs and signal my wishes so that only that one moves or acts. However, in sheep work I try not to use hand signals or facial signals, for I do not want the dog to keep taking its eyes off the sheep. It would be the same with scent discrimination in Obedience or tracking in Working Trials – the dog needs to concentrate on the task in hand. In training, there is a place for everything and everything must be used in the correct place.

ESTABLISHING YOUR POSITION

Many times over the years, people have asked for advice because their dog did not look at them. The poor dog is a very lost and confused animal in this situation. Even if my dogs seem to be asleep, their ears are so well tuned in that I cannot sneak in or out of the house without them knowing. Like many Border Collies, they play a great deal with each other, but there is not the slightest doubt which of us is most important, their playmate or me. I do not need to say a single thing, but the two main dogs are with me before I have gone a couple of yards. Even the outside dogs watch me a great deal: Who am I going to invite in? Who is going to get brushed? Who will get the first retrieve?

So many people do not start to notice their dogs before they start training. The dog is left to 'develop', but, in fact, the opposite is more likely to occur. The puppy, maturing into the adult dog, must regard you as *the* most important thing in its whole life. To your dog, you must be God – if you are not, then you are not Alpha Leader. This means that you are not in control and you will have trouble at some stage, if not all the time. If your dog does not watch you, then you must embark on a programme of education to establish your relationship on the right terms. (See Chapter Three: Problems in Training – Attention exercises.)

The bulk of your training is completed by the time your puppy is twelve weeks old. After this, you merely expand on what the puppy has already done and learnt. You can also be sure that if you are not teaching your dog, then, as certainly as the world is revolving, the dog is learning from you or from another animal – and this is achieved by watching. Dogs learn and manipulate their environment, so it is better to teach them what they are to learn, and to teach them to watch you for the clues. A dog who watches you (except in sheep work, scent discrimination and tracking) is not distracted by what is going on and is therefore more likely to succeed in the given task.

RECALL

All my puppies come to me by four weeks of age because they find I am a fun person. I also feed them, but this is not the most important factor. Trapper will sit scrounging bacon from my husband with her mouth drooling, but one move from me and she is immediately alert. She loves food, but she is more interested in being with me. This sort of dog will always respond to the recall. If your

Encourage your puppy to come to you by sounding exciting, so the exercise is viewed as fun.

dog does not have this instant response you should be asking yourself: 'Why isn't my dog motivated like that?'

It could be that you have a very sensitive dog who hates being grabbed and forced into a straight sit in front. Unintentionally, you may have hurt your dog when doing this, and so the dog is now frightened to come up. Perhaps the dog does not understand what is required? There are many factors which can influence the recall. Do you play with your dog? This does not mean a riotous session of chasing and rough-and-tumble. It means sharing activities without formal commands. These should be fun activities but, nevertheless, they are an important part of building a strong foundation. Hide-and-seek games, for example, are great fun and they are also highly educational. Watch a litter of puppies at play and observe all the manoeuvres that make up their play. These are skills that will be useful later on in their life, but at this point of time it is just pure fun.

Are you a tall person with a sensitive dog, or, even worse, are you using a gruff voice? The solution is simple: bend down, make yourself smaller, less forbidding, more accessible, and put a some enticement into your voice – few dogs can resist that. Are you one of those people who have a monotonous, dull voice which is exactly the same whether you are cross with the dog or pleased with the dog? No wonder there are recall difficulties – if I were a dog I would think twice before I came. The answer is obvious. So if you have a recall problem, ask yourself: 'What am *I* doing wrong?'

Each of my dogs has a 'work-only toy'. This is something they really crave for, and it is only given as reward, alternated with tidbits. My dogs all have toys, and it soon becomes evident which is favourite to a particular dog. This toy is then taken from the toy box and into the training bag. From then onwards, the dog is never allowed to play with this toy except for a reward. This is alternated with giving tidbits so that the dog does not always have the toy as a reward. Dogs are like humans: something which is rationed quickly becomes a craving.

The 'work toy' is invaluable when teaching the recall. Call your dog in a really enticing voice, bend to a crouch position, knees slightly apart so it is easy for the dog to come in straight, and hold the toy close to your face (reinforcing face-watching). The dog should be used to sitting for reward, and so as you call, the dog comes in straight (after all, you have made a runway for guidance), and the work toy is positioned at the face for a sit. If your knees are correctly placed, the dog cannot help but sit straight, and so a perfect recall is achieved with no need to grab the dog. There is no need to finish to heel at this stage. The aim is to get your dog really keen to do a recall because it is fun. Substitute a tidbit instead of the toy, and once in every three recalls, do not give a tidbit. As the dog becomes more confident, you can raise your position to a slightly higher crouch. However, even with my trained dogs, I still crouch from time to time, to take the formality out of the exercise.

THE SCRUFF METHOD

This is not a method I use very often, but done gently yet firmly on the odd occasion, it can be very useful. Like all negative actions, it is at its most effective on its very first application, and the effectiveness decreases rapidly each successive time that it is used. It is not used as a punishment but merely as a way to get attention. It says: "Hey, stop and listen to me!" The pup's mother will use it in the same way. It therefore needs to be applied with an attention communication as well. For example, give a firm, quick scruff and a growled "Hey, listen!" – and once you have the dog's attention, you growl "No". The complete action has to be carried out in a couple of seconds maximum. It certainly is not the answer to all the problems, but it can be most effective on a slightly older dog who has got a well-established bad habit, e.g. barking at other dogs, and has never had any real control training.

At the side of the dog's head on the cheek, the hair is usually long and dense. You can take hold of this firmly and just give a quick, firm but gentle tug and at the same time a growled "No" or "Hey, listen to me!" I use this latter reprimand when I am not getting the dog's attention and I want to modify the behaviour, whereas "No" is used when the dog is trying to get it right but does not quite make it. In this instance, the dog is not really being disobedient. If the dog is barking at other dogs I would use the "Hey, listen to me!", and as soon as I had got the dog's attention, I would give the command "Quiet".

When the dog is trying to get the exercise right, the "No" should be said in a more mellow tone and used as an aid to help the dog to try a little harder and get it right. When you say "No" in a sharp tone of voice, this means that the dog's behaviour is way over the mark and must cease immediately. The tone in which you give a command helps the dog to get it right more easily.

REWARD

If a dog is doing the work for which it was bred, then that is all the reward that is needed. Real, natural work is self-rewarding and fulfilling for the dog, who asks no more of life. Other such activities are Greyhound hare

The 'scruff method' of correction. This should be enforced with a gentle tug at the dog's cheek, and a growled "No".

coursing or Terrier ratting. In the modern dog activities I would also include Flyball and Agility as self-rewarding, but Obedience and Working Trials are much more frustrating for the dog – that I would think is obvious to most people.

Whatever the discipline is going to be, the basics do need rewarding. One very vital reason for this is that we have a language barrier with our dogs, but the tidbit is a universal language. The dog may be a little hesitant in being sure we are pleased/satisfied (we give so many conflicting signals to the dog), but the tidbit reassures that the action is correct. However, you need to be sure you are rewarding an action done correctly, and not the complete opposite. I watched a man at a training club who was having problems trying to stop his dog barking. Everytime the dog barked he gave a tidbit. The owner thought this was to quieten the dog – the dog thought it was to continue barking!

A reward has to be something that the dog really craves for, otherwise it is of little use. If someone tells you to use dried cat food and your dog is merely interested in it, that is not enough. If you know your dog gets really excited when playing with one particular toy, then use the toy. The 'work toy' is then taken out of circulation and kept as a special training reward. I use a mixture of toy and food reward so that the dog does not become bored with the reward. You may have to change the toy as a reward, for if the dog has become dis-interested in it, it is useless.

I never go anywhere without a few odd tidbits in my pocket. This is usually dried cat food, as my dogs' obsession to steal the cat's food means that this tidbit is regarded as a real treat! It also has the advantage of being dry and very small. A tidbit should be a mere taste of a treat, or the dog will get bored with it. The same applies to the 'work toy'. The dog must be restricted to a quick play with it so that the toy keeps its attraction.

In the very early stages I give the reward every time the dog achieves success. I then start reducing this, offering it only twice in every three times, then once every three times and eventually only giving it on the odd occasion. However, even the oldest of my dogs is allowed an occasional tidbit, just to keep them interested and happy.

TOYS
Border Collies are the most playful of dogs, and for them, toys are a necessity. However, they must always be under your strict control. My dogs have quite a large number of toys, but only a few are available at a time, so they do not become bored with them. If your dog is under proper control and is giving you no problems then it is safe to leave the toys with the dog. If there are any problems over aggressiveness or possessiveness, the toys must never be left down. The possessive dog will assume he has 'won' the toys from you, and this means he is of a higher rank than you. Before long, you will not be able to touch the toys or go near them – and then you have real troubles brewing.

THAT'LL DO/ENOUGH
Teach your dog from the start that "No" means that the action is not acceptable. Use another command which says to the dog that the action is alright, but you do not wish to continue with it at that point of time. A useful command is "Enough". I use "That'll do" which is used by most sheep people. It means: That is all the sheep work for the moment, so come off the sheep and away with me. It is also useful if you are playing a game and then want to end it. I say "That'll do", and the dog knows the game is finished.

TIMING
Whatever branch of training you are involved in, the efficiency of what you are trying to teach is

directly related to your timing. Timing is extremely difficult to explain to a person who does not have it naturally. There is an excellent method, which I call the 'McCleavy four seconds', which was worked out by an extremely experienced dog instructor to help beginners. If you have not rewarded or modified a particular action within four seconds from the dog's first twitch of movement, then the dog is unlikely to associate your follow-up with the action just completed.

For example, with a dog beginning to break the stay, the four seconds starts from the first sign, e.g. altered ear position or drop of head – *not* once the dog's rear end is lifted off the floor. Ask a friend to time an action that you do, stopping you at four seconds. You will find that this is an incredibly short period of time. However, you have got to get your timing down to this finest level (and even better), and this means watching and studying your dog. All dogs give signals of their intentions to carry out an action. Do not forget that the four seconds includes not just your follow-up command, it also applies to the giving of tidbits.

STRESS

This type of behaviour is shown in a number of different ways. A dog who may be suffering from stress may display any of the following:

Insecurity
Unusual behaviour
Haunted look in eyes
Frustration
Aggression
Trying too hard to please
Guilt
Sudden fears
Unreliable actions
Variable response.

A dog suffering from stress will show this in a sudden failing in work. This could be due to many causes such as:

Too much pressure
Illness
Tiredness (variable)
Strange place
Change in routine
Changes in equipment (jumps, whistles etc.).

CASE STUDY OF TRAPPER
The early education of a Border Collie puppy

I have singled out one of my dogs, Trapper, in order to detail the progresss and development of a youngster and the training that is required. All dogs are individuals and a variety of different problems may arise with every dog you train. However, Trapper's case study gives a general picture of what you can expect from a young, lively, intelligent dog, and how to cope with difficulties as they arise.

I bred Trapper, so she started her training a little earlier than many puppies. Education really

A tidbit is used to teach the puppy the Sit exercise.

In the second stage of teaching the Sit, the tidbit is in the hand, but is not given until the puppy has gone into the Sit.

The puppy is now sitting on command.

does start at the nest, and the mother, assisted by the breeder, should have given the puppy an excellent grounding for adult life. The breeder will have stimulated the litter by playing with them. The puppies will also be used to running to greet the breeder, and so the recall has been started. The bitch will have taught the puppies their lines of demarcation, and it would be a foolhardy puppy who would ignore this, and so discipline has already started before the puppy goes to the new home. Your training starts from the second you take ownership.

Trapper lived partially outside for the first six months, but this made little difference to her education because she was in the house with me every morning and every evening. She was already coming when called. Therefore, this initial keenness was nurtured and encouraged so she was performing the exercise without realising it was a lesson.

FIRST LESSONS

Trapper's first piece of formal education was learning the Sit position. I always have a few odd tidbits in my pocket for adults and youngsters, but when I have a youngster coming on then the number increases. Puppies frequently sit because they are so small that sitting helps them to look a little higher. I always utilise this, and each time Trapper started to sit I would give her the command "Sit", praise her once in that position and give her a tidbit – one hundred per cent success for dog and owner! Learning rate is magnified if success is always achieved, and within a day Trapper was sitting when requested. Feeding time is a must for the Sit instruction, but on this occasion the puppy gets the food rather than a tidbit.

Once Trapper was sitting each time I asked, I would slip in the command at all sorts of odd times throughout the day. When she had proved to be completely reliable for three or four days, I started teaching the Down command. I selected a day when I would be about all day and could have Trapper with me, and could watch her closely all the time. Whenever I saw her start to go into the Down position, I would give the command "Down" and give her a tidbit. At other times I would hold a tidbit in my hand, Trapper would sit, and then I let her head follow my hand down towards the floor, holding the tidbit in front of her nose. This encourages the puppy to sink into the Down position and as soon as she started to go down I would give the command "Down", and then praise her and reward her with a tidbit.

It took Trapper about a day to catch on and go down as soon as she was told, so now she was responding to the "Sit" and "Down" commands. During these early days and weeks when I am educating a young puppy, I always sit on the floor, knees apart or on a low chair, knees apart, and encourage the puppy to come right up as close as possible and when the pup's head is in my lap, I make a big fuss and give a tidbit. Here, I am developing a correct recall position. The puppy does not know it, but I am forming the habit of always coming into me.

TEETHING

Puppies, like all young animals (and humans), go through a teething stage when they start to chew and use their teeth on all manner of objects. Trapper was no different. She would pull at trousers, tug at the longer washing on the line, and she would attempt to chew at my fingers. However, this type of behaviour was quickly stopped. You cannot allow a puppy to chew fingers and play tug-of-war at seven weeks old, and then suddenly clamp down on this behaviour at seven months when it has become unacceptable. Imagine the puppy's confusion when one day she is allowed to do something and the next day she gets punished for it.

If the mother has had plenty of contact with the puppies, she will have taught them a great deal of respect, and they will know that a warning growl means stop what you are doing. All you need to do is to develop a deep, growling voice to discipline the puppy. I woud growl at Trapper, and as

The Down is a natural development of the Sit exercise. Again, a tidbit is used to encourage the puppy to go into the correct position.

soon as she stopped chewing, I would give her one of her toys. If you do this once, you will probably never have to do it again. However, if you turn a blind eye you have condoned the action as being acceptable, and so it gets progressively harder to stop.

Dogs and puppies who have been reared naturally understand a deep growl. If the trainer thinks like a dog and uses their mode of communication, the puppy will learn quicker. How can a puppy or a dog find out what is acceptable and what is unacceptable, unless they try it on the people and animals they live with? After all, if the puppy was being reared in the wild there would be no harm in chewing a wooden object, such as the branch of a tree, but the rest of the pack would very certainly stop the puppy chewing at their ears and tails. The growl you develop must be deep and rumbling; it is quite easy to do – the main problem is that people feel self-conscious about doing it!

Whenever Trapper picked up something I did not want her to have, I would either sit on the floor or on a low chair and encourage her to come to me. I would then praise her, take the object from her, and give her a tidbit followed by one of her own toys. The puppy soon learns to bring things for a tidbit. This is the start of the retrieve, and because the puppy is bringing the object to you, there is no interest in chewing it. I have used this technique with all my dogs, and I rarely have problems with chewing. In fact, the older dogs sometimes bring a 'forbidden' object to me, just to get my attention – and this is always rewarded with a tidbit.

RETRIEVE GAMES
Retrieve games – and for many months they are no more than games – are taught as an extension of the puppy's natural behaviour. However, I note where the puppy likes to run to with a chosen toy and then position myself at the door of the room, facing inwards, with the puppy also in the room. The puppy, holding the toy, runs straight up to where I am waiting – and we have a perfect retrieve. With Trapper, I would wait in the lounge, facing inwards. I would sit on the floor with my knees bent outwards so that she would run straight into the correct present finish, and I would give her plenty of praise.

The puppy comes running up with a toy, and, with encouragement, you have the beginnings of a retrieve.

Retrieving must always be taught as a fun exercise. You can encourage your puppy to become enthusiastic by having a game with the retrieve toy.

It is many months before I introduce the "Wait" or the "Sit" command to develop the recall or the retrieve exercises. It is important to guard against a dog losing enthusiasm – too much nit-picking has been the downfall of many a competition dog.

SEARCHING

During those very early weeks, when Trapper was keen on her toy, I would let her see me hide it so that she had to search for it. Then, gradually, very gradually, I would make the task slightly harder. She had one special ball which she would hardly ever be parted from. If she lost it, she would wander around like a lost soul. When she was out of sight, I would hide the ball, and she very quickly learnt to walk into a room and locate it. There is one very important factor: the puppy must always succeed in finding the toy, and if sometimes she had trouble, I would help her to locate it. It is vital in this type of education by natural sources, that success is one hundred per cent.

THE STAY

Once Trapper was completely reliable on the Sit, I started to work on the Stay. I always choose feeding times to start this lesson. The puppy has already learned to sit before the bowl is placed down, so now I ask for the Sit, and with the dish in my right hand and my left hand fully open about two inches in front of her nose, I give the command "Wait" and place the dish on the floor. Make sure the puppy is steady for a second or two, then praise her and let her eat. The flat hand, held so close to the face, usually puzzles the puppy for a moment – just long enough to achieve what I want. This is gradually built up to slightly longer and longer waiting periods. Once I can do this, using the food dish, for a few seconds, then I repeat it elsewhere in the house area.

You will notice that I use the command "Wait" rather than "Stay" and there is a good reason for this. Have you ever considered how perplexing it must be to a dog if she is told to "Stay", which means remaining staying still and not moving off the spot, and then the next time the command is given, the dog is expected to come to the handler or perform a different task. If the dog gets it wrong she knows she's in trouble. But how does she know if this is a long stay where she is not allowed to move, or whether this is just a temporary halt?

Therefore, if I want the dog to move and do something else, the command is "Wait", whereas, if I give the command "Stay", I mean just that – do not move from that spot. The puppy/dog soon learns the difference between the two commands, and responds better for knowing what is expected.

THE RIGHT APPROACH

There are numerous control lessons that your puppy must be taught in the early stages of education, and most of these involve 'house rules'. The puppy must learn not to push ahead of you when going through doors; the pup must learn to wait quietly while the lead is put on, and to wait the obligatory few seconds once the lead has been removed until the release command is given.

While it is essential to teach all these exercises, it is equally important to decide on what method to use. Every dog is different and requires a slightly different approach. It does not matter how closely two dogs are related – mother and daughter or even brother and sister – they are all different. I consider the complete dog, and I weigh this up with various training methods, and then make a decision on which is *probably* the correct one for that particular dog. However, you must remain watchful and sensitive at all times, for there is a distinct possibility that you may need to modify your approach.

THE EXTENSION LEAD

In the early weeks when taking Trapper (or any other puppy) out on road exercise, I used the extension lead. This allows the puppy to have a great deal of freedom, while I have maximum control. It teaches the puppy to follow you, to relax and learn about the road and respect it. No matter where you live, your dog must learn about traffic and learn to respect the road. This must become ingrained as a way of life. Whenever Trapper strayed near the kerb, I would use the anchor on the extension lead and give the command "No". I would walk out to the front gate with the lead slack, and if she did not stop and wait for me before reaching the point where we joined the footpath, on would go the anchor, plus the command "Wait". In the early days whenever we reached the kerb, Trapper was made to sit. I would then pick her up and carry her over the road, instilling in her mind that roads are a taboo area.

There is nothing worse than seeing someone drag a reluctant puppy along the road because it does not like the lead. This situation does not occur if you use an extension lead, as the puppy will not want a wide gap to develop between the owner and themselves. When Trapper dug her heels in

Car drill is an essential part of a puppy's early education. This four-month-old pup is learning to wait in the car without jumping out.

on the first few outings, I merely let the line out and carried on walking, calling in an encouraging way. Trapper took a couple of days and was soon keeping up with me.

CAR TRAVEL

Trapper travelled in the car from birth, but training in car manners did not start until she was about six weeks old when she could travel in the back on her own. Each of my dogs has their own place in the back area, which has been agreed and sorted out by them. Trapper was quickly made to understand where she could have her spot.

The dogs are never allowed to get in or out of the car without the appropriate command to do so. In the case of Trapper, who was too young to know the command, she was kept on a lead so that she did not have the chance to disobey. Once in the car, the lead was removed, but it was attached again before she was allowed to get out. This has a double function. It reinforces the Alpha roll, and it prevents a dog dashing out and getting caught by a passing motorist. I also insist that the dogs only respond to my command to get in or out of the car – not to any other member of the family or a visiting friend. I always take great care to check the way is clear, and to watch out for any possible distractions. Few people do this automatically, yet is so easy to give a careless command and so put your dog's life at risk.

PLAY

This is the most overlooked aspect of dog training, with too many handlers fearing that a dog who plays will not take its work seriously. In fact, the wolf is one of the very few wild animals which indulges in play other than sexual or with young, and the dog is a near descendant. All youngsters learn through play. In the wild the youngster would not be leaving either parents or the pack until a much older age than the average puppy going to a new home, and so play as a process of learning would have gone on for some considerable time. The average dog will live for twelve to fifteen years, and will work until ten or twelve years old, so what is the hurry?

Mentally and physically the youngster is not going to be able to do much work until eighteen months to two years of age, so again there is no hurry. My top working dogs have been those who have also played the hardest and are still enjoying relaxation with play when twelve years old. If the breeding is right, there is no way that a really good dog will ever give play a thought while working.

Watch two dogs play together, especially if one is older and the other considerably younger, and observe all the skills that go into a simple game, such as a tussle over a ball. A typical game between Trapper and my older dog, Trim, would start with Trim taking Trapper's ball and taunting her into a game. This would develop into a series of twists and turns, avoiding contact and involving control of the body. These manoeuvres are a preparation for game catching, working sheep, etc.

After a while, Trim would lie in front of Trapper and drop the ball between her paws. It did not matter how quickly Trapper moved, Trim always got to the ball before her, showing formidable accuracy and speed. After a bit of teasing, the game would be kept going by Trapper managing to get the ball or, in truth, Trim letting her get it.

Trapper and Nell have a different game. Nell will try to get Trapper's ball from her by lying down quite close by, and slowly, so slowly you scarcely notice, she manoeuvres up until she is touching the ball, showing tthe stealth of a predator after its prey.

Watch out that the dogs do not become too canine-orientated by spending too long playing together. All that you need to do is to distract the puppy from the game and inject some human-dog activity in place of it.

BACK YARD TRAINING (BYT)

Before long, Trapper started widening her education to incorporate Backyard Training, which I term BYT. To my mind, this is *the* most vital part of control education. Show me any dog who is having a problem away from home, and I will prove to you that that dog is also experiencing the same problem in a modified form back on its home territory – even if this is undetected by the handler. If your dog is not totally reliable on home ground, then you cannot expect reliability away from home.

BYT forms the major part of my control work, and as I have several dogs (nine at present), they all act as testers or tempters for each other, which makes BYT even easier. It does not matter that each dog is of a different age and at a different stage of their education. A five-minute session every day is an essential part of my training routine – BYT should be a way of life for both yourself and your dogs. It does not matter whether I correct a mistake during work or not, I still do the major part of the correction at home. With my sheepdogs the most common problem is getting a sloppy recall off sheep or problems with the stop. The next time I am dealing with the dogs at home I take particular note of just how quickly that dog is carrying out any command I have issued, and the answer is always the same, sloppily.

Let us take an example. Each dog is called into the run by name. I may call "Todd" after all the others are in. If he hesitates, I call again – and there is the problem: two commands for one action. This might only happen occasionally and so I have not noticed doing it, but the dog has certainly noticed and logged it in the brain. The first week it may only happen once, and the next a couple of times, if you are busy and in a rush; it slips by unnoticed as the dog quickly obliges at the second command – but the rot has set in.

The dog is excited because you have just come home, and in all the enthusiasm you give a second command, thinking the dog did not hear and it does not matter because the dog was over-excited. However, the truth is that the dog did hear the first command and chose to ignore it. All handlers make these mistakes from time to time. The important thing is that you realise what is happening and put a stop before it develops into a problem. Throughout the dog's life, there will always be times of testing when the dog is ascertaining what it can get away with. This can be insidious, starting very gradually but developing into a severe problem – and *you* let it happen. At first, you may give an extra command because you are busy or preoccupied, but the dog logs it. This scenario occurs more frequently until you are always giving two commands, and then the day comes when your command is met with complete refusal.

BYT goes on from weaning and runs side by side with foundation training. They are broadly similar except that one is in the house and the other takes place in the back yard. Foundation training is a one-to-one relationship, whereas BYT involves interaction with the handler and all the other dogs present. It starts either as soon as all the puppies have gone to new homes, with the exception of the one I am keeping, or when a young adult joins the team.

The essence of BYT is to be unpredictable, never sticking to a routine. If the dogs do not know what to expect, they will be on their toes and listening for commands. You must be at your most observant, detecting problems as they arise and then finding ways of solving them. Remember, even with BYT it is important to help the dog to get a command right. This is the time when you are establishing your control and your authority and, if necessary, going back to basics with a dog who is having problems in work. If you use BYT effectively, you will never regret the time you have spent. The rewards will be evident not only in your dogs' work, but also in an improvement in your relationship with each individual dog.

Chapter Three

PROBLEMS IN TRAINING

WHO IS DOMINANT?
Does the dog push through the doorway/gateway first in front of you?
Does the dog sleep in the bedroom?
Does the dog insist on a particular sleeping place?
Is the chosen bed/lying-place high up, e.g. top of the stairs?
Does the dog pester for attention and will not stop when asked?
Are you having aggression problems with the dog?
Does the dog resist being groomed?

If the answer is Yes, then you have got to put yourself back as Alpha Leader and demote the dog.

PUTTING YOURSELF BACK IN CONTROL
1. Remove all the dog's toys and only allow access to them for short periods. The dog must not be allowed to keep any of them.
2. When going out for a walk, the dog must not be allowed to pull and must not be allowed to sniff anything, except if locating the spot to relieve himself.
3. The dog must also be allowed to cock his leg only once.
4. At no time is the dog allowed through any doorway/passage-way/gateway in front of you. The dog must be told to wait until you give the command.
5. The dog must not be allowed upstairs.
6. The dog's bed must be in some quiet place out of the main stream of the household activity.
7. The dog must have limited access to rooms.
8. Never raise your voice to give a command.
9. Do not ask the dog to do something – you command.
10. Only give one command and then make the dog do what you want.
11. The dog must eat when everyone else has eaten.
12. Do not give any tidbits from your plate.
13. The dog must sit and wait while you prepare the food (fasten the long line to some tethering post if you need to force control), put the dish down and do not allow the dog to eat it until you give the command.
14. The kitchen is generally a taboo area.

The dog must learn that anything pleasurable in life comes from you, at your invitation. Your voice must always be firm and definite with authority when needed, and should be light and

The Border Collie is a highly intelligent breed, but it is essential to provide plenty of stimulation to keep your dog happy and fulfilled.   *A. Wells.*

playful when the dog is obeying and behaving. You decide when to start a game or to give a tidbit; play with other dogs is banned. Gradually, the dog will learn that you are the centre of life. The dog will learn to respect you and to look to you for everything.

WHY DO PROBLEMS DEVELOP?

More often than not, problems start when the pup is still young. Like babies which tend to be treated differently, the puppy gets treated differently "because he is too young to know any better". However, the dominant puppy will have been manipulating brothers and sisters from the very start. This puppy will always be feeding on the best teat – and this is not accidental. If a lesser puppy is on that teat, the dominant puppy will push it out. By the time they are weaned, this puppy will be quite skilful at this. In fact the only difference between a six-week-old puppy and an adult is the physical ability; the pup certainly has the mental ability.

So, if you don't want an adult dog that bites your hand, do not allow the pup to do this at two months of age and say it is because of teething. Do not allow a seven-week-old pup to make a grab at the food the moment you put the bowl down. A seven-week-old puppy can be taught to sit properly, possibly aided by a gentle restraint with the collar. The pup must get used to giving up food and toys at your request, and never allow the puppy to retain a toy after you have been playing together.

There are many problems for dogs living in the nineties, and one of these is open-plan houses. In older houses it is comparatively easy to confine the puppy to the back quarters. These days, with the house opened up, a puppy as young as seven or eight weeks old is more likely to have learnt to climb the stairs. Naturally, the pup wants to follow 'the boss' upstairs and it is not long before this

When problems arise in training it is important to establish your position as Alpha Leader. One of the ways of doing this is to return to basic training exercises, making sure the dog does what is required. Here the Down is being taught by easing the front leg forward and slightly inward with the right hand, while the left hand pushes on the dog's shoulder.

The combination of the left hand on the front leg and pressure on the shoulder results in the dog going into the Down.

The full Down position has been achieved with little trouble, and the owner has put herself firmly in control.

is considered right. To the dominant puppy, this is the perfect opportunity to select the highest point in the house to sleep in. It is important that you establish where the puppy is allowed to go, not only to protect best carpets and furniture but to establish control.

I had an older house, and I removed the back-room door so that we had a walk-through straight into the lounge. However, as far as the dogs were concerned, it was as though there was an electric fence on the section of the doorway. I never had to correct any of the dogs for going over that line; they would often lie, nose touching that imaginary line, but they never crossed it. To us, this is an imaginary line, but to a dog obeying the natural laws, it is clear as a solid, wooden door. In the wild, all territory lines are invisible to us, but to all other creatures living in that area, they are as clear as daylight. A well-mannered dog, who knows that you are Alpha Leader and accepts a subordinate status, will obey the laws of demarcation. All dogs are governed by natural instincts – the laws of nature endowed at birth. If these laws do not suit us, then we must modify them with a set which is consistent and which every member of the family uses.

MAKING THE PROBLEMS WORSE

We have discussed the major problem as to why dogs get it wrong, but this needs to be taken a little further. Certain activities actually accentuate the problem, especially if you have a dominant puppy. Rough-and-tumble games is one such activity. Personally, I cannot see a need for this type of behaviour in any aspect of living with dogs. Tug-of-war games, which can be an extremely useful training aid, are potential trouble if you allow the puppy to 'win' the toy at the end of the game.

Inconsistency is one of the most common faults in human/dog interaction – on the part of the human, not the dog. We are sloppy by nature; we give two orders instead of one, we give one order and before the dog can carry it out we give a counteracting order, thus allowing the first order to be disobeyed. We give different commands for the same action, e.g. "Lie down" and "Get down" mean the same in our language, but this does not apply to the dog, who hears two different words. You may give the command "Sit" with emphasis on the 'S' or on the 'T'. It sounds the same to us, but not to the dog. Looking at our inconsistencies, it is amazing that the dogs understand us at all!

Another diabolical fault is that when we get excited we screech, and that is about the biggest sin we can commit. When things are going wrong in training, get control of *yourself* first, and then of the dog. Drop your voice to a whisper, go back a few lessons and end with something that the dog can do easily. Raising the tone of your voice only spurs the dog on with more enthusiasm, and so you are basically telling the dog that what you consider a wrong action is, according to your voice tone, correct – and you therefore reinforce the action. Women have a worse problem than men, as a woman's voice automatically goes up in excitement, while a man's voice usually becomes deeper. This is a matter of self-training. Remember to lower the voice and deepen it, even though this is not always easy when you also are all steamed up.

Border Collies get completely absorbed when carrying out an activity, and sometimes the activity takes one hundred per cent control so that the dog genuinely does not hear the command. In this situation, you need to ask the dog to carry out a command which has become so natural and habit-forming that it has become part of the subconscious.

I have watched my best bitch working when she is completely intent on the job in hand. I give her a flank or down whistle, and she just sways her body with no apparent acknowledgement of hearing, except through body movements. The command is obeyed as though I had guided her on a piece of elastic. Over the years, I have noticed that the best dogs never seem to hear a command, they just seem to obey it as though it is a completely subconscious action.

PROGRAMME FOR INDEPENDENCE

1. Teach the dog short Sit-Stays several times a day, first in sight and then just the other side of the door.
2. Leave an item of well-worn and scented clothing in the room where the dog is to be left. Leave the dog for a few moments, and as long as no barking takes place, go back in, give a tidbit and plenty of praise. Repeat this several times a day, gradually extending the time the dog is left.
3. When you are planning to go out, ignore the dog for a period beforehand. Then, quietly shut the dog in the designated area, say nothing, slam the front door shut, and wait to ensure that no barking takes place. Leave the dog for a short period, go back, give a tidbit and plenty of praise. Build this programme up gradually, slowly increasing the time the dog is left. It can help if you feed the dog beforehand; exercise can also help, as the dog will be tired and more likely to settle. Some people leave a radio on. If the dog barks, return, growl a reprimand, and leave again. Be careful with your timing. Try to leave just long enough to ensure quietness, but at the same time working towards extending the dog's independence. The completion of this programme will take a long time, but if you stick to it, the effort will be worthwhile.

ATTENTION EXERCISES

Attention exercises are needed if your dog is not watching you, wanting to be part of your life. This applies to the dog who fails to take notice of you, prefers to pursue its own interests, even when given a command. A correctly brought up puppy, who has been properly educated and is under good control, will rarely need these exercises.

1(i). Take the dog for a brisk walk. Walk for fifteen minutes without stopping, and do not speak to the dog at all. Then stop and play with the dog for three to four minutes.
(ii). Take the dog for a fifteen minute walk as before. Stop, and play with your dog's favourite toy for two to three minutes. Do not let the dog have the toy.
(iii). Start to walk home and two-thirds of the way home, stop and play with the dog for three to four minutes, continuing home briskly, in silence, and without stopping. This needs doing daily until your dog starts taking notice of you. Continue with this programme on a once-weekly basis.
2. From time to time, prepare the dog's meal and instead of giving it to the dog, put it up on a high shelf, letting the dog see what you are doing. After a period of time, feed the dog.
3. Periodically, get your dog's lead, and let the dog see you place it in your pocket. Then walk out without the dog. A couple of hours later, take the dog for a walk.
4. When involved in an outside job (hanging the washing out, doing small repair job etc.), tie the dog on a short lead where you are working, and occasionally throw a tidbit.
5. Do a few mini Stays. If the dog is not reliable in this exercise, use a lead to tie the dog up, ensuring that the dog cannot move. This exercise can be done in the park or at home. Keep on the move so the dog watches you. Do not use the "Stay" command in this situation. The correct command is "Wait".
6. Give the command "Watch me" and get your dog's attention with a tidbit.
   Try and invent other watching activities and use these. The more you work on this, the better your dog will become.

BEHAVIOURAL PROBLEMS

It is only possible to touch on the subject superficially, but even so, it should help you to think of ways of helping yourself, or at least help you to become aware of problems and seek additional assistance. If you have a behavioural problem, then you have three choices:

1. Get rid of the dog.
2. Change to suit the dog.
3. Work out a solution, which could mean that either you or the dog will have to adjust.
Generally, both of you will need to make some adjustment – but not necessarily to the same extent.

It is important to bear in mind that the dog does not carry out an action to annoy you. The dog is merely obeying natural instincts; the action maybe unacceptable to you, but unless taught otherwise, the dog is doing nothing wrong. The dog really cannot understand why it is unacceptable to wet on your best lounge carpet. After all, in the wild there would have been no restrictions. It is no use saying that dogs are domesticated; they still obey the primitive canine laws. In order to modify a behavioural problem you must really want to do it, and all the household has to be involved.

In some instances a dog crate will be suggested. This is not to be used as a punishment cell, but it is a useful aid to training as long as the dog spends more time out of it than inside it.

SIX STEPS TO PROBLEM SOLVING
1. Recognise that, as far as the dog is concerned, existing behaviour is normal.
2. Define the problem: where, when and why?
3. List all the possible solutions.
4. Collect information to add to your list of solutions.
5. Select and put into action the best solution/s.
6. Evaluate the results.

PLANNING YOUR CORRECTION PROGRAMME
It is essential to ensure that the dog really knows what it is being corrected for, and that the correct behaviour is rewarded. You also need to learn to read your dog's signs and what is being communicated to you.

Start off by getting a sheet of paper. At the top write the name of the problem, and then divide the page into four columns. The first column should be labelled 'When it Occurs'; label the second column 'Possible Reasons for Occurrence', label the third column 'Possible Solutions' and label the fourth column 'Results'. Keep this programme and fill it in truthfully as you progress. Obviously, columns one and two require observation of the dog, and the third column demands some hard thinking and research.

VOICE
Misuse of voice is often one of the major contributors to a problem. Remember, a dog's hearing is very finely tuned, and high-pitched screeching, or loud shouting can have an adverse effect on behaviour. When dealing with dogs, women and children in particular, need to drop the level of their voices, as increasing it only incites a dog. Many of the attacks on children are caused by their hysterical reaction – screaming, running and waving their arms. Arguments and rows really upset and hype up a dog, or they can do just the opposite and make the dog worried and frightened.

BACK-UP HELP
While you are trying to sort out behavioural problems with your dog, it is highly advisable to enrol at a really good dog training club and to embark on a general obedience training course. The

whole family should be consistent in following the training methods, as this will ensure that the dog knows its place is in the human pack – right at the very bottom.

In the limited space available, I have decided to cover some of the most common problems which crop up; of these aggression is the biggest and most variable behavioural problem.

AGGRESSION

This section is divided into six sub-sections, but they all result from *one* human-generated problem – the dog has not been taught where to interact in the pack status. Even with one dog you have a 'pack' situation; with more than one dog, you have a more complex pack situation. Problems with aggression require a firm but steady restructuring of the dog's role within your human pack and of your role as Alpha Leader.

POSSESSION AGGRESSION

This may be with toys, kitchen, bed, food, a member of the family, or maybe with one of these or several. It is usually shown when the dog is 'in possession' of the desired object and then growls in resentment if any attempt is made to interfere. Before starting on correction, ensure that the aggreesive reaction is not due to a physical cause, e.g. an older dog in pain through arthritis, or becoming deaf with age and so easily startled when wakened up suddenly from a deep sleep.

REMEDIES
1. A dog training club to learn to control the dog.
2. Demote the dog's rank.
3. Attach a training lead (a light line several feet in length) and leave this on the dog until such time as you are no longer having a problem. If the dog is on the bed and growls as you approach, take the line, growl at the dog and say "No". Call the dog to you (use the lead if necessary), praise once the dog is at your side, and then command the dog to go to its bed area.
4. If the problem is with the food dish, you will probably need to enlist the help of a second person who will hold the lead for you. Give the command "Sit", and allow the dog to feed from the dish while you are holding it. When the dog is part-way through the meal (your partner controlling the dog if necessary), give the command "Sit", remove the dish and put it up out of reach. The dog, who is still sitting, is then praised. Use the same technique, feed the rest of the food to the dog while you still hold the dish. If the dog growls at you, growl "No", as your partner pulls the dog away. Then put the dish up, command "Sit", and as soon as the dog responds, praise, and go back to feeding.

When the dog is on the line, you have more control and so you can approach the dog with more authority and confidence. There is no hurry to take off the line; it is not doing the dog any harm and they soon become used to it and forget it is on.

PREDATORY AGGRESSION

This is where the dog chases anything moving. Border Collies are one of the worst offenders in this behaviour, because until the dog will chase sheep, it will not work sheep. However, the difference between working and chasing is control. If the first signs of this type of aggression had been stamped on when the pup was seven to eight weeks old, it would never have become a problem. At the first sign of a puppy stopping and watching something moving or going into a creep position, growl "No", call the dog and praise when at your side. If the behaviour takes root, it is more difficult to cure.

REMEDIES
1. Restore control and lower the dog's rank.
2. Enrol at a training club for basic control and obedience.
3. Attach a long training lead and every time the dog pulls away to chase, correct with a "No". Call the dog back to you (use the lead to enforce the command if necessary), and praise the dog once at your side.
4. As the dog sets off, sound a screech alarm or blow a horn, call the dog back (using the lead if necessary), and praise once at your side.

AGGRESSION OVER GROOMING

Again, a puppy should be accustomed to being handled from an early age (see Chapter One: A Puppy in your Family), so that this should not present problems. However, some dogs show resentment when being groomed and this is a situation which cannot be tolerated. Not only does it mean that you have lost your status as Alpha Leader, it will also cause serious problems when your dog has to be examined by a vet or when you have to give medication.

Problems can develop with grooming if a dog has not been handled from an early age. This Border Collie has been tied to a gate to give the owner greater control.

REMEDIES
1. Tie the dog up on a short lead to a table leg or a post, so you can groom in safety. Make the dog stand still, and give plenty of praise and encouragement.

AGGRESSION WITH OTHER DOGS

This is not so easy to stop and will require a great deal of hard work. Enlisting at a training club is essential in this programme of correction, as the dog will have to get used to working alongside other dogs in controlled circumstances.

REMEDIES
1. Encourage the dog to gain an interest in a toy or toys. When you are out exercising the dog in an open space, use the training lead so the dog has freedom and you have control. At the approach of another dog, call your dog to you, attract his attention with the toy, diverting his attention from the

other dog with the toy, and then give lots of praise. Gradually you should be able to call your dog back to you, command "Sit", and praise and give a tidbit. If your dog is distracted by the other dog, growl "No", and when you are back in control, praise, and move off in the opposite direction.

2. At the dog training club you will have dogs working in front of you, behind you and to your sides. The Instructor will help you to stop the dog paying attention to other dogs.

3. You will also need to restore your position as Alpha Leader, and in this situation, attention exercises are a valuable aid. If your dog becomes more interested in watching you, there will not be the same temptation to be distracted by everything else – including other dogs. This does not happen overnight, but the success will be directly proportional to the effort you put in.

Do not be in too much of a hurry to take off the training lead, and never hesitate to put it back on again if the dog's behaviour deteriorates.

AGGRESSION OVER PEOPLE
In this context, I am referring to the dog who tries to prevent people coming into or going out of the house.

REMEDIES
1. Attach the training lead, command "Sit", and ensure the dog stays in that position. You may need to enlist someone else's help to do this. Now, let the 'visitor' through the door, and as the person comes in, give them the dog's favourite toy and ask them to throw it to the dog.

2. If the problem is with people leaving, the toy is not used. Attach the dog to the training lead, give the command "Sit", ensuring the dog stays in position. If you cannot enlist the help of a friend, tie the dog to a firm object.

Do not forget the praise, even if the dog has been physically prevented from disobeying. Before long the dog should sit with little restraint and then the praise will be fully justified. The praise in the initial stages is to let the dog know that is the behaviour you want.

AGGRESSION TOWARDS ANOTHER DOG IN THE HOUSE
I have a mixed group of nine dogs and bitches, and we have no arguments – not even when the bitches are in season. Each dog knows exactly where it lies in the pack social system and because of this I can enjoy a carefree dog-ownership. Dogs have to respect each other as they have to respect their human family. The problem often starts when a young pup is introduced into a household where there is already another dog. The pup annoys the established dog (pups have to find out how far they can go), the older dog growls a reprimand, the puppy makes a loud scream and the owner rushes in, shouts at the older dog for bullying and picks up the pup for a cuddle. In fact, the pup was not hurt, but merely trying it on – and has won. The owner should have growled at the pup and removed the dog to its bed.

Dogs displaying place authority will rarely damage the other dog or dogs concerned. Border Collies, in particular, make amazingly loud, aggressive growls which sound deadly. They will often appear to snap, but ninety-nine per cent of the time it is merely a threat. Unless actual bodily harm is being inflicted, you should not interfere in these authority assertions. The loud, aggressive noises are just the one dog saying to the other: "Hey! you're over-stretching your place, back off!"

REMEDIES
1. The top dog (the established dog) must always be fed first, must have the lead put on and taken

off first, be allowed to get in the car first, and be praised first. You must follow pack law and support the top dog's position.

As the established dog gets older and infirm, or maybe is not really bothered about being the boss, the young upstart will try to gain supremacy. Sometimes, it is best to allow this to happen and to treat the younger dog as Boss. My oldest stud dog has never wanted to be the top dog, and his great, great grandson has taken over as the lead of the dogs which live outside. Inside, his mother, the oldest bitch, leads.

Bitches in whelp and in season can be a little moody, and normal friendly relationships can slip during these times. If this happens, keep the dogs apart, or, at least, never leave them alone together. After it is all over, the old, friendly relationship will be resumed. Unless you are really sure of your dogs, never leave them together on their own. It takes time to develop a totally reliable relationship.

LIVESTOCK CHASING
This is a form of predatory aggression but, on the whole, this problem is a great deal more serious. Again, if the dog had been educated correctly when young, the problem would not have arisen. Generally, if you have a sheep-chaser you must seek professional help. I spend a considerable amount of time teaching people and dogs to work sheep, but I also do a good deal of sheep aversion. I have also had considerable success with stopping confirmed sheep-chasers, but it is skilled work.

If you do not want your dog to work sheep, and this is the case for many Border Collie owners, then the puppy will need educating when quite young. When I am teaching, I always advise owners to prevent the dog seeing sheep until the day when we tackle this part of the training programme. As stated previously, each time a correction occurs, the less effective every subsequent correction will be. If the dog sees sheep regularly and nothing untoward occurs, then your set-up education is not going to be as successful. The best time to introduce your puppy to sheep is at four months when the Recall has been learnt, the meaning of "No" is fully understood, and the puppy has built up a good relationship with you.

If your dog is already chasing livestock, you will need to take more drastic action.

REMEDIES
1. Find someone who does sheep trialing in your area, explain exactly what you want to do and ask for their help. You need to equip yourself with a strong training lead (fairly light) and a half check-collar. You start with your dog roaming on the line, coming down a lane, a hedge, or a wall, so the dog cannot see where the sheep are. Then suddenly turn into where the sheep are positioned. The dog will almost certainly take some notice, so check as hard as you can, growl "No", and then pleasantly call the dog to you and give a reward.

I make no apologies for the harsher than necessary action, for, ideally, the dog wants a once-only correction to hammer the lesson home for the rest of its life. The dog usually identifies the sheep as being the cause for this harshness, for the attempt to make contact with them had unpleasant results, whereas when the dog returned to you, the greeting was pleasant.

2. If you have not used a screech alarm before, you could try using one. Walk around the field, with your dog on the training lead, pretending that you have not seen the sheep. Unless the dog pays the slightest attention to them (even eye contact), treat this as a normal, enjoyable walk in the country. If the dog takes any interest in the sheep, sound the screech alarm, and then call the dog back to you, giving lots of praise. If this is done correctly, I have never had to repeat the exercise,

and the dog has gone on to be totally reliable with livestock. It is worth the time and effort of setting up this training programme for the security that it gives.

URINATION
Much of the following also applies to defecating, and the same principles apply. There are many reasons why this problem may arise, and it is vital that the real cause is understood. It can be and often is, a combination of causes. In the wild, a dog would urinate anywhere except in its own bed area. So, as far as the dog is concerned, there is no built-in inhibition. The need to be clean in the house is just another example of the major modifications a dog has to make to its basic instincts in return for living in the human pack. It is interesting to note that the dog has to give up far more than we humans.

SUBMISSION URINATION
This is different from other problems with house-training, and, with help, the dog will grow out of it. Many sensitive young dogs have this problem and, on the whole, most will grow out of it by the time they are around nine months of age. In the wild, a dog will show willingness to co-operate with the higher-ranking members of the pack by urinating. The young dog is displaying the same type of behaviour and, unless harassed about it, these dogs make excellent adults, being extremely biddable. A number of my best workers have had this as an early inconvenience.

REMEDIES
These are based on building up confidence and helping to prevent the problem from arising.

1. Before any excitement, or any situation which is likely to produce this action, make sure the dog's bladder is empty.
2. Encourage the dog's confidence with plenty of outings and a variety of experiences.
3. If the dog does urinate, do not shout. You will destroy the dog's confidence, and dashing out to mop up the mess will only draw the dog's attention to it.
4. Often the dog will be completely unaware that it is doing it; it is a subconscious action.
5. Do not make an issue out of it.
6. Try to arrange for situations where you know the dog will urinate or defecate in a place where it doesn't matter, i.e. dog greeting you in the garden.
7. Try a diversion technique, such as throwing a toy as the dog comes to greet you. This helps to calm the dog. Generally, it happens as a result of excitement combined with slight apprehension. Remember, to a youngster, you appear very big and tall, which must be quite daunting.

This problem can be a nuisance but usually, with sympathetic handling, it disappears in a matter of months. I had a bitch who would always do it as soon as she was lifted on to the vet's table, even though she had relieved herself moments before going in. The vet understood but it was still embarrassing. However, it all stopped when the vet moved his table near the window. The bitch would be lifted up and immediately look out of the window. This diversion solved the problem.

OTHER CAUSES
There are eight other reasons why problems with being house-clean may arise. These will never solve themselves, and you must make an effort to sort out the problem. If the dog is young, your task will be easier. However, if the dog has got into a really bad habit, then, as with most established habits, I reckon that it takes twice as long to break it as the dog took to gain it. The

most common causes of the problem are as follows:

CAUSE 1. The dog has never been taught or fully understood what is required.

REMEDY
You need to teach the dog a trigger word; mine is "Hurry up". Go back to first lessons in house-training, taking the dog out at specific times, using the trigger word, and rewarding with lavish praise and a tidbit. This applies regardless of the age of the dog. Remember, you must stay with your dog until success has been achieved. Once the dog has really got the idea, you can probably stand at the door, telling the dog to "Hurry up" while in the relative warm and dry of the doorway. If an accident happens – it is *your* fault.

CAUSE 2. The dog is subjected to long periods of being shut in, so it is impossible to be clean. This applies to dogs kept by people who are out at work all day.

REMEDY
This should be very obvious: you need to find some way of letting the dog out more frequently. I have a dog-door on the back door, and on the odd occasion that we are away for a few hours, the dogs can go out and relieve themselves. If you are out all day, ask a neighbour or friend to call in. If necessary, put this arrangement on a financial footing, and then it is more likely to be reliable. You could provide a kennel and run in the garden for use when you are out. Whatever arrangements you make, the dog must have outside access.

CAUSE 3. Bad feeding regimes – meals are given at the wrong times, too much water or milk is given; milk is very prone to make a dog wet more.

REMEDY
Do not give any water or food after about 6pm at night, and certainly no milk. This will give the food and drink time to work through the dog's system before being shut up for the night. A change of diet might help in some situations.

CAUSE 4. Marking.

REMEDY
This requires strict observation and immediate correction applied by the Scruff Method (see Chapter Two: Early Education). The aim is to prevent the situations arising which stimulate the activity, and to discourage further problems by carefully cleaning down any areas which have been marked. Never use ammonia for cleaning a urination patch as this will only encourage the dog to go there again. A strong alum-in-water solution can be used for de-scenting, or you can use a strong salt solution or white vinegar. The dog must also be demoted to bottom rank.

CAUSE 5. The dog is upset and making a point.

REMEDY
This happens when a normally house-clean dog starts to mess, and it is usually in exactly the same spot. Something has occurred to upset the dog's security, such as a new baby in the house, a new dog in the household, or you may have changed the dog's routine. In order to solve the problem,

you need to find the underlying cause. It will require a modification on both sides to solve the problem, but in most cases, you need to restore confidence so the dog feels sure of its place in the household.

CAUSE 6. Hormone related.

REMEDY
Spayed bitches or older bitches will sometimes make quite large pools of wet, and they are usually completely unaware of doing it. One old bitch of mine only noticed what she had done when she leapt up and looked round at herself. If a bitch who is normally clean starts doing this, consult your vet. The problem can be controlled with medication.

CAUSE 7. The pattern to life is inconsistent.

REMEDY
Dogs need a structured pattern to their lives, and if you do not follow this basic rule then you can expect trouble. The dog has an amazingly good internal time clock, and by nature they are creatures of habit. Feeding at different times, letting out at different times, all lead to poor house-training.

CAUSE 8. The dog dislikes the surface allocated for urinating.

REMEDY
Bitches, in particular, can be very fussy about where they will relieve themselves. I once stayed with a friend in the city and I had to walk half a mile every time my bitch needed to relieve herself as she would only go on rough grass – even their lawn was not considered suitable. Sometimes a rescued dog is used to going on concrete and will not go on grass. Some bitches will never relieve themselves away from home without a great deal of encouragement. It is not easy to change a pattern, and it needs much sympathy and carefully re-training. Dogs are rarely as difficult.

RECALL PROBLEMS
This is not really a behavioural problem, but to a great number of people it actually becomes one. It is particularly difficult with re-homed dogs. The problem should be tackled at home first; a dog who will not come in the home, will not come anywhere. It is obvious that your dog does not have a very high opinion of you and has assumed higher ranking, so control training is the start, with enrolling at a good training club as a continuing activity.

REMEDIES
1. You need to carry out the programme of attention exercises and make your dog aware of you.
2. Equip yourself with a whistle and some tidbits, and keep them with you all the time. At any time during the day when you see your dog is coming towards you, give the whistle command (3-4 short peeps), and when the dog responds give a tidbit and praise. It does not matter that the dog was coming anyway, the main thing is that you have rewarded success.
3. Carry out the following series of training exercises that teach the recall.
   Blow 3-4 blasts on your whistle, for the first few times especially, as the dog will almost certainly come to see what you are doing. Do this in the house when there are no other distractions. When your dog responds, reward with a tidbit and praise. Repeat this twice more

during the day. At this stage, the dog will need to be quite close by when you attempt the exercise. The following day, repeat this procedure for two sessions of three recalls, and continue with this pattern for a further three days. On the fourth day, try the exercise when the dog is a little further away from you. These sessions need to be carried out in the house and garden area for two weeks before you try outside.

When trying the exercise outside, go to a completely new place so that the dog feels slightly unsure and does not want to lose sight of you. Make sure there are no distractions, give your whistle command, and then run off in the opposite direction. As soon as the dog catches up with you, reward with a tidbit and praise. Repeat this exercise twice more during the period of half an hour.

This programme should be built up gradually and used in conjunction with the attention exercises and the back-up classes at a dog training club. It may help if you go back to using a training lead, along with the whistle and tidbits, to enforce the command. It will take quite some time to achieve complete reliability in all situations, but in the end you should be back in control and will have gained the dog's respect for your authority.

CHEWING
A dog chews for one of six reasons, of which the most common is boredom.

1. Teething
2. Continuation habit
3. No education and lack of attention
4. Over-dependence
5. Boredom
6. Hyperactivity.

TEETHING
Puppies, like their human counterparts, suffer much discomfort at the time of cutting their milk teeth, and again, a short time later, when they cut their adult teeth, which is worse.

REMEDIES
1. When the youngster is teething, give plenty of juicy bones, raw-hide chews, and other such items. Do not give the puppy old shoes, for this can encourage a habit of moving on to shoes that you do not want to be chewed.
2. Every time your puppy takes something that is not allowed, encourage the pup to come to you, and then gently remove it from the puppy's mouth. Then, give a tidbit and one of the puppy's own toys. This prevents problems when you are teaching the Retrieve at a later date.

CHEWING FROM HABIT
Sometimes the habit of chewing grows stronger and does not pass off with puppyhood. It is also frequently associated with boredom. The dog must be educated, and if you have done a thorough job in the early stages, there should be no problems later on.

REMEDIES
1. Do not leave items unattended which the dog is likely to chew.
2. Cover surfaces that are likely to be chewed in an anti-chew solution (such as alum-in-water).
3. With a compulsive chewer, purchase an anti-chew solution (such as Bitter Apple), apply a little

on a tissue and place the tissue on the dog's tongue, holding it there for a few seconds. Then cover items which are attractive to the dog with the same solution (this will be ineffective if the tongue treatment has not been applied first).

BOREDOM CHEWING
This involves some re-organisation of your lifestyle in order to give your dog more stimulation.

REMEDIES
1. At least two walks a day with the opportunity of some free-running exercise.
2. Play a daily game with your dog – just five minutes play with a ball will be rewarding for the dog.
3. Organise one training session a day. This does not have to be very long – five to ten minutes is adequate.
4. If you are out at work all day, return at lunchtime to exercise and play with the dog.
5. Hire the services of a dog walker.
6. Leave the dog at a friend's or relative's house while you are out. Some kennels will care for dogs on a daily basis.
7. Try feeding the dog an hour before you go out (if you go out at a regular time). This gives the dog a chance to be clean, and hopefully, the dog will be more content to sleep the period away.

ATTENTION SEEKING
(See Barking)

HYPER-ACTIVITY
This applies to the dog who has been exercised so much that periods of inactivity are unacceptable. There is a tendency to think that if you give a Border Collie extensive exercise, the dog will then sleep all day and evening and cause no trouble. In fact, all you achieve is an ultra-fit dog with a very active brain who cannot settle for extended periods.

There is a current craze for feeding dogs on a high-protein diet. Farm dogs, in general, are fed on a lowish protein diet and they still carry out vast amounts of work for long periods without any problems. A pet dog does not need a high-protein diet, and neither do those dogs competing in Obedience, Working Trials, Flyball, or the majority of Agility dogs.

REMEDIES
1. Cut down the exercise, keep it low-key and give several short walks instead of one long one.
2. Check the level of protein you are feeding. If it is over twenty-one per cent, change the brand or use a lower protein feed.

OVER-DEPENDENCE
(See Barking)

BARKING
This is one of the most common causes of friction between neighbours, and in most cases it is caused by boredom. Once the barking habit has become well-established, it is extremely hard to break, for any reaction from the owner is a reward for the dog. If the owner returns, even to reprimand, the dog has won attention and has relieved the boredom, and in no time you are in a vicious circle.

This habit starts from early puppyhood, and it needs stopping immediately. Even if the pup is only seven weeks old you must reprimand for barking. In fact, much of the advice given on chewing applies equally to the barking dog. Shouting often encourages the dog to bark more, for it becomes a game: the dog barks, the owner barks, and so it goes on.

REMEDIES
1. Prevent the problem from arising by stopping your puppy from yapping or attention-seeking barking at the very first sign of it.
2. Teaching to bark on command helps, for then the dog will understand the command to cease.

CAR BARKERS
Dogs bark in cars for two main reasons, guarding or excitement. A barking dog is a good protector, but it takes a good deal of patience to educate the dog into carefully controlled guard barking, i.e. selective barking. If you have a car-barker, do not make the mistake of shouting reprimands.

REMEDIES
1. Enrol at a dog training club in order to establish control. The dog can then be commanded to be quiet.
2. A water-pistol is quite a useful aid, particularly for the dog who barks while you are in motion. You will need to enlist the help of a passenger to squirt it at the dog the moment the barking starts.
3. Fit a cage in the car so the dog has a safe, secure place to travel.
4. If the problem only occurs when the dog knows a walk is in the offing, command the dog to be quiet. If the dog does not obey, just drive the car home and take the dog out. It does not take a bright dog long to realise that barking results in no walk.

PHONE BARKERS
This is a very common problem. The phone rings and you dash to answer it. This looks like fun, and in no time the dog is dashing to beat you to the phone or barks as soon as it starts to ring.

REMEDIES
1. Stop running to answer the phone.
2. Put the dog in the Down-stay (fastening if necessary).
3. Pre-arrange phone calls with a friend, and ensure the dog is fastened when the phone is due to ring. Walk slowly to the phone and pretend to answer it (unless you wish to pay your friend's phone bill!). You can make a tape-recording of the phone ringing.
4. Squirt a water-pistol the moment the dog starts barking.
5. Throw a toy to distract the dog.
6. Step up the control training.

ATTENTION BARKERS
This is when the dog barks to gain your attention, and any reaction from you serves as a reward. The solution is to react by doing something which does not reward the dog.

REMEDIES
1. Get up and walk out of the room as soon as the barking starts, shutting the door on the dog.
2. The Scruff Method (see Chapter Two: Early Education) can sometimes work, but not always.

Some dogs will even be glad of this attention. This also applies to using a water-pistol; it usually works on the more sensitive dogs.
3. Command the dog to go to bed and lie down, only rewarding when the dog is quiet.

OVER-DEPENDENCY
We teach our dogs to develop this problem by never leaving them on their own for periods.

REMEDIES
1. A programme of independence needs to be embarked upon (see 33).

DIGGING

Border Collies are notorious for this activity, and they really get a great deal of pleasure from it. Maybe it is possible to leave a small area in the garden where this activity can be carried out. Insist that the dog does keep to it, and then each night, push the soil back in place so the 'digging pit' is ready for the next day. However, most people will not want to go to such lengths and so training must be given. Just occasionally, the gruff growling "No" will work, especially if it occurs the very first time the dog is caught digging, but it usually requires more strenuous training.

REMEDIES
1. A hosepipe directed at the dog will often work. Do not give any command or shout at the dog. Pretend that you had nothing to do with that jet of water, and then divert the dog's attention.
2. If caused by boredom, then follow the suggestions relating to chewing caused by boredom.
3. Cordon off an area, concrete/paving-stone the area, and let the dog have that section as its part of the garden when not being supervised.
4. The Scruff method of punishment can sometimes work (see Chapter Two: Early Education).

FAECES EATING

In the wild dogs would often carry out this activity, so a domesticated dog needs to learn that this is unacceptable behaviour.

REMEDIES
1. The first, and most obvious, is that all dog mess should be cleaned up immediately, thus preventing the problem from arising. Bitches often develop the habit, as it is a natural thing for them to clean up after their puppies. Sometimes the situation arises when one of the pups is kept and she continues with this activity. Again, the answer is to clean up.
2. Some brands of dog food include an inhibitor to discourage this activity.
3. It could be caused by worm infestation or a mineral deficiency. Ask your vet for advice.
4. More roughage in the diet might help (e.g. bran without sugar added).
5. The screech alarm or hosepipe can be employed if you catch the dog in the act, but it is much easier to clean it up.

JUMPING UP

This is more of a nuisance, as most people do not appreciate being pounced on by a dog, regardless of whether the feet are clean or dirty. This behavioural trait is a typical example of a problem which starts off in puppyhood. The tiny puppy is so small that everyone bends down to give a cuddle and make a fuss of the new arrival. The puppy becomes used to this type of contact, and so jumping up is not so much learnt as taught. A puppy which is never allowed to start jumping up will never need correcting. It is particularly hard on the half-grown youngster who is suddenly corrected for something which has previously been encouraged – but it does happen frequently.

REMEDIES
1. Teach the dog to Sit on command and only praise in the Sit position.
2. Use the water-pistol technique, and when you shoot, say nothing. As soon as the dog sits, give plenty of praise.
3. For persistent offenders, hold their front legs firmly, and when the dog starts to struggle to get down, continue to hold on firmly, ignoring the dog. Hold for a short period, and when the dog gets down, give the command to Sit and then praise. This is usually very effective.
4. You can try using the screech alarm, but I prefer to use it outside and only keep it in reserve. The more it is used, the less effective it becomes.
5. A puff device has been manufactured which, when squeezed, sends out a puff of unpleasant but safe powder.

JUMPING UP AT VISITORS
This is a most annoying problem, and a sure way of losing friends!

REMEDIES
1. When the visitors arrive, shut the dog away first and let the visitors in. When they have sat down, allow the dog to come in. The dog must be sitting before any fuss and attention is given.
2. You could keep a toy at the door, and when the visitor comes in they give the dog the toy, and tell the dog to go to bed.

This form of excessive excitement takes a while to break. It is a matter of working on the dog gradually to achieve control. Do not expect overnight success – this is a longterm project.

OVER-EXCITEMENT ON RETURNING HOME
Some dogs get really get very excited when the family returns home, and this can develop into a problem.

REMEDIES
1. Walk in, saying nothing to the dog. Walk into the kitchen and put on a pan of water and wait for it to boil, then ask the dog to Sit and praise. Putting the water on can be replaced by any small task; the idea is to be occupied and to let the dog see you are occupied. After this short wait, the dog has calmed down and will greet you without excessive enthusiasm!

MOUNTING
This type of behaviour is not only annoying but also embarrassing. Again there is no need for it, for it should never have started. I have three dogs and seven bitches, and even when the bitches are in season we do not have this problem from the dogs. *The key is never to allow it to start.* However, if it has, correction will be necessary.

REMEDIES
1. Work on establishing your position as Alpha Leader, and make it clear that this type of behaviour is not acceptable. The dog must be demoted and privileges withdrawn.

2. Make a note of the situations which start this pattern off in order to prevent it starting. In most cases, this means keeping the dog calm and not allowing him to become over-excited.

3. Try distracting the dog by giving a toy or a raw-hide chew.

4. Take the dog by the thick hair at the side of the cheek, and shake very firmly, growling "No" in your gruffest voice. Command the dog to Sit, and then praise.

5. Castration does sometimes help with this problem, but success is not guaranteed. Ask your vet for advice.

SOCIAL SNIFFING

Dogs live in a world of scents, and they are more important to the dog than any other stimulus. Watch two dogs greet each other and, straightaway, each goes through a ritual of sniffing. As far as the dog is concerned, humans are merely an extension of their canine pack and so they also get sniffed. As with all problems, do not allow it to develop and then it never needs stopping. A youngster only needs correcting with a gentle, gruff "No". This form of correction should also be sufficient if an older dog forgets himself. If the dog does not respond, you have a control problem which needs working on. Dogs should not be allowed to sniff the smells along a walk. Teach the dog that, unfortunately, in the human pack, this is not acceptable. Not only is it a nuisance, but disease can also be transmitted by this activity. Do not allow your male dog to mark *any place at all* on his walk.

REMEDIES

Use the same remedies that apply to Mounting problems.

Chapter Four

FEEDING

There are as many ways of feeding dogs as there are dog/human partnerships, and no two people feed exactly the same way. It is therefore preferable for one person in the household to be responsible for this aspect of caring for the dog or dogs. Dietary requirements may vary according to different situations, and they also need to be adjusted throughout the various phases of the dog's life.

PRINCIPLES OF FEEDING
It is necessary to understand the principles behind feeding to be able to understand what is needed to suit each individual. Factors to take into consideration include:

1. Palatability to the dog.
2. Age of the dog.
3. Health of the dog.
4. Food storage arrangements.
5. The digestive ability of the dog in relation to the food.
6. The dog's metabolism.
7. Quantity.
8. Work-load (or otherwise) of the dog.

Once you have found a good diet to suit your dog, do not start swapping and changing, as it does a dog no good. Storage facilities are an important consideration. These must be dry, air-tight and rodent/dog safe. Fresh meat cannot be kept out of a freezer for very long, whereas canned meat can be stored anywhere that is relatively cool. If you have good-size container bins for dry feed, you can buy in bulk; otherwise you will have to buy in small quantities. Dogs and mice are expert at finding their way into food – it is amazing how small a hole a mouse needs.

A dog's food needs change during the period of growth and development, and then the mature dog's needs vary according to work-load and age. Metabolism varies from dog to dog, even between littermates. Some dogs have a natural tendency to put on weight whereas others will always stay as thin as a rake. The breed is not thought of as being fussy over food, but many Border Collies are so work-oriented that food is a low priority, and they will only eat sufficient to keep body and soul together. These dogs may start off as really good feeders in early puppyhood, and then from around three to four months old, as their horizons broaden, they seem to lose interest in food.

With dogs who are working, food can vary in quality and protein content almost on a daily basis, depending upon what they are doing. Food quantity also needs varying, and this is dependent on the weather. In extremes of temperature – in intense heat or in the freezing cold – the dog requires more food than when the weather is more moderate. I would double the quantity at these times. Young, growing dogs require twice to three times as much as an adult, and it needs to be good-quality food with plenty of protein. Poor-quality food is a waste of money and, in the long run, you do not save money. Many of the expensive diets only require small quantities, whereas the cheaper foods require a much larger quantity to be fed.

Dogs appreciate a slight change of diet rather than feeding exactly the same, year in year out. However, this does not mean you need to make drastic changes; just add some leftover gravy or vegetable water, and that is enough to make the food taste a little different. I always add a little hot water in order to serve the food warm, unless it is a period of very hot weather. I do not think it is good idea to serve food totally dry, so that the dog needs to drink large quantities of water. Mix water or gravy with the food at the time, and you will find the dog is not desperately thirsty after eating, and you are providing a more natural meal.

It is not only age and work-load which affects feeding regimes. These also need to be varied when a bitch is about to come into season and be mated, when a bitch is in whelp, and when she is nursing a litter.

QUANTITY TO FEED
This is probably the most difficult part of it all, for every dog is different and also at different times they require varying amounts – so how can you resolve the problem? If the dog is a puppy then you start by asking the breeder how much she/he advises. The best indication that you are feeding the correct amount is to observe the dog's motions. The motion should be properly formed and firm; any sloppiness may indicate that too much has been fed, so you will need to cut back.

Sometimes you find a dog with a poor digestive system, particularly so with poorly reared dogs, and they need a much larger amount than the system can tolerate. The only solution is feed two or three feeds a day to make up the required quantity. This is particularly so with a young puppy, and this regime may need to be continued well into adulthood.

Some food can be too rich for a particular dog, so adjustments may need to be made. In the case of a puppy, always find out what the breeder has been feeding and make sure that you have a supply of it before you take ownership of the puppy. After worming, especially in the first three months of a puppy's life, the digestive system may be upset. So, after you have wormed the puppy/dog, just cut back on the food quantity for twenty-four hours. Always listen to what nature is telling you; a wise person will never ignore the warning signs.

THE OBESE DOG
There are two ways of tackling this situation. The first is to use a diet manufactured specifically for obese dogs; there are a number of good brands on the market. The other method is the old-fashioned one which I tend to prefer. It requires feeding bran which is sugar-free. If the dog is on 8oz of food a day, feed only 4oz of the normal rations and add 4oz of bran. Bran has little nutritional value so it does not result in the dog gaining weight. However, it bulks up the food and the dog feels full and is therefore contented. Continue with this until the dog is nearly back to the correct weight, and then change the proportions to 6oz of normal rations and 2oz of bran. Obviously this can be adjusted according to the individual dog's requirements.

Bran is an amazing substance and it can correct apparently conflicting problems. If a dog has a digestive upset and is suffering from diarrhoea, bran will invariably correct the problem. Conversely, if a dog is suffering from constipation, this can also be corrected by using bran. Bran is a digestive balancer; it is a completely natural product which is free from chemicals.

TRAVELLING

It does not matter how good a traveller the dog is, it is far better to starve for twelve hours before travelling, and to wait thirty to forty-five minutes after the journey before feeding again. Make sure fresh water is available in the period before the journey.

OLDER DOGS

An older dog needs two smaller feeds a day of a good protein diet, and this is where the top-quality complete diets fit in well, for you feed smaller quantities. There are now several good diets by the leading dog food firms on the market for dogs in this age group.

WORKING DOGS

Dogs who are in continuous work are easier to feed than those who perform high activity work, but only on odd occasions. This includes dogs competing in Working Trials and other similar competitive activities where the 6ft scale and the 9ft long jump have to be tackled, and the dog needs an active mind for tracking.

   The night before the trial, I would only feed the dog one-third of the normal rations. On the night after the trial has been completed, I would again feed one-third of normal rations. Then for the next week I would feed the standard quantity, plus one-third extra. This means that by the end of the week the dog has made up the short-fall with a little extra to compensate for the increase work-load. It is totally unfair, and possibly disastrous to ask a dog to work on a full stomach, particularly if jumping is involved. When a dog has been under the stress of competition, their whole system is still tense and so a light diet is beneficial and more easily digested.

FUSSY EATERS

If the puppy/dog is really playing you up over food, then you must stop the habit immediately. Give the dog a few minutes to eat the food, and if it is not consumed within that time, take the bowl away. I have never known a dog wilfully starve to death, but I have known many who have been so pampered that they became neurotic about their food. Do not fall into this trap, regardless of the 'agonised' looks your dog gives you. Border Collies are second to none in the art of play-acting!

Chapter Five

HEALTH CARE

KNOWING YOUR DOG

Fortunately, the Border Collie is among the most hardy of breeds, and your dog should, hopefully, live a long and healthy life. However, we, as owners, have responsibility for our dogs' physical well-being, and so it is important to understand what constitutes a healthy dog. In fact, the signs of a healthy dog can vary slightly from one dog to the next, and even among littermates, so it is vital you get to know and be sensitive to each of your dogs.

GENERAL OBSERVATION
Observation of general condition and behaviour is the best way to judge a dog's state of health. Your Border Collie should be lively and alert, with no signs of listlessness, dullness, crying, or constantly trying to get comfortable.

BREATH: Your dog's breath should be fresh and sweet smelling, and the teeth should be free of excessive discolouring – an early indicator of problems. Bad breath is a sign of many disorders, such as worm infestation or digestive problems, and warrants further investigation.

TONGUE: The tongue should be a healthy pink colour; it should not be furred over.

NOSE: The coldness and dampness of a dog's nose also varies from dog to dog, and so if you have more than one dog, it is important to know each of your dogs' norms. The nose should not be cracked, and there should be no evidence of a discharge. A warm nose is acceptable for short periods. However, if it remains warm for prolonged periods, particularly if you notice this in conjunction with other symptoms, something is likely to be amiss and you should consult your vet.

EYES: The eyes should be bright, alert and shining, with the correct membrane colouring. Beware of any sign of eyes discharging or eyes flickering.

EARS: These should be clean and sweet-smelling, with no evidence of discharge or discomfort.

COAT: The coat should be sleek, flat and glossy. When it is brushed backwards, it should fall immediately back into place. The coat should not appear dull or appear to stand out from the body.

UNDER-TAIL: No evidence of swelling or redness; no hair gummed up with faeces.

LEGS AND FEET: Your dog should move easily with no suggestion of pain or lameness. The dog should not flinch when legs and feet are gently felt, and there should be no evidence of excessive heat. The pads should not be cracked or appear to be sore.

STOMACH: No evidence of pain, distension or hardness.

URINE: This should be of normal quantity and colour.

FAECES: These should be correctly formed and of a normal colour, with no oppressive smell. Watch out for constipation, diarrhoea, blood-staining or mucus.

APPETITE: Your dog should have a normal, healthy appetite – not excessively greedy, nor excessively lacking in interest.

ADDITIONAL CHECKS
MEMBRANE COLORATION: Make sure that you are familiar with the colour of the membranes of the eye and mouth. These should be a pale salmon-pink colour at rest; they will be slightly darker when the dog is excited. They should neither be too pale nor too deeply coloured, and so it is important to know what is normal for your dog. You can do this by gently exposing the gums, and by very gently exposing the lining surrounding the actual eye, which is hidden from easy view by facial skin.

TEMPERATURE: Choose a time when your dog is relaxed and well, and then take the dog's temperature over a period of several days. This is done via the rectum, using a stubby bulb thermometer. Like humans, dogs can have slightly differing normal temperatures. The temperature ties up with the colour of the membranes, these being a deeper colour if the temperature is raised, in proportion to the degree of temperature. The normal average temperature for a dog is 101.3 degrees Fahrenheit, although it can be within the range of 100 to 102.5 degrees (38.3-39.2 degrees Centigrade) and give no cause for concern.

PULSE-RATE: This does not vary from one dog to another, but it does vary according to age, and so a constant update of this needs to be kept. To find the pulse-rate, your dog must be in a relaxed mood, placed in the standing position. You may need someone to hold the dog still. When the dog is steady, slip your hand on the inside of the hindleg, and with your finger, gently locate the major vein which runs down just behind the front part of the inside hindleg. Once this is located, wait for a steady pulse vibration and record these, preferably for a minute, otherwise half a minute and double it. The pulse-rate is usually somewhere between 60 and 120, hence the need to know what is the norm for each dog.

KEEPING RECORDS
It is a good idea to have your dog's details recorded. This is for two reasons:
1. If you have more than one dog, a written record will ensure that you do not get mixed up or panic in an emergency
2. If you are not available at the time of trouble, someone else can refer to the records for the vet.

CONSULTING YOUR VET
Never hesitate to take your dog to the vet if you think help is needed. The bill from the vet pales

If tartar accumulates on your dog's teeth, you will need to clean them. This can be done using a toothbrush and a canine toothpaste; it should present no problems if your dog is used to being handled.

Liquid medicine should be given using a syringe. This procedure should be practised so that there is no struggle when the dog actually needs medication.

into insignificance compared with the suffering you could inflict on your dog through lack of expert attention. If your dog becomes ill during the night, such as blood coming from the mouth or rectum, or problems arising with a whelping bitch, it is plainly negligent to delay until morning, just because the bill might be higher.

ALTERNATIVE TREATMENT
If I need glasses, I go to an optician; if I have a high fever, I consult the doctor; if I have sprained a muscle, I need a physiotherapist. It is the same with an animal – different conditions require different areas of expertise. If your dog requires specialised help, your vet may be able to refer you to the relevant practitioner. Alternatively, you can seek information from those involved in your breed – at dog shows, sheepdog trials, or any other competitive event.

HERBALIST
Herbalists treat diseases and other problems by using the appropriate herbs. If you want to use the services of a herbalist, make sure you go to someone who is well qualified – there are good and bad practitioners in all professions.

HOMOEOPATHIST
With more people becoming disenchanted with conventional medicine, homoeopathy is now becoming more widely recognised as an alternative method of treatment. If you are lucky, your vet may be qualified to practise both conventional medicine and homoeopathy. If not, most veterinary practices will be able to put you in touch with a homoeopathist.

Very simply, homoeopathy works on using a substance which, when tested on a healthy individual, produces the symptoms. An infinitesimal dilute potency is used and it activates the body to correct the problem, a little like the conventional vaccinations. The difference between conventional and homoeopathy/herbal treatments is that the latter are completely natural, whereas the conventional rely on chemicals – even natural cures used in conventional treatments are reproduced chemically.

Treatment involves using a potency, and you might as well use a different remedy altogether if you do not use the correct potency. For example: Urtica urens (stinging nettle), is used to control the bitch's milk secretion: Urtica urens 6c decreases the milk supply after the bitch has finished rearing the pups, but a bitch with insufficient milk requires Urtica urens 30c. If these two potencies are mixed, it can result in a drastic situation, i.e. dried up milk supply for the tiny puppies. Potency 6c is available from many chemists, but any other potency usually has to be obtained from an homoeopathic pharmacy.

Much care must be taken with these remedies. They should not be stored in extreme temperatures, nor alongside strongly scented substances. Do not swap bottles about; keep each one to its own container, and always use a spoon when handling the tablets.

To administer, humans suck the tablets under the tongue, which is obviously not applicable to the dog. You will therefore need to crush the tablet between two spoons and place the powder on the tongue. This should be administered half an hour before food/drink, and nothing else should be given for half an hour afterwards. Obviously, with some first-aid situations this is not always possible, but if you can, try to keep to this timing, if possible.

I have referred to all homoeopathic remedies by their Latin names, as well as by the names that are generally used in retail outlets, and so there should be no difficulty in obtaining the remedies required. (See Appendices for major supplier in the USA.)

CHIROPRACTOR

These practitioners treat mainly spinal problems, which encompass lameness, back and neck problems and sciatica pains. Working sheepdogs, Agility dogs, Flyball competitors and any active running or jumping dogs are liable to a great deal of wear and tear on the spine. If you have a dog who competes in one of these activities, you will prolong its active working life by having the dog frequently checked over. It is tragic how many working dogs have to be retired early because of lameness/back problems.

The spine is a series of vertebrae, with the major nerve running through the centre, which are somewhat flexible in their movement. If any vertebra is slightly misplaced, the nerve is also misplaced, and the vertebrae above and below are also misaligned – possibly extending to several both above and below the offending problem vertebra. You can deal with this problem in two ways. One method is to push the offending vertebra into place, which uses a certain amount of force and does not correct the other misplaced ones. The alternative and preferable method is to start right at the head and slowly work downwards, realigning each vertebra in turn. This means that by the time the offending vertebra is reached, it is almost back into position by being gradually manoeuvred into place as the ones above it are corrected, and so it is a much more gentle and complete operation. The sooner this is done after the problem arises, the better will be the response to treatment, for the longer the vertebra is out of place, the more damage is being done. Before starting a course of treatment, ask the chiropractor which method is used and opt for the method which treats the whole spine – not just the damaged part.

ACUPUNCTURE

This type of treatment can be used for injuries and other complaints. Basically, it works on the principle of transferring energy from areas with a large amount of energy to other areas of the body which have little. Many successes have been claimed in both humans and animals. Needles are sometimes used on animals, but it is more usual, with animals, to use the electronic pointer. Like all the disciplines, I feel that it has a place and should not be disregarded. Like the other forms of alternative treatment, no chemicals are used.

BACH AND GEM REMEDIES

These work a little like homoeopathic treatment, and are mainly used for the treatment of emotional problems. It has proved to be particularly effective in treating fear.

SUMMARY

A homoeopathist/herbalist usually has an eighty-five per cent success rate, and this is invariably on subjects which could not be cured by conventional medicine. This is an extremely high rate for these treatments, which are becoming better-known by the general public.

Many conventional practitioners will claim that the success rate of alternative treatments can be attributed to mind over matter. However, in the case of the dog, this does not apply, and so any success can justifiably be claimed for the method of treatment. It is important to bear in mind that a vet does not always produce a cure with the first, second or even the third treatment tried. If you are having your dog treated by an alternative method and it is not working, do as you would with your conventional vet – go back, so that another approach may be tried

I have studied homoeopathy, and I use standard homoeopathic remedies as needed, and I have found them invaluable over the years. However, you must never take a chance. If you have the slightest doubt regarding your dog's health, consult your vet (conventional) or homeopathic vet, who has to be both a qualified conventional and homeopathic practitioner.

COMMON AILMENTS AND CONDITIONS

ANAL GLANDS

The anal glands, situated on either side of the anus, occasionally become too full, causing discomfort to the dog. This becomes evident when you see your dog rubbing its backside on the ground. The glands can be emptied, either by a vet or by an experienced dog handler. Fortunately, this is not a common problem with Border Collies, but many years ago, a number of my dogs seemed to be suffering from this problem. I quickly realised that the more often the glands were emptied, the more frequently they needed emptying – it was a vicious circle.

I soon came to the conclusion that prevention was better than cure, and correct feeding would prevent the condition from arising. Roughage in the diet is required. This should take the form of natural roughage, such as natural bran, without sugar in it. Homoeopathically, there is quite a lot which can be done for this condition, but in extreme cases, it would be advisable to consult a homeopathic vet.

ARTHRITIS

In many working dogs, especially those involved in shepherding, agility and working trials, arthritis is likely to occur in later life. As yet, a cure has not been found, and so treatment consists of help to relieve pain and inflammation, and to keep the joints mobile. I have found that Denes Greenleaf tablets (or a mixture of dandelion and nettles) certainly seem to help stiffness, Hypericum 6c (St John's-wort) is a straight pain-killer which even allergic dogs can tolerate, and for the inflammation, Bryonia 6c (wild hops) and Rhus Tox 6c (Rhus toxiodendron – poison ivy) given daily are extremely beneficial.

If you do not want to use these remedies, an aspirin tablet is recommended by most vets. This has the effect of dulling the pain. This human medication is safe for dogs, but beware of many similar products used for humans, which are unsuitable for dogs. Cod-liver oil sometimes helps to ease the stiffness, as does Oil of Primrose. Cortisone injections can be beneficial, but they carry many side-effects and so careful consideration must be given to their use. There are now a number of anti-inflammatory drugs which your vet can prescribe, but they often contain stomach irritants which many dogs cannot tolerate.

Try and prevent the dog from doing things which aggravate the condition, such as jumping, twisting and turning, and any uphill work. An arthritic dog can still do a little work for many years if you miss those three activities out, and this makes all the difference to the dog, who will still feel needed and useful.

BITES AND STINGS

If your dog is stung by a wasp, treat externally with Hypercal (Hypericum and Calendula mixture) ointment; for internal stings, use Ledum (Marsh tea). If you have a bee-keeper living nearby, give your dog a single dose of Apis Mel 200c (Apis Mellifica – honey bee) at the very start to the season, and this will protect the dog for the season. For immediate action, use Hypercal ointment and Ledum. If there is swelling of the area or it appears red and sore, give Apis Mel. Calamine lotion and, if needed, antihistamine cream is recommended. For nettle stings apply Dermidex or a similar treatment. There are several excellent sprays on the market which ease the pain of stings. Your pharmacist will advise. If your dog is stung by a bee, do not attempt to remove the sting with tweezers as this spreads the venom. It is better to use your fingernails.

Snake bites need very urgent attention. If you suspect your dog has been bitten by a poisonous snake, contact your vet immediately.

BURNS

Dogs do not often get burnt, but whether the burn is superficial or a little more serious, the quicker something is put on to the area, the quicker it will heal. Immediate attention will mean little or no blistering results. Hypercal (Hypericum and Calendula) placed on the affected area immediately will often be all that is needed. In severe cases give immediate first-aid, and seek professional help quickly.

COLIC

This condition is rare in the Border Collie. However, if your dog appears to be prone to it, try to avoid the problem arising by feeding carbohydrates and proteins separately. Colocynthis (Bitter cucumber) or Nux Vom 6c (poison nut) can help a mild attack. If colic is caused by over-eating, try Nux Vom; if wind is the cause, try Carbo Veg 6c (Carbo vegetabilis – vegetable charcoal); if it is the result of teething, try Chamomilla 6c (German chamomile).

CRACKED PADS

Working dogs are used to working on rough surfaces, and so Border Collies rarely have trouble with cracked pads. However, if your dog has this problem, it is usually the result of a lack of fat in the diet. If this is the cause, then all that is necessary is a teaspoon of sunflower oil (cooking variety) placed on the food. The pad can be softened with a little Neats Foot oil or Olive oil. Black Pudding is also a useful dietary addition.

Sweaty feet can usually be cleared up by bathing in salt water, dry off and use athlete's foot powder.

DIARRHOEA

This is probably the most frequent problem that dog owners encounter. In effect, diarrhoea is the body warning that something is wrong, and so you really need to find out what has caused it. With puppies, diarrhoea is often the result of over-feeding, but it can also be caused by a bad worm problem, too high a protein diet, by food that is too rich food or the inability to digest milk. It could also be a symptom of a far more serious condition such as parvovirus.

The best solution is to cut out all food for twenty-four hours and give boiled water only. Dosing with kaolin may help to settle the stomach. Indian Brandee (rhubarb tinct, capsicum tinct) obtainable from many chemists, is good for young dogs. The correct dosage is one teaspoon in water three times daily, reducing to twice daily, and then once a day. If the problem has been caused by over-eating, try Nux Vom 6c. If your dog is not showing improvement within twenty-four hours, then professional help is needed.

EARS

Border Collies do not usually suffer from ear problems, but some do seem to be more prone to them than others. The following ear powder can be made up at a good chemist:
15 gm Boric Acid Powder (Boracic Acid)
15 gm Zinc Oxide Powder
4 gm Iodoform Powder (Tri-Idomethane).

These must be mixed very thoroughly. To treat your dog, use a cotton wool bud, dip it into the powder, knock off the excess and then carefully apply inside the ear. Check from time to time that the ears smell sweet; if not, a couple of days treatment with the powder will usually work. If the dog has a lot of wax in the ears, clean this out with Eardrex (one third Arachis oil, one third

Almond oil, one third Rectified Camphor oil) or Waxol (Docusate sodium 0.5 per cent in water-miscible base). There are a number of other treatments available – ask your vet for advice.

Obviously if there is not a vast improvement within three to four days then professional help is required.

EYES

Like feet, eyes are subject to summer problems, such as dust, and the occasional grass seed which must be removed very quickly. Border Collies are play dogs and can from time to time get knocked in the eye. If it is only a slight knock, then the eye will be merely a little bloodshot. The eye can be eased by using Eyebright (Euphrasia), available from a homoeopathic pharmacy, or there is a superb lotion you can make up yourself. Collect the chickweed plant when it is in flower, place it into a container, cover with boiling water, cover and allow to steep for 24 hours, strain off the liquid and put into ice-cube containers and freeze. This lotion doesn't last too long and the flowering season is short. Whenever you need it you merely take a cube out of the freezer and thaw it out. It is useful for all animals and humans.

HEAT STROKE

Border Collies are very active, and therefore it is not uncommon for a dog to suffer from over-heating. This sometimes happens on the trial field in the hot sun. Competitors who tie their dogs up between events are advised to ensure they are in the shade, and preferably in a quiet place where they cannot be stimulated by seeing other dogs competing. Sometimes a dog will lie in the sun and become over-heated, so it is always wise to ensure that summer quarters are shaded. A dog suffering from heat stroke must be immersed in cold water as quickly as possible.

Give Aconitum 6c (Aconitum napellus – Monk's Hood) every ten minutes until an improvement shows and then increase the time interval. Wet towels draped over the dog can prevent over-heating. My dogs, who are very thick-coated, are shaved off completely smooth for the summer, and I am sure this extends their lives.

KENNEL COUGH

This is an extremely infectious disease, typified by a dry, harsh, hacking type of cough, which is dreaded by anyone who has heard it. The disease can vary from area to area, and like all viruses there seem to be many different mutations of it. It is spread through contact with other dogs, and therefore all dogs who attend training clubs or shows, or go to boarding kennels are vulnerable. If you have more than one dog in the household, it will spread to all the dogs, unless you are able to isolate the affected dog immediately.

The intensity of the disease is very variable but it can be life-threatening, particularly among young and old dogs. There is vaccination available, and most boarding kennels will insist your dog is vaccinated against the disease. The homoeopathic remedy is to give four to six garlic tablets a day, and if the cough is troublesome you can administer Benylyn Expectorant, which is a human cough mixture, and is available over the counter from most pharmacists. It contains Diphenhydramine hydrochloride, Ammonium chloride, Sodium citrate and Menthol. However, if the cough continues to get worse after forty-eight hours, consult your vet. The quicker you start treatment – even with the garlic tablets – the better the response will be.

MANGE

It is unusual to come across mange in Border Collies. There are several types of this skin complaint and it can be very difficult to clear up. Ask your vet for a suitable treatment. If available, Benzyl Benzoate is extremely effective in simple cases.

MOUTH ULCERS

Just occasionally this will occur. If it is more than a 'one off', you should be finding out the cause. Sponge the linings of the mouth with diluted Hydrogen Peroxide in accordance with the instructions on the bottle.

NAILS

For split nails give Silica 6c (Silicea – pureflint). For infection in the nail bed, give one capful of Stergene (or one level teaspoon of Potassium permanganate) to a standard washing-up bowl containing water; soak the foot in this so that the dewclaw is just covered for several minutes; repeat twice daily for two weeks and allow the foot to dry off naturally. If the pads go soft, stop the treatment until they harden. A diet of chicken and dog biscuits, plus two cubes of jelly will help to harden the nails.

NERVOUS PROBLEMS

I have found that homoeopathic remedies are very useful when treating dogs who have nervous problems. Alternatively, you can consult your vet, who will be able to prescribe some form of tranquilliser. Homoeopathic remedies include:

Dog which is hyped-up over bitch in season: Agnus castus 6c (the Chaste tree) three times a day for a week.

Fireworks (start a fortnight before): Borax 3c (Borate of sodium) and 4 drops of Rock Rose (Bach flower remedies), given three times daily.

Fear of vet: Phos 200c, 1 hour before visit.

Fighting amongst other dogs within household: Chamomilla 200c.

Homesickness: 2 doses of Ignatia 200c (St Ignatius Bean), 2 hours apart.

Attention-seeking, e.g. soiling bed and other activities: 1 dose Pulsatilla 200c (wind flower), and if not completely effective, 3 days later one dose of Platinum 200c.

Barking: Phos 30c.

Chewing: Pulsatilla 30c, or the pet shop will stock products which may be suitable.

Upset by new things: Argentum nitricum 12c (Nitrate of silver). Single dose for a few weeks.

Timidness: Kalium Phosphoricum 12c (Phosphate of potassium).

NETTLE RASH

For the first-timer owner, this condition is really alarming. The dog will suddenly – literally within seconds – become covered in huge lumps all over the body. This a reaction to some substance, often nettles (hence its name), but it can be caused by many other things, such as the salt in the sea air. Sometimes it is a reaction to some food or chemical within the food. Treatment is usually easy, a few doses of Apis Mel 3x every 10/20 minutes and cold compress of a solution of a cupful of vinegar to a litre of cold water. For a few days keep your dog on a scant diet, and even a little kaolin in the food can be beneficial. However, if this condition occurs on a more regular basis, you must find out what the cause is and eradicate it.

PARASITES
ROUNDWORMS

All puppies need to have the programme outlined in the puppy section for worming, and thereafter, the use of garlic and the control of fleas and lice, means they should not present too much of a problem. Your vet will prescribe a suitable treatment. There are homoeopathic remedies for worms; all homoeopathic remedies work on the basis of 'non-killing' and likewise with worms. The homoeopathic method is to strengthen the intestinal tract so that the worms are excreted. For Roundworms give Abrotanum 3c (Southernwood) for seven days.

TAPEWORMS
Give Cina 4c (Cinchona officinaliis – Peruvian bark) for 7 days. There are occasions when tapeworms are not completely cleared up and a product such as Droncit (or a tapeworm treatment that covers all tapeworms – some only cover a few of the species that dogs can get) will be needed to get on top of them.

FLEAS
Fleas are a host for tapeworm and the dog can infect itself by catching the flea and eating it, so external parasites must be kept under control. Herbal flea collars are really extremely effective and do work and are completely non-chemical and safe. If you have a flea problem and a cat in the house, then that is probably the cause of the trouble. If you keep the cat free of fleas, the dogs will be free. There are herbal flea collars for cats; they can be safely left on the cat all the time and need renewing about every four to five months. It is important to remember that if you have a flea problem, then bedding and carpets need regular attention, otherwise the eggs will hatch and start the cycle over again.

TICKS
Ticks are usually picked up in sheep-grazing areas or where there is a local population of deer. A weekly spray with an anti-parasitic spray will give your dog protection, but make sure you ask your vet to recommend a spray which will act as a tick repellant, as many brands only act on fleas. If your dog does pick up a tick, you will need to remove it. Do not make the mistake of trying to pull the tick from your dog's body. This will leave the tick's mouth-piece embedded in the dog's skin, which will result in an infection. The best method is to apply some cotton-wool soaked in a mild antiseptic, and this will force the tick to release its hold.

LYME DISEASE
This is a well-known and dreaded problem in North America, and in recent times it has come across the Atlantic to Britain. In North America the disease has spread extremely rapidly, but, to date, its progress in Britain has been relatively slow, and it seems to be confined to an area around the New Forest. The problem with the disease is that it is so hard to diagnose, as it mimics other problems. It is carried by a tick, and several animals are known to be carriers; the deer is a common denominator in both Continents. It is not only dogs that are affected – cats, horses, cows, sheep, goats and even humans can catch the disease. In North America a vaccination against Lyme Disease is now available, but this is not currently the case in the UK.

Symptoms include elevated temperature, depression, loss of appetite, eye problems, lameness in one or more legs, joints swelling, encephalitis, disorders of the kidneys, arthritis and stiffness in the joints. An affected dog may have one or several symptoms. Although it can be treated, it does seem to re-occur. Antibiotic treatment has to be of a high dosage and must be continued for some time; so vaccination appears to be the most effective method of treatment.

POOR APPETITE
Border Collies are, on the whole, a greedy breed and they feed well. However, there is a

percentage who do not put food at the top of their priorities and they can certainly cause a great deal of worry. To start with, it is a rare dog who will get close to starvation. The poor feeder will eat just sufficient, but the owner becomes over-anxious if the dog looks lean. This can become a very emotive issue, and the more you make an issue out of it with this type of dog, the greater the problem becomes. The best solution is to find something which the dog will enjoy and eat and then start to feed it in very small quantities – just fractionally smaller than the dog would eat of its own free will – and give it no more. You then alter the balance, the dog is hungry and would like to eat more, you praise the dog for eating that up and wait for the next day, continuing with this programme for a couple of weeks.

Once you have got the dog feeding well and wanting more, just increase the ration slightly, but if, at any stage, the dog starts leaving food, reduce the ration. Ignore the "I don't want it", remove the dish and go about your normal duties. Sometimes the dog's main objection is merely to the type of food being offered. Most dogs can be easily persuaded to eat cat food, so start off with that and gradually introduce dog food. Never make an issue out of it.

In the case of some bitches, poor feeding is hormone-related. If the bitch also has a false pregnancy, however slight, then you will probably find that treating for a false pregnancy will also sort out the eating problem.

TORSION/BLOAT
This is a condition which some breeds are prone to. Fortunately, it rarely occurs with Border Collies. The signs are the stomach beginning to swell, and *you must call the vet without delay, as surgery is essential if you are to save the dog's life*. Prevention is better than cure, and if you are unlucky enough to have a dog who is prone to this condition you should avoid feeding one large meal a day. Try feeding two or three smaller meals a day. It has also been suggested that protein and carbohydrate should be fed separately. Do not exercise the dog after a meal, and wet the food, if possible, to avoid the food expanding once digested.

TRAVEL SICKNESS
I always used to believe that this condition was caused by the owner not taking sufficient care to accustom the puppy to travelling. However, there seem to be a few Border Collies who have been trained correctly from the start, but still seem to be prone to the problem. Further enquiries have revealed that either the sire or dam has also had the problem, so it is possible that there may be a genetic link.

Travel sickness varies from pacing the area, to dribbling, whining, to vomiting. Your vet can prescribe travel sickness tablets and these are usually extremely effective. If you want to use a homoeopathic remedy, try Nux Vom 3c (Nux vomica – poison nut) for restlessness/pacing, Cocculus 6c (Indian cockle) for vomiting/salivating.

In each case give a tablet half an hour before the journey and then repeat at hourly intervals (if a long journey). After a couple of months you will probably find that they can be stopped for the return journey and then gradually stopped altogether.

SPRAINS
Any dog can suffer from this injury, but it is obviously more likely to occur in a working dog. The best treatment is rest – for at least a month. It is counter-productive to give a pain-reliever, such as aspirin, as this will encourage the dog to be more active. Cold water bandages help; your pet store or your vet may suggest an embrocation, which can be rubbed into the affected area. If the joint is swollen, then Bryonia 6c; if the tendon is inflamed and is worse for rest and better with gentle

movement, then Rhus Tox 30c three times a day; Arnica 3c (Leopard's Bane) and Rhos Tox 8c for a straight strain; cold compresses help stimulate the blood and so help heal the area; if the ligament is torn Ruta Grav 4c can be beneficial.

WHELPING/HORMONAL PROBLEMS
(See Chapter Eight: Breeding Border Collies)

WOUNDS
The first task is to clean the area thoroughly. For this use salt-water, or a few crystals of potassium permanganate diluted in cooled, boiled water. Calendula ointment (Calendula officinalis – Marigold) is a brilliant promoter of cell growth and is my main wound treatment. However, as it promotes cell growth, I do not use it if there is infection in the wound as it seals it in.
Puncture/bite wounds: If sensitive and warm to the touch, use Hepar Sul 6c (Hepar sulphuris calcareum – calcium sulphide); if sensitive and cool, use Ledum 6c (Marsh tea).
For shock after an operation: Arnica 30c every four hours for three days.
Infected wounds – if leaky and difficult to heal: Staphysagria 6c (Stavesacre); if not quite such a long-term problem, the Black Jack – Ichthammol (Ammonium ichthosulphonate or Ammonium sulphoichthyolate) is useful for drawing splinters and the like and for all slightly infected wounds.

HEREDITARY DISEASES

Like all breeds, the Border Collie has a couple of inherited conditions which all owners should be aware of. No matter how careful you are, there is no guarantee that you will not either breed or purchase a dog which is affected by an inherited condition. This is not necessarily due to a lack of vigilance. I know of one breeder who bred twelve generations that were free of Collie Eye Anomaly (CEA) and the breeding stock were always tested. Then, like a bolt from the blue the condition cropped up in her breeding line. No blame can be attached to the breeder, but it shows that responsible owners and breeders must never relax their efforts to eliminate inherited conditions.

Before purchasing stock, ask the breeder if they have certification for the parents. Farmers usually test for eye diseases, but not for hip dysplasia. However, a dog who has had a hard working life and at the age of five-plus is still sound, can be reckoned to be free of this hereditary problem.

COLLIE EYE ANOMALY (CEA)
Unfortunately, this condition appears to be on the increase among Border Collies, and it is by far the worst of the inherited conditions that can affect this breed. All my puppies are tested for CEA between six and seven weeks, and by far the majority of breeders are now doing this, as the condition can be picked up at an early stage by a specialised eye vet. Puppies who are not tested clear should be sold with endorsed papers, which should be lodged with the national Kennel Club and the ISDS.

CEA appears to be caused by a simple recessive gene, and for every case that is found, there are approximately eighteen cases that go undetected. It can show up in the full grading from very minor blindness to compete blindness. This condition can be present at six weeks of age and then it may have disappeared by two years of age – hence the need to test at a very early age. If there is a puppy in the litter with CEA, then the littermates have a three in four chance of carrying it – even if they are tested free on examination.

PROGRESSIVE RETINAL ATROPHY (PRA)

The breed first known to be affected by this condition, nick-named night blindness, was the Irish Setter. However, this was found to be Generalised PRA, whereas the Border Collie is affected by Centralised PRA. This condition was very prevalent at one time, but the incidence has been reduced following the ISDS scheme of voluntary eye testing for a reduced registration fee.

PRA is thought to be caused by a dominant gene, but its mode of inheritance is far from simple, and is still not fully understood. In some cases the problem does not surface until the dog is eight years old, which, in the case of breeding stock, means that extensive damage can be done before the condition is detected. Affected dogs will suffer from total blindness. It is advisable to have your stock tested at two years, three years, and every couple of years after that.

HIP DYSPLASIA (HD)

Breeding stock should be tested for HD, and breeders should provide certification of both parents when you are buying a puppy. The mode of inheritance of this condition is very complex, but the incidence has certainly been reduced by using animals with low hip scores for breeding. However, two low-scored parents can occasionally produce a puppy with a high hip score.

HD produces a malformation of the hip ball-and-socket joint, so that the two do not fit closely together. The result is varying forms of lameness, from very mild to the dog being a complete cripple. Puppies who are born with a slight problem can aggravate the condition by being overweight or by being over-exercised.

In Britain dogs should be tested at twelve months of age; in the US the tests are carried out at twenty-four months for certification, and earlier for preliminary evaluation.

CEROID LIPOFUSCINOSIS (CL)

Also known as Storage Disease, CL affects the nerve cells. It is thought to be inherited by a simple recessive gene. It was first seen in the early 1980s, and to date only twenty cases have been recorded.

CL is a disease which in animals does not become evident until the animal is eighteen months of age. The signs are unusual apprehension, lack of concentration, abnormal gait, rage and hyperactivity. The dog may begin to show some or all of these. CL needs to be kept strictly in perspective. Considering the large number of dogs born, it appears to be very rare indeed.

THE AGEING BORDER COLLIE

This is a subject that few people consider sufficiently, because with age comes a whole new set of problems, especially for the working Border Collie who is very likely to be suffering from arthritis and therefore slow, sometimes grumpy and often in pain. In his book, *The Dog's Mind*, Bruce Fogle writes that an older dog's brain is twenty-five per cent lighter than a younger one– I can well believe that. The whole system slows down and clogs up.

Older dogs may revert to puppy behaviour, they may become stubborn and seem to think that the rules which have applied all their lives now no longer apply to them. They lose concentration and can only do activities for a short period of time. A command takes much longer to register before they can act on the command. This is not being stubborn, it just takes longer to get to the brain and for the brain to send out the signal to the appropriate part of the body. They get muddled more easily and forget more easily.   As far as the owner is concerned, tolerance must be the order of the day. Most people are aware that the internal organs wear out, but stiffness and arthritis make it difficult for the dog to carry out your wishes. Hearing or sight or both, can become weaker and so sudden movements towards the old dog (a child running past quickly) might make the dog over-react and snap. They might even be slow to recognise the person, or pain might make the dog irritable and therefore a little more prone to snap out.

All these things must be considered and allowed for. Make a new place for the old dog to lie in. This should be a haven, away from the main stream of activity so that the dog can be quiet and more secure, as well as being warm and out of draughts. If your dog has been a faithful companion or a tireless worker for you, you owe a debt by being considerate and showing understanding in the twilight years.

It is better to feed two smaller feeds in the day rather than one main meal, and use an easily assimilated, good-quality, crunchy complete diet, such as those provided by the leading manufacturers. This maybe expensive, but the dog does not require so much bulk. Keep a check on the teeth; they get worn down and can give rise to problems and abscesses.

There can be problems with the hard-working Border Collie once old age forces retirement. If a dog wants to work, it is mental cruelty if you deny this instinct. It would be awful to leave your old faithful worker at home feeling unwanted and neglected. It is far better to take the dog with you, and allocate a few easy, effortless tasks. A very limited work-load will not do much physical harm, and it will considerably improve the dog's mental state. Most dedicated dogs would prefer to suffer a little pain rather than be left at home. Even in infirmity, the quality of life must be balanced.

Chapter Six

THE BREED STANDARD

The Breed Standard, as it is laid down, is a reasonable assessment of a true, working Border Collie. However, the problem comes in interpretation of the wording. So few people involved in the show world of Border Collies really understand what a true Border Collie is. This seems to me to be a great pity, for it was the working Border Collie which drew them to the breed in the first instance. This is one of the very few breeds which is fashioned from the job of work it does – from conformation and colouring to facial markings and the way the ears are held.

THE BRITISH BREED STANDARD

GENERAL APPEARANCE
Well proportioned, smooth outline showing quality, gracefulness and perfect balance, combined with sufficient substance to give impression of endurance. Any tendency to coarseness or weediness undesirable.

Ma Biche of Whenway working sheep. 'Polly', owned by Bruce and Sheena Kilsby, is one of the very few show-bred Border Collies who have qualified in the ISDS/KC Working Test. Border Collies should be bred so that they are physically capable of working, even if this function is not required.

Cories Lara at Norvellyne: A well-known breed and trial winner.

Nij Vyas.

Lienheath So Smart: A highly successful competitor in Agility. The Border Collie's natural athleticism makes it ideally suited to this discipline.

CHARACTERISTICS
Tenacious, hard-working sheepdog, of great tractability.

TEMPERAMENT
Keen, alert, responsive and intelligent. Neither nervous nor aggressive.

HEAD AND SKULL
Skull fairly broad, occiput not pronounced. Cheeks not full or rounded. Muzzle, tapering to nose, moderately short and strong. Skull and foreface approximately equal in length. Stop very distinct. Nose black, except in brown or chocolate colour when it may be brown, in blues nose should be slate colour. Nostrils well developed.

EYES
Set wide apart, oval shaped, of moderate size, brown in colour except in merles where one or part of one or both may be blue. Expression mild, keen, alert and intelligent.

EARS
Medium size and texture, set well apart. Carried erect or semi-erect and sensitive in use.

MOUTH
Teeth and jaws strong with a perfect, regular and complete scissor bite, i.e. upper teeth closely overlapping lower teeth and set square to the jaws.

NECK
Of good length, strong and muscular, slightly arched and broadening to shoulders.

FOREQUARTERS
Front legs parallel when viewed from front, pasterns slightly sloping when viewed from the side. Bone strong but not heavy. Shoulders well laid back, elbows close to body.

BODY
Athletic in appearance, ribs well sprung, chest deep and rather broad, loins deep and muscular, but not tucked up. Body slightly longer than height at shoulder.

HINDQUARTERS
Broad, muscular in profile sloping gracefully to set on of tail. Thighs long, deep and muscular with well turned stifles and strong well let down hocks. From hock to ground, hindlegs well boned and parallel when viewed from rear.

FEET
Oval in shape, pads deep, strong and sound, toes arched and close together. Nails short and strong.

TAIL
Moderately long, the bone reaching at least to hock, set on low, well furnished and with an upward swirl towards the end, completing graceful contour and balance of dog. Tail may be raised in excitement, never carried over back.

GAIT/MOVEMENT
Free, smooth and tireless, with minimum lift of feet, conveying impression of ability to move with great stealth and speed.

COAT
Two varieties: 1) Moderately long; 2) Smooth. In both, topcoat dense and medium textured, undercoat soft and dense giving good weather resistance. In moderately long coat variety, abundant coat forms mane, breeching and brush. On face, ears, forelegs (except for feather), hindlegs from hock to ground, hair should be short and smooth.

COLOUR
Variety of colours permissible. White should never predominate.

SIZE
Ideal height: dogs 53cms (21 inches); bitches: slightly less.

FAULTS
Any departure from the foregoing points should be considered a fault and the seriousness with which the fault should be regarded should be in exact proportion to its degree.

NOTE
Male animals should have two apparently normal testicles fully descended into the scrotum.

Reproduced by kind permission of the English Kennel Club.

In both Canada and America full registration of the Border Collie has been vetoed by a vote.

OFFICIAL STANDARD OF AMERICAN REGISTRIES

All three 'official' Border Collie Registries in the United States, the North American Sheep Dog Society (NASDS), the American International Border Collie Association (AIBC) and the American Border Collie Association (ABCA) are opposed to a written conformation standard. Their only standard is WORKING ABILITY.

SIZE
Large, Medium or Small.

COAT
Rough, Medium or Smooth.

COLOUR
All colours accepted.

EARS
Prick, Semi prick or Drop.

THE AMERICAN BORDER COLLIE STANDARD

Approved June 1980 by the Border Collie Club of America (Amended January 1985)

GENERAL APPEARANCE
The general appearance of the Border Collie is that of a medium-sized, alert, well-proportioned dog, with the strength, stamina and agility to endure long periods of active duty in its designated task as a working stockdog. The double coat may be rough or smooth and the colouring offers a wide variety of individuality in each specimen. Soundness of structure and movement, and freedom from exaggeration of coat and type are of utmost importance in a working breed such as the Border Collie. Dogs should be presented in their natural, untrimmed coats and be in a hard, working condition, without excess finish.

CHARACTERISTICS
The Border Collie is necessarily extremely intelligent and very responsive to training for a wide variety of tasks. A well bred dog will instinctively circle wide around livestock with no training, will control it with its keen and intent gaze or "eye", seeming to hypnotise its charges, and is ready for instant action should they try to break away. The breed exhibits a remarkable dexterity in stopping, turning, and dropping and possesses unusual speed and stamina for a dog of its size.

HEAD
Skull basically box-like in shape, broader between the ears, giving ample brain room, and narrowing slightly to the eyes. Muzzle moderately blunt, with length slightly less than or equal to the length of the skull. Stop moderate. Lips tight and clean. Nose is black, except in the case of red or red merle coloured dogs, which have a matching brown nose.

TEETH
Strong, well developed, meeting in a perfect, regular scissors bite, with upper teeth closely overlapping but touching the lower teeth and set squarely in the jaw. Teeth broken by accident not to be penalized.

EYES
Fairly large, oval shaped, and set well apart at an almost imperceptible slant. Colour may be brown, blue or amber. Preferred colour is medium brown, except in the cases of blue or blue merle coloured dogs, where one or both eyes may be blue, and red or red merle dogs, which may have amber eyes. The expression should be mild, yet keen, alert and intelligent.

EARS
Should be of medium size, set well apart, tapering to a rounded tip, and sensitive in their use. Ear carriage varies from drop to prick, however, usually carried from one quarter to three quarters erect, with the upper portion of the ear breaking forward to protect the entrance of the ear canal from sleet, snow and insects.

NECK
Of good length, strong and muscular, broadening into the shoulders, and carried level with the back in motion. When standing at attention the head and neck is raised alertly.

FOREQUARTERS
The shoulders are long and well angulated, meeting the upper arm at a right angle, with the elbows close to and parallel with the body. The forelegs are well boned and straight when viewed from the front or side. Pasterns show a slight slope when viewed from the side.

BODY
Body moderately long, ribs well sprung, tapering to a deep and moderately broad chest. Back strong and level in its topline, loins broad and deep with a slight muscular arch. In profile the croup slopes slightly to the set on the tail.

HINDQUARTERS
The hind legs are longer than the forelegs and set on wide. Thighs long, broad and well muscled, and well bent stifles, and strong, well let down hocks, showing no signs of weakness. Viewed from behind the hind legs should be parallel from the hocks to the ground.

FEET
Oval in shape, with well arched toes and pads tough enough for heavy field work. Nails short and strong. Feet and legs are judged by having the dog walk into a natural, unposed stance.

TAIL
Long, reaching at least to the hock joint, set on low and carried low, in line with the curve of the hind legs, swirling upwards slightly at the tip. The tail may be raised in excitement but not carried over the back.

COAT
Double, with a dense, medium textured topcoat, and a short, soft undercoat, making weather-resisting protection. Rough coats are moderately long maybe wavy or slightly curly with more abundant coat to form a mane, breeching brush and feathering on the backs of the forelegs. Hair short on the face, fronts of the forelegs and from the hocks down. Smooth coated dogs have a short, dense, smooth topcoat over the entire body.

COLOURS
A variety of colours are permissible. Black and white most common, followed by tri-colour (black, white and tan, with black body retained). Other colours are blue and white (any shade of grey), blue merle and white (body colour light red or fawn with broken patches of chocolate), or mottled (black or red with white markings that are speckled or spotted, causing a roan effect). Tan markings on the face and legs, as in the tri-colour, are permissible in all of these colours. White markings common and desirable as: full or partial ring around the neck, tail tip, blaze up the face, forechest, and belly. Predominantly white individuals do occur, but are undesirable, as sheep do not respect a white dog as much as they do a dark one, mistaking it for another sheep.

SIZE
Height varies from 17 to 26 inches at the withers, weight from 25 to 65 pounds; however, most dogs average 19 to 22 inches, bitches 18 to 21 inches. Average weight is 30 to 50 pounds. Size varies with type of work. No preference providing bone and musculature is that of a dog quick on its feet.

MOVEMENT
Action should be free, smooth and tireless, with a minimum lift to the feet, conveying the impression of ability to move with great stealth. The action viewed from the front should be straightforward and true, the feet tracking comparatively close together at the ground, without weakness at shoulders, elbows or pasterns. Viewed from behind the quarters thrust with strength and flexibility, with the hind legs straight, tracking comparatively close together at the ground. Any tendency toward stiltiness, cow or bow hocks in motion or weakness at the shoulders or pasterns is a serious fault.

FAULTS
Exaggerated type, long-narrow head, tail carried above the back, excessively long and abundant coat, stilty or unsound movement, coarseness, over-refinement, predominately white colour, shyness, lack of angulation, any deviation which would adversely affect the working ability of the dog.

DISQUALIFICATIONS
Bob-tail; any dog showing evidence of being cross-bred with any other breed; any dog which attacks or attempts to attack the judge, its handler, or another dog, albino colouring, overshot or undershot jaw, lameness, deafness or blindness.

NOTE
Male animals should have two apparently normal testicles fully descended into the scrotum.

ANALYSIS AND INTERPRETATION

THE HEAD
I have never seen a really good working Border Collie who has not had a good head. In fact the shape of the head, and in particular the skull, is one of the criteria on which I select my dogs for work. I have been told by veterans in the breed that the width of the skull is proportional to biddability and power. You might just get away with a bitch who has a narrow width of skull, but a dog of this type would be useless for work. A dog with a broad skull will probably cope, providing he has a strong-minded handler, but a bitch with a very broad skull would probably be too 'pig-headed' to be of use.

As in all breeds, the male's skull is broader than the female's, but both must be in proportion to their gender. It is also important to bear in mind that the brain is housed within the skull area, and a Border Collie without a brain is no better than a Toy dog. So, when picking a puppy or even an older dog, the skull has tremendous significance. A definite stop between the foreface and the skull is necessary, dividing the head into two equal parts. The occiput, located on the back of the skull, should not be too pronounced. Snipy muzzles seem to be a common fault with Border Collies. I am not too keen on this, but it does not influence the dog's ability to work and so it has a lower 'rating' for me than many other faults.

EYE COLOUR
There seems to be a growing obsession regarding eye colour, and dark eyes are becoming increasingly prevalent in the breed. However, this preference is based on a basic misunderstanding regarding the working sheepdog. A great deal of the inner thoughts and feelings pass through the eye – it never ceases to amaze me how an organ full of tissue and fluid can relay so much

The male should have a slightly broader skull than the female, and there should be a definite stop between the foreface and the skull.

The female's head is slightly finer and more feminine than the male head.

information. But it is not only humans who read the dog's eyes; so do the sheep, and therefore dogs with the wrong eye colour are not so easily understood by sheep.

The ideal eye for a Border Collie is medium-sized, and a nice, warm brown colour – not too dark and not too pale. Light eyes, which are frequently seen today, often come down through John Thomas' Don (108889), and these have a very hard, harsh look. The eyes in tri-colours are of a paler shade than in black and whites. Reds often have quite a yellowish eye, but it varies between many shades of yellow and even green, and blue dogs usually have a slate colour eye. Merles and black and whites can have wall eyes, also known as china or blue eyes. This eye colouring is more common in the merle than in black and whites, but on average, one black and white in every hundred will carry the colour, with some strains producing a greater percentage than others.

The very dark eye, now becoming fashionable, fails to convey the dog's inner thoughts and they are virtually unreadable. This applies equally to Border Collies working in Obedience or Working Trials, and even to the companion dog living in the house, for when you have a good relationship with your dog, you will find that you can understand much from looking into the eyes.

Many years ago I had a little bitch who, on one particular day, kept coming up to me and just looking at me with an odd look in her eyes. As the day wore on, I was sure it was a look of need. She showed no sign whatsoever that she was in anything but tip-top health, but, nevertheless, the look in those eyes got to me. I took her to evening surgery and told my vet that I thought the bitch was very ill. He replied that she looked in great shape, but he knew me well enough to appreciate that I would not be concerned without reason.

He spent some time examining her, and suddenly exclaimed that he knew what the problem was – and if I had I left her another two hours she would have been dead. She was suffering from

Wall eyes, also known as china eyes, are more common in blue merles, but, on average, one black and white in every one hundred will carry the colour.

internal haemorrhaging, a complaint with ninety-five per cent mortality because it had no external signs. If this bitch had failed to convey her feelings through her eyes (which were the correct colour), she would have been dead. She was the finest working sheep bitch I have ever had, and was the foundation for the next six generations in my breeding programme. So, again, I make the point: listen to nature – she knows what colour the eyes should be.

NOSE AND NOSTRILS
These should be a good size, so that the dog, when working extremely hard, can intake sufficient air.

FACIAL MARKINGS
Your own sheep soon get to know dogs for what they are worth, and so in this instance I am referring to working strange sheep. Over the years I have noticed that sheep have less respect for a dog with too much white on the face, and they are frightened by a dog with too little white (a dark face). Sheep understand a balance between the black and white, and, ideally, neither colour should predominate.

EARS
Ear carriage also affects the sheep's behaviour. Dogs with pricked/upright ears seem to frighten the sheep, whereas dogs with low, dropped ears tend to be ignored. It is the tipped ear carriage that the sheep react to best. A dark-faced, prick-eared dog can experience problems in a trial situation when trying to work unfamiliar sheep.

Border Collies with low-set ears (left) can be ignored by sheep. However, dogs with erect ear carriage (right) tend to frighten sheep.

It is the tipped ear carriage that sheep are most likely to react to, as shown by one of Maxine Netherway's Border Collies at work in Ontario. Ranier Leipscher.

BODY AND SUBSTANCE

Why do breeders think that big bone is good? Disastrous is the word I would use for it. A dog who needs to run for miles, going up hills, jumping the scale, competing at flyball etc., will be severely penalised by heavy bone, becoming much more tired than the medium-boned dog.

Another very common fault with Border Collies is poor front shoulders. I do not think this has too drastic an influence on dogs running flat lands, but it needs to be watched in dogs required to run hilly land. Those involved in working trials, agility or flyball also need to take note, for poor shoulders will mean early retirement for your dog.

The length of body should be slightly longer than it is high at the point of the shoulder blades. The important word is 'slightly' – the Border Collie should not be like the sausage-shaped Dachshund! There seems to be an increase in the number of dogs with short legs – some could even get stranded running over a large rock – and an extreme length of coupling. Coupling is the piece of spine which goes between the last rib and the points of the pelvic girdle (hips). Balance a length of paper between two supports and then balance another piece twice as long – that will show you the effect on a dog. Because Border Collies twist and turn a great deal, they are more prone to back problems later in maturity than other breeds . However, the poor dogs with very long couplings will suffer long before they ever reach maturity. I assess the coupling as being the width of my hand-span plus a little extra – about seven inches in total.

HINDQUARTERS

The hindquarters are, for me, of equal importance to the head. The hindquarters are the Border Collie's power pack. The dogs who have a long second thigh seem to be more agile, and they do not seem to have such a tendency to back problems. For a very active dog (and this applies especially to Agility, Working Trial and Flyball competitors), the second thigh length should be an important consideration.

A working Border Collie needs to have a balance between speed and endurance, and the pastern

The smooth-coated Border Collie has no fringe hair on either its front or its rear legs.

joint is a deciding factor in this. I like to see the pastern joint about four and a half inches in height. Obviously, the size of the Border Collie has to be taken into consideration, but this is about the normal Border Collie dimension. The longer hock joint gives quick bursts of speed, whereas the shorter hock produces endurance.

FEET

Feet in both back and front legs are important, as without good feet a dog cannot travel far. They should not be large saucer-like structures; they should be oval, deep, strong, muscular, and well-arched. The hair should be left untrimmed between the pads as it acts as a cushion and prevents slipping.

I always remove dewclaws on the hind legs, for they are big and tend to catch and cause problems. I do not remove dewclaws on the front legs as I find that Border Collies make a great deal of use of them.

The working Border Collie, and those competing in Agility, has to twist and turn a great deal, and therefore correct conformation is essential in order to avoid back problems.

The tan marking on a tricolour are very variable, both in the extent and in the colour density.

Blue merle Border Collies are more likely to have wall eyes.

The red colouring on a red and white Collie is very variable in shade.

White Border Collies are not common, and there are those who believe that the sheep do not react to them. However, this dog is a good worker.

TAIL

The tail is the dog's rudder and balancer. It should reach down to the hock, although this is easier in a higher-hocked dog, and so hock joint length should be taken into consideration. There is a common belief that a Border Collie who flies its tail (carries it high) is no use. I have my own feelings on this, but it is certainly true to say that the Border Collie who flies its tail on seeing sheep or when working sheep is at fault. The novice dog will often get excited and will momentarily fly the tail, but most of the time I want to see it kept low. When meeting other dogs in a show ring situation some dogs will fly their tail, especially males, as it asserts their dominance and these situations are often exciting and provoking.

COAT

Coat is another obsession of the show breeder, and again it comes from a failure to understand the real Border Collie. I fail to see how a good, natural, well-looked-after, working coat can be any less attractive than the very heavy coats often seen in beauty competitions. Heavy-coated dogs are absolutely miserable in hot weather, and in the winter snow-balls can get tangled up in the dense fur. Obviously, not all Border Collies competing in the beauty ring have this wealth of coat, but it is on the increase.

COLOUR

There are few predominantly white Border Collies who work sheep; I suspect that this is mainly because farmers do not keep them. Personally, I do not mind how the white is distributed, and I do not object to half or all-white faces, although for real preference I do prefer the slightly darker colours.

To me the true Border Collie is the loveliest creature in the world, not only for its work but also for its aesthetic beauty.

Chapter Seven

PRINCIPLES OF GENETICS

UNDERSTANDING GENETICS

Planning a litter is never an easy job, but it is possible to make it a little simpler, and the results more reliable, by understanding and employing the science of genetics. This is the only way to remove chance from the equation, and with a good working knowledge of the breed and genetics, it is possible to be able to predict with ninety-five per cent certainty what a litter will be like. To the breeder, this knowledge is essential. However, many people seem to be wary of the subject and fear it is too complex for a basic understanding – but this is not the case. In my time as a teacher, I taught the principles of genetics to young children, and when these were presented in a straightforward manner, there was never a problem in acquiring rudimentary knowledge.

Genetics is a little like using a barometer to forecast the weather. You do not need to understand all the words and numbers – it is the way the needle moves up and down that is the key. With regard to genetics, you do not need to know all the technical terms, you just need to know how to apply the rules.

DOMINANTS AND RECESSIVES

Genetics is the relationship between dominant and recessive characteristics, and although much of it is applicable to most breeds, some individual factors are relevant to a particular breed. For example, hind dewclaws are dominant in some breeds but they are recessive in Border Collies.

The dominant factor is the stronger of the two. For example, the colour black is a stronger colour than blue; consequently black is dominant and blue is recessive. Geneticists give letters to represent the characteristics. Most accept those introduced by Clarence Little, so I will use those in this context. The dominant characteristic has an upper-case letter and the recessive always has a lower-case letter, which keeps matters straightforward.

Symbols applicable to Border Collies are:

Characteristic	Symbol	Dominant	Recessive
Black	B	*	
Red	b		*
Tricolour	$a^t a^t$		*
Merle	M	*	
Blue	d		*
Black/Tan	a^y		*

Brown Eyes	Ir	*	
Wall Eyes	w		*
Classical White Markings	S^i		
All White	S^w		
Semi-Pricked Ears	H^a	*	
Pricked Ears	h		*
Sensitivity to Sound	NN	*	
Sensitivity to Touch	SS	*	
Ticking (mottling)	TT	*	

The dominant characteristics are those which appear most frequently. Life was developed on dominants, and I do not believe in mating two recessive factors together if I can possibly help it – such as mating tricolour to tricolour. Recessive characteristics are often weaker. The pale pigmentation on the pads of red and white Border Collies and yellow Labrador Retrievers often gives these dogs a great deal of discomfort when working in nettles, which does not affect the black pigmented pads of these breeds. Mating blue merle to blue merle produces a lethal factor: pups are born either blind, deaf, or white – or any combination of these three conditions. These examples show why we need to understand genetics and to have a good knowledge of the breed.

A sire passes on to his offspring two choices for each characteristic, and the female does likewise. This means that when the sperm meets the egg, four choices of each characteristic meet, but only one of these from the male and one from the female make the offspring. You can therefore have one of three combinations for each characteristic, which are as follows:

1. Two dominant genes
2. Two recessive genes
3. One dominant and one recessive.

Both dominants and recessives are of equal importance in opposing ways. Every characteristic – eye colour, coat colour, ear carriage, working 'eye' – is a genetic factor in two parts, one you see, and one you cannot see. Recessive factors are more difficult to get to grips with, especially as they can lie dormant for many generations. There is a vital message that you must understand: *for every dog you see with a particular fault, there are eighteen other dogs which carry that fault without showing it.* The hereditary eye diseases fall into this category.

Hardy Weiberg produced a law to prove this:

81% BB + 18% Bb + 1%bb

BB dogs do not show the recessive characteristic and do not have it.
Bb dogs do not show the recessive characteristic but are carrying it.
bb dogs show the recessive characteristic and carry it.

With a good knowledge of a breeding line, you can build up a picture of the 'hidden' recessive factors, which helps with predicting the outcome of future matings.

For example, if Trapper, a black and white bitch, was put to a dog who had both the visible and the hidden coat colour factor as black. The result could only be black and white puppies. However, when mated to a black-coated dog with a hidden red factor, she will throw red and white puppies, for she carries the hidden red factor – her father was red and her mother was black. Lad, her grandfather, could be mated to any bitch, including red, and never produced red and white puppies, so he does not carry red as an unseen characteristic.

USING GENETICS

If you have four degrees of a characteristic, you have four possible ways in which they can join up. In genetics, the term homozygous (homo means similar/same) is when you have the same letter, e.g. BB or bb. The term heterozygous is where you have a mixture, e.g. Bb. The following examples relate to the bitch mentioned above.

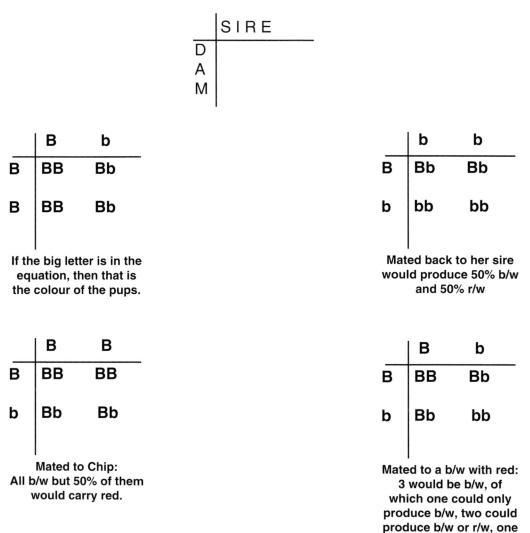

	SIRE	
D		
A		
M		

	B	b
B	BB	Bb
B	BB	Bb

If the big letter is in the equation, then that is the colour of the pups.

	b	b
B	Bb	Bb
b	bb	bb

Mated back to her sire would produce 50% b/w and 50% r/w

	B	B
B	BB	BB
b	Bb	Bb

Mated to Chip:
All b/w but 50% of them would carry red.

	B	b
B	BB	Bb
b	Bb	bb

Mated to a b/w with red:
3 would be b/w, of which one could only produce b/w, two could produce b/w or r/w, one would be red.

Both the sire and the dam are Bb. The dam's B can join up with either the sire's B or his b, and the same goes for the dam's b, which may join with either the sire's B or his b. Ideally, in a litter of four pups you would have three who were black and white (three in the equation carry a B) and one puppy will be red and white. From the three black and white puppies, two will carry a hidden red factor and one will only produce black and white puppies. When I am working out what I might get from a litter, I draw diagrams, for although I know the theory I find that the visual impact carries more weight with my mind.

This one simple method for working out the chances is exactly the same for every characteristic, and with a little skill and practice, you can have more than one characteristic in the equation at a time. You would therefore use this equation to work out ear carriage, sensitivity to sound and touch, or any other factor which you were interested in producing.

SENSITIVITY TO SOUND AND TOUCH

SOUND TOUCH
NN   SS – under-sensitive
Nn   Ss – medium sensitive
nn   ss – over-sensitive

Many of the characteristics are either/or, but some, such as ear carriage and sensitivity have a middle range. These two aspects of sensitivity are extremely important in the balance of the dog, influencing the working qualities and live-with-ability qualities very considerably. Over-sensitivity can produce a dog who is terrified by thunder and gunfire, but it can also produce the opposite. For example, hand-clapping at an event when the dog snaps and grabs at anything close by. Under-sensitivity produces a dog who is stubborn and self-willed, which is not at all desirable.

The degree of sensitivity needs carefully matching to the temperament of the owner. Nn produces the highest percentage of quality worker, but can be a type quickly spoilt by an insensitive owner. The nn type are prone to quit if a voice is raised. SS and NN types produce the worst workers in general, although a possible liaison might be achieved with a hard and totally insensitive owner – but generally not a type to breed for.

EYE COLOUR
This characteristic is like that for sensitivity in that dominance is incomplete. Therefore you get an intermediate stage:

Ir Dark Chestnut
ir Hazel
rr Pale Yellow

In Border Collies there is also the wall eye, often called 'china eye' or sometimes 'glass eye'. This is recessive, so only 1 in 100 will have it, 18 will carry it and 81 will be free of it. In my personal experience, the characteristic can lie hidden for fourteen generations and then suddenly appear when the right two parents are mated. Lines carrying this are: Purdies Old Line, Richardson's Cap (15839), sire of Wiston Cap, Frames Nell (9885), who is Cap's (15839) great grandmother.

Some shepherds believe that dogs with this eye-colouring can see better, others dislike it; it is a matter of personal preference. There is a theory that light eyes produce or go along with high intelligence, but this has not been proved genetically. However, the obsession for dark eyes in the show ring is definitely detrimental to the working dog. Through the eye a great deal of expression is transmitted. This is best achieved through a hazel eye; dark eyes mask expression from both human interpretation and the sheep's interpretation.

THE WORKING 'EYE'
The amount of 'eye' a Border Collie shows influences the working of that dog very considerably. Too much, and the dog stares at the sheep instead of moving them; too little, and the dog tends to rush the sheep. Assessing the genetic degree of 'eye' is difficult, for this can be modified with work, either extra work in the case of a 'strong-eyed' dog or less work with a 'loose-eyed' dog.
  The 'eye' is described in two parts:
1. Tendency to watch eagerly and follow any moving object.
2. Checking movement at a certain distance from the moving object.

In experimentation when a non Border Collie was mated to a Border Collie, all the resultant puppies had some degree of 'eye'. For my assessment of eye, I use the scale drawn up by R.B. Kelly in his book, *Sheep Dogs: Their Breeding, Maintenance and Training*:
1. No eye: bustle their sheep into position.
2. Weak-eye: seldom drop their heads or pull up.
3. Light-eyed: barely drop their heads.
4. Free-eyed: will sight sheep, have some eye but the eye will move around the group one after the other, may pull up but will run on.
5. Medium-eyed: control sheep by eye, fixes first one and then another. May hold, but moves on.
6. Strong-eyed: great control over sheep, remains flexible under command.
7. Over-eyed: dogs become fixed and immobile.

EARS
An emotive subject to all show people, but only a handful of trial people worry unduly about ear carriage. Ears have several genes, which is why there are so many variations of a type. There are also other factors which influence the type of ear carriage, such as size and texture. These additional factors make it extremely difficult to work out the possibilities and even the geneticists are not in agreement. The only way to use genetics here is to cut down the possibilities.
Semi-pricked: H^a
Drop ears: H   Dominant to Pricked: h
Pricked ears: h

POSSIBILITIES

1. Semi-pricked (double gene) to dropped with recessive for pricked.

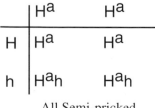

	H^a	H^a
H	H^a	H^a
h	$H^a h$	$H^a h$

All Semi-pricked

2. Semi-pricked (double) to pricked (double).

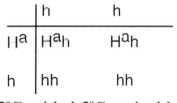

	h	h
H^a	H^ah	H^ah
H^a	H^ah	H^ah

All Semi-pricked

3. Semi-pricked (recessive for pricked) to pricked (double).

	h	h
H^a	H^ah	H^ah
h	hh	hh

50% pricked, 50% semi-pricked

4. Pricked (HH double) to Dropped (hh double).

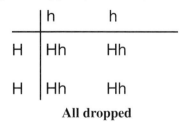

	h	h
H	Hh	Hh
H	Hh	Hh

All dropped

COAT COLOURS
Black and white is dominant to all other coat colours in the Border Collie, but you can have a BB or a Bb: both will be blk/wt, but one can only produce blk/wt, the other can produce a different colour. To produce red, therefore, you must use a dog who is Bb. An example is Sh. Ch. Tork from Whenway, who is BB, but his sire Roy is Bb: so if you wanted these lines and you also wanted red, then it would be no use using Tork, you would have to use his sire.

The red comes through Cap (3036) who has in five generations no less than twelve lines to red, making a total number of red lines an amazing 1,752. Red is recessive, and I make no apologies for repeating yet again: recessive characteristics need to be treated with respect and caution – it is unwise to mate red to red.

TRICOLOUR ($a^t a^t$)

There are two tricolours: the one most people think of is black, white and tan, but there is also red, white and tan. The large numbers of tricolours seen today are basically the result of extensive breeding to Wiston Cap (31154), himself a tricolour.

MERLE

This is a vital characteristic to understand, for it carries with it a semi-lethal factor. Mate merle to merle and you produce white, blind and or deaf puppies in a twenty-five percentage. This semi-lethal factor is carried on the MM.

				Shep*
			Shep	
				Tamsin
		Buck		
				Flint*
			Cloud	
Rhys (Bb)				Gillie*
				Wiston Cap*
			Bill	
				Nan
		Wisp		
				Glen*
			Jenny	
Copper				Dawn
				Dave*
			Roy (Bb)	
				Fly*
		Tork (BB)		
				Coon*
			Belle	
Fly (Bb)				Smut*
				Sweep*
			Tweed	
				Meg*
		Candy (Bb)		
				Spot*
			Nan	
				Fan

Known CAP (3036) lines off this pedigree*

	M	m
M	MM	Mm
m	mM	mm

1. Homozygous MM with the double lethal.
2. Heterozygous Mm which are normal blue merles.
3. Homozygous recessive mm which is usually some other colour, often black and white or tricolour.

Blue merle is a different type of gene to blk/wt and is recessive to blk/wt; therefore to produce merle, one of the parents must be a merle. From time to time you hear of reports where two apparently blk/wt parents have produced a merle, but this cannot be the case. The answer is that occasionally you come across a puppy who has only the slightest merle marking, which fades with maturity, giving what appears to be a blk/wt dog. It is vital that these puppies are registered as a merle and the new owner must understand that the dog must be treated as a merle for breeding purposes.

WHITE (S^p) (s^w) (s^i)
Three types of white influence the Border Collie, the most usual being s^i which produces the classic black and white markings. The sp produces dogs who are basically piebald. The s^w produces the self-white, which is occasionally seen. Despite the theory that a white dog cannot work sheep, as the sheep do not respect a dog of this colour, this does not appear to be the case. There were two very famous white dogs – the old White Bitch of Wale, and Ann (4545), grandmother of Gilchrist's Spot (24981) – a line through which most of the modern white dogs come.

TICKING (mottling) (TT)
This spot/ticking characteristic seen in many Border Collies is an inherited characteristic, the ticking being TT and no ticking tt.

BLUE (dd)
I have spent a vast amount of time trying to trace where this colour originated from. It does not appear to come through the normal Old Hemp lines but appears to come through non-registered lines. The colour blue is a dilution, hence slate noses and smoky-coloured eyes are characteristic of blue dogs. There are very many shades in the blues and the reason for this is not totally known. It is probably caused by the D not being totally dominant to the d; possibly the dark blue ones are Dd.
I find it rather interesting that in the ISDS Stud Book Volume 1 there are more blues registered

than reds, and the colour was common and owned/bred by most of the top people of that era. It appears to come from the old cattle dogs. It would seem the best way to produce blue is by mating clear blk/wt parents with blue lines in them.

COAT LENGTH

The length of the coat appears to be controlled by a number of genes, which results in grades of length from short to long. Short coat appears to be dominant over long coat. Short coat to short coat will produce both long and short-coated dogs. Long coat to long coats will produce dogs with long coats. Short coat to long coat produces pups with coats longer than the short-coated parent, hence the intermediate length.

    Professional geneticists prove theories by mating outside the breed e.g. a smooth-coated Border Collie would be mated to a breed which was dominant for short coat and to another dominant for long coat, and the results would be plotted. By doing this you remove the problem of the hidden recessive gene. When test matings are carried out within the breed you cannot be quite so sure, and the matings from out-crossing produce some extremely interesting genetical information.

HIND DEWCLAWS

This characteristic is recessive in the Border Collie. There is very little early documentation on this characteristic. The hind dewclaws tend to be rather large in Border Collies and as they are very much active dogs, they can easily get torn. It is therefore best to remove them when the puppies are two to three days old.

Chapter Eight

BREEDING BORDER COLLIES

SELECTING BREEDING STOCK

Planning for a litter should start when you either breed or buy the mother-to-be. Before purchasing a bitch for breeding, you should have studied her pedigree and made in-depth enquiries about the puppy's dam and sire, and, hopefully, you will have seen one or other or, preferably, both dogs in action. The quality of the bitch far outweighs that of the stud dog, for she will be bringing up the pups. It has been found that inherited factors contribute twenty-five per cent to the puppy's make-up, while environmental factors contribute seventy-five per cent. The proof of quality is in the resulting puppies, and you will find that good breeders never have to advertise their stock; they always have a waiting list.

So how does a novice acquire the necessary information and knowledge to start a breeding programme? Quite simply, by doing your homework and not being in too big a hurry. Go to the larger Championship shows, talk to breeders and exhibitors and, even more importantly, go to sheepdog trials and speak to the competitors. The majority of competitors are extremely helpful, and will give you the benefit of their knowledge and experience. Watch the runs carefully and observe how the dogs handle each situation – this tells you a great deal about that dog. It will be helpful to jot everything down in a notebook, as you will not remember everything in detail. As well as recording notes about a particular dog, include any information about the parents, and if possible, details of any other stock they have produced.

You need to find out about particular lines of both dogs and bitches that suit your style of working. There are numerous slight variations in the breed, and it is essential to be aware of this, for when working a dog, each individual's needs are just slightly different. You must decide what your needs are, and your personal preferences, before you start searching for the most suitable animal. It is no use buying from real hill material if you have small lowland fields, for the dog will be frustrated and your resultant pups very likely hyperactive. Obviously, the same situation applies in reverse.

Potential breeding stock should have been eye-tested, and hip-scored as well. Farmers may not have had their dogs hip-scored, but I do not consider that a justification for not using a good line, *providing you can see that the dogs are still working hard after a number of years and are showing no real movement problem.* In their everyday work sheepdogs take a great many knocks and strains, and they need to be fit and sound to carry on with the job. Dogs may suffer back problems following bad knocks from the sheep, but their hips could well be perfectly sound. I have a six-year-old bitch who is on retirement work because of back problems, but she was hip-scored 3 : 3, so be cautious what you read into things. Buy the best bitch you can afford – not the one who has won vast numbers of prizes, but a bitch of really sound conformation and temperament who is from good, sound breeding lines.

Once you have acquired your prospective brood bitch, start on her work schedule, whatever her age, even if is only very simple. It is important that you learn to understand your bitch, getting to know what her nature, temperament and what her style is like. You will need this information when it comes to selecting the sire, for he should be carefully selected to complement the bitch's good points, and to counter-balance any faults she may possess. Selection of stud dogs is an on-going activity. The serious breeder will continuously work on the form of stud dogs and what they produce, for although a dog may not be suitable for the next litter you are planning, he could easily be suitable for a subsequent match. A breeder who has most of their stock booked in advance can, with skill and knowledge, slightly adjust the characteristics in a litter according to the needs of the booked customers – especially if the breeder does not intend to keep a pup for themselves.

IN-BREEDING VERSUS LINE-BREEDING

Much has been written on this subject and the views are wide-ranging, mostly because what one person calls 'line-breeding', another calls 'in-breeding'. In fact, all line breeding has a degree of in-breeding, but the problem goes deeper than that.

Many formulae have been worked out to give the pedigree a mathematical figure representing the amount of line or in breeding. These are generally worked out on the basis of the sire contributing fifty per cent and the dam contributing fifty per cent. The four grandparents contribute twenty-five per cent each, the great grandparents contribute twelve and a half per cent, and the great great grandparents contribute six and a quarter per cent. It would appear that the dilution after this has no real effect on the dog, but in my strain the wall eye which occurs has come from twelve generations back. It is also true to say that some dogs leave a greater legacy than others. This can be proved in practical terms in a great many cases.

PEDIGREE OF BEN: IN-BREEDING OR LINE-BREEDING?

If you look at the pedigree of Ben, some people would say that in-breeding took place to Spot and Fan, for the maternal grandsire is a litter brother to the sire. There are others who would claim that

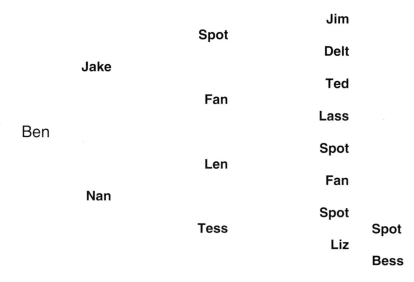

he was line-bred to Spot, while it is also possible to prove that he was line-bred to Fan and in-bred to Spot, depending on what system you are following. However, the vital factors are what qualities the dogs produce, and whether these qualities are sound or harmful. The best policy is to draw up a step-by-step breeding programme:

1. Decide on a few traits regarded as a) essential and b) intolerable. Obviously, consideration to disease, defects and abnormalities is vital.
2. Produce a scoring system for values of importance and rarity.
3. Not scored are well-established good points in each of the individuals.
4. Once the rare factors become more established, their score is down-graded.
5. Always line-breed to the best dog.
6. To keep an outstanding dog going after his death, he must be in-bred to whilst still alive, but *only* if he has exceptional qualities with no outstanding faults.
7. Because you get poor litters from in-breeding, this does not mean the favoured dog is bad, just that it should be used in a less close relationship.
8. Accumulation of characteristics does occur with in-breeding – these are both good points and *bad* points.

WHEN TO BREED?
Much is said and written about the correct age for mating a bitch. No bitch under eighteen months old should have a litter. However, there are a few very immature bitches who are not ready at two or even at two and a half years old. The best advice is to watch what nature is telling and showing you. A brood bitch needs to be both mentally and physically almost completely mature. There should also be an upper age limit after four and a half to five years old, bearing in mind that a maiden bitch runs much higher risks. It is also a sound practice never to mate a maiden bitch to a maiden dog. It is important that at least one of the pair knows the procedure, but it does not matter whether this is the bitch or the dog.

MATING THE BITCH
Preparation for the mating should start early on in the bitch's life: watching each season she has, noting its pattern, the time between seasons, the duration of the season, and when she seems ready to receive the dog. If you are familiar with your bitch's cycle, you will know what to expect and when. Before mating your bitch you should have her eye-tested. This can be done at two years of age.

About six weeks before the bitch is due to come into season, give her a good protein diet and some Vitamin E supplement. This stimulates the body and the reproductive organs, which is known in farming circles as 'flushing'. If it is over three months since you last carried out routine worming, then about four weeks before she is due to come into season, give her a thorough worming. By this stage, you should have selected the stud dog, and told the owner when the bitch is likely to be in season. The day she actually comes into season, contact the stud dog owner and give the date when you think she will be ready for the dog. Tradition has it that the bitch always goes to the dog. This is because the male will usually perform better on his home territory, and he may also have other bitches to accommodate, but occasionally other arrangements can be made.

All my bitches are taught from an early age to roll over, to allow me to inspect them regularly. I make into a game, frequently giving a tidbit afterwards. This means that when a bitch is in season, there is no problem about daily inspections, which are a must if you are not to waste everyone's time. It is the vulva, which is triangular in shape, which must be closely observed at this time, as

Served January	Due to Whelp March	Served February	Due to Whelp April	Served March	Due to Whelp May	Served April	Due to Whelp June	Served May	Due to Whelp July	Served June	Due to Whelp August	Served July	Due to Whelp September	Served August	Due to Whelp October	Served September	Due to Whelp November	Served October	Due to Whelp December	Served November	Due to Whelp January	Served December	Due to Whelp February
1	5	1	5	1	3	1	3	1	3	1	3	1	2	1	3	1	3	1	3	1	3	1	2
2	6	2	6	2	4	2	4	2	4	2	4	2	3	2	4	2	4	2	4	2	4	2	3
3	7	3	7	3	5	3	5	3	5	3	5	3	4	3	5	3	5	3	5	3	5	3	4
4	8	4	8	4	6	4	6	4	6	4	6	4	5	4	6	4	6	4	6	4	6	4	5
5	9	5	9	5	7	5	7	5	7	5	7	5	6	5	7	5	7	5	7	5	7	5	6
6	10	6	10	6	8	6	8	6	8	6	8	6	7	6	8	6	8	6	8	6	8	6	7
7	11	7	11	7	9	7	9	7	9	7	9	7	8	7	9	7	9	7	9	7	9	7	8
8	12	8	12	8	10	8	10	8	10	8	10	8	9	8	10	8	10	8	10	8	10	8	9
9	13	9	13	9	11	9	11	9	11	9	11	9	10	9	11	9	11	9	11	9	11	9	10
10	14	10	14	10	12	10	12	10	12	10	12	10	11	10	12	10	12	10	12	10	12	10	11
11	15	11	15	11	13	11	13	11	13	11	13	11	12	11	13	11	13	11	13	11	13	11	12
12	16	12	16	12	14	12	14	12	14	12	14	12	13	12	14	12	14	12	14	12	14	12	13
13	17	13	17	13	15	13	15	13	15	13	15	13	14	13	15	13	15	13	15	13	15	13	14
14	18	14	18	14	16	14	16	14	16	14	16	14	15	14	16	14	16	14	16	14	16	14	15
15	19	15	19	15	17	15	17	15	17	15	17	15	16	15	17	15	17	15	17	15	17	15	16
16	20	16	20	16	18	16	18	16	18	16	18	16	17	16	18	16	18	16	18	16	18	16	17
17	21	17	21	17	19	17	19	17	19	17	19	17	18	17	19	17	19	17	19	17	19	17	18
18	22	18	22	18	20	18	20	18	20	18	20	18	19	18	20	18	20	18	20	18	20	18	19
19	23	19	23	19	21	19	21	19	21	19	21	19	20	19	21	19	21	19	21	19	21	19	20
20	24	20	24	20	22	20	22	20	22	20	22	20	21	20	22	20	22	20	22	20	22	20	21
21	25	21	25	21	23	21	23	21	23	21	23	21	22	21	23	21	23	21	23	21	23	21	22
22	26	22	26	22	24	22	24	22	24	22	24	22	23	22	24	22	24	22	24	22	24	22	23
23	27	23	27	23	25	23	25	23	25	23	25	23	24	23	25	23	25	23	25	23	25	23	24
24	28	24	28	24	26	24	26	24	26	24	26	24	25	24	26	24	26	24	26	24	26	24	25
25	29	25	29	25	27	25	27	25	27	25	27	25	26	25	27	25	27	25	27	25	27	25	26
26	30	26	30 (May)	26	28	26	28	26	28	26	28	26	27	26	28	26	28	26	28	26	28	26	27
27	31 (Apr)	27	1	27	29	27	29	27	29	27	29	27	28	27	29	27	29	27	29	27	29	27	28 (Mar)
28	1	28	2	28	30	28	30	28	30	28	30	28	29	28	30	28	30 (Dec)	28	30	28	30	28	1
29	2	29	3	29	31 (Jun)	29	1 (Jul)	29	31 (Aug)	29	31 (Sep)	29	30 (Oct)	29	31 (Nov)	29	1	29	31	29	31 (Feb)	29	2
30	3	30	4	30	1	30	2	30	1	30	1	30	1	30	1	30	2	30 (Jan)	1	30	1	30	3
31	4			31	2			31	2			31	2	31	2			31	2			31	4

Whelping Table.

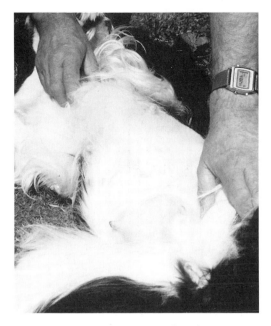

The bitch should be trained to lie on her back for examination. This bitch is just about to come into season.

Day three of the season: the vulva has become swollen and enlarged.

this will be the best guide to your bitch's readiness for mating. It is impossible to predict with certainty when a bitch will be ready. A bitch may show a pattern of being receptive to the male on the eleventh day and then suddenly, for no apparent reason, she appears to be ready on the third day. This happened to one of my bitches, who had a season of only five days, but she was successfully mated on the third day and went on to produce a litter.

When a bitch is in season, the vulva starts to swell and there will be a discharge, light at first and then heavier and redder as the season progresses. However, many bitches are so fastidious with cleanliness that you may scarcely notice the discharge. The swelling increases daily and the base of the triangle (the root) becomes hard and firm to the touch. This swelling increases until one day you notice that it starts to decrease. The root turns soft and flabby (a bit like jelly), and the bitch is ready for mating between twenty-four hours to thirty-six hours after this change has taken place. It is better to mate slightly later, rather than too early.

THE MATING

The only thing you can be certain about in breeding is that there is no such thing as the 'average' or the 'normal'. To add to the problem, the bitch can alter from one mating to the next. Some bitches like to be courted; others are so natural that they do not want any courtship and cannot wait to get on with the job. Observe what the bitch wants and go with her, her way; it is far better in the end. It is advisable for one of the dogs to be knowledgeable in the procedure – and also one of the humans.

When a mating is to take place, someone very close to the bitch should be with her at this time.

It is no excuse to say you are embarrassed; if you are, then you should not be breeding from the bitch. A bitch and dog should never be left unsupervised when mating; a great many things can happen, and one of the pair could be damaged for life. Equally, the dogs do not want too much interference. They may need reassurance, and they may need some assistance; again, they will tell you if you keep a receptive mind.

The dog will mount the bitch and penetrate her. Shortly after the early thrusts he will lock or 'tie', as it is called. However, this does not always occur; the dog might penetrate and withdraw – and there has been many a litter from this type of mating. The 'tie' can last from fractions of a second to over an hour; the duration is decided by the bitch, who often has about the same length of 'tie' at each mating. But as with all things, she can suddenly change from a forty minute normal to a couple of minutes, and still produce the same size litter. Heredity seems to play an important part. A bitch often has the same time lapse between seasons, the same length of season, and the same length of tie as her mother.

Once the tie has taken place, most males will turn themselves. However, if he fails to do this you can assist by carefully helping his hind leg over bitch's back, so that they can stand in a more comfortable position for the duration. Sometimes the pair will both lie down, perfectly relaxed; let them decide what suits them. Once the dogs break free, give each a drink of water and put them away. Often the bitch will return for a second mating, and if this is to be the case, make sure there is a thirty-six hour gap between matings, and not longer than a forty-eight hour gap as this might give rise to whelping problems. The stud fee is usually paid at the completion of the service, and the necessary paperwork is signed by the stud dog owner. Most stud dog owners will give a free service at the next season of the bitch if she fails to come into whelp, but this is at the stud dog owner's discretion.

The bitch will still stand again to any dog, and so a very careful eye must be kept on her until the end of her season. When a bitch has been mated, the vulva often remains slightly enlarged. If your bitch should experience any hormonal problems connected to her seasonal cycle, you may find that the following homeopathic remedies are useful:

Sepia 6x: Given three times a day for three weeks before the season is due, if the bitch has rejected the dog at the previous attempt.
Pulsatilla 200x: Given on the first day of the season and continued for twenty-one days to prevent false pregnancy.

FALSE PREGNANCY
This is a hormonal condition which has a devastating effect on the racing Greyhound, but it affects all bitches to some degree and many become quite useless for work. It usually continues for a period of some nine weeks after a bitch has come into season. Those involved with Sheepdog Trials, Working Trials and any competitive activity will often have to plan their events around the bitch's season.In the most extreme cases, the bitch will produce milk and she may even have false contractions, but at the other end of the spectrum she may just lack concentration so that her performance is slightly below standard. If something unexpected occurs in your bitch's work, ask yourself when was she last in season?

MANAGING THE STUD DOG
Just like bitches, males vary in the age when they become mature, and like the prospective brood, the stud dog needs to be both mentally and physically mature. Although the dog cannot be officially eye-tested before he is two years old, if he is used for mating before this age, he should

undergo an unofficial test. You must also make sure that both you and your dog are correctly registered. For example, if your dog is registered with the International Sheepdog Society (ISDS), then make sure you also are a member. Members' dogs must only be used on members' bitches in order for the puppies to be registered.

It would be feasible to use the young dog from about ten months to thirteen months old for his first stud, and then rest him for a few months. The majority of dogs are not going to be over-used, but if you are lucky enough to have a very popular dog then you should restrict matings to one a week, and preferably less. You may have no bookings at all for months and then have a couple with barely a week between them. This is acceptable, providing there has been a considerable time-gap beforehand. Dogs who are used too frequently often fail to get bitches into whelp.

Do not arrange a mating just after the dog has been fed; wait until after the mating has taken place and the dog has had a chance to rest. If you have several bookings, make sure you are feeding good-quality food, with an occasional supplement of Vitamin E. The dog should be kept fit, clean, and free from fleas and any other parasites, but he does not need any other special treatment.

It is a good idea to keep a few copies of your stud dog's pedigree in hand, and endorse them right across the centre with 'For stud purposes only'. It is also worth featuring a good photograph of the dog.

A little thought needs to be given as to where the mating will take place. It is helpful if you have somewhere under cover, with lighting. It often pays to have a small container of Vaseline and just grease the bitch's vulva to aid penetration. Assisting at a mating can be a back-breaking job, especially with a long tie, so make sure you provide a couple of seats – and a cup of tea is always welcome.

Once the mating has taken place, give your dog a drink of water and put him away to rest. You must then make sure that you have completed all the necessary paperwork for the Kennel Club or the ISDS.

THE GESTATION PERIOD

Good food and reasonable exercise is basically all the bitch needs for the first six weeks after mating, with one exception. I always give a supplement of raspberry leaf, in liquid, powder or tablet form, starting from the day after mating and continuing through the pregnancy. There is considerable evidence to suggest that this supplement results in a more troublefree whelping, and it seems to cleanse the bitch after the litter is born. It is a completely natural product and cannot harm the bitch at all.

Many farmers will continue to work their bitches throughout this period, but there is a risk, as a bitch can take some bad knocks from belligerent ewes. The working bitch will also twist and slip a fair bit in everyday work, and the same risk applies to Agility and Flyball dogs. I would be the last person to suggest a complete break from work, but at the same time, I would advise sensible, limited running and exercise, and the allocation of easier work jobs around the farm. By the time the bitch is six weeks in whelp she will be beginning to feel the extra weight, and it is unfair to ask her to cope with a long outrun or to overtake lively sheep.

If your bitch is on a good-quality food, there is no need to provide additives. In fact, calcium and vitamin supplements can do more harm than good. There has been a great deal of research into eclampsia, a potentially fatal condition for breeding bitches, which is caused by calcium deficiency. It appears that bitches who have been poorly fed and not given additives are rarely affected by it, and bitches who are richly fed are more prone to the condition.

Eclampsia can occur at any time from just before the puppies are born until after they have finished feeding. It has been discovered that the bitch may have plenty of calcium stored in her body, but it becomes unavailable to the blood, resulting in eclampsia. There are a number of signs which herald the onset of the condition:

Restlessness
Stiff walking in the hind limbs
The bitch may go into a coma
Convulsions
Paralysis or partial paralysis of the hind limbs.

If your bitch shows any of these signs you must rush her to the vet without delay – it is a life-or-death situation. The vet will inject intravenously a large dose of calcium directly into the vein, and if caught in time, the recovery from coma is miraculous. In no time at all she will appear completely normal. However, she must not be treated as normal and must not be allowed to take over milk-duties with her puppies.

If you use homeopathic remedies, the bitch will need a top-up of the Big 5, so that the puppies will gain early immunity through their mother. (See Chapter Five: Health Care.)

ULTRA-SOUND
I have had considerable cause to be grateful to scanning technology. On one occasion a scan of my in-whelp bitch showed that a caesarean would be necessary, and on another occasion the scan showed one very large puppy. In fact, this did cause minor problems at whelping – but at least we were ready for it.

Of the three types of scanning, only the diagnostic type will produce a picture. I have had several bitches scanned each week from the third week of pregnancy, and it is fascinating to see the development of the whelps. The bitch can be scanned at any time, but three weeks after mating is a good time and will certainly show up the puppies and number, providing you have an experienced operator who can interpret the picture on the screen. Ideally, I have the bitch scanned twice: at three weeks, and then two to three days before the whelping date. In this way, I know the bitch is in whelp and the size of the litter, and the second scan will alert me to any problems that may arise at whelping. If restricted to one scan, I would opt for the one just prior to whelping.

I had one bitch who was scanned three weeks after mating, and she was found to be carrying six whelps. When she was scanned again a week later, there was only evidence of four pups, and the scan before birth showed only two whelps – which was what she actually produced. This shows why the last scan is the most important. If I had relied on the findings of the first scan, I would have been waiting for the other four pups – and called the vet to find out what had gone wrong. In the case of a bitch who fails to produce puppies, the scan will help you to discover whether it was a false pregnancy, the stud dog being (on that occasion) infertile, or the bitch reabsorbing the puppies. I also have the bitch scanned after she has finished whelping, which is no more costly than a visit to the vet. The vet has to rely on feel to ensure all is well, whereas the scan will show you if this is the case.

PREPARING FOR THE BIRTH
If you take the bitch's temperature every day for the last week it will be constant, then it will suddenly drop a couple of degrees. This is the sign that the birth will take place in the next twenty-four hours. Once you are more experienced, and you know the bitch in question, you will observe other signs, such as restlessness, digging, and other nest-making behaviour. Some bitches continue

with this type of behaviour for a couple of days before whelping. The majority of bitches will refuse food shortly before they start to whelp – but not all. Just like the seasonal cycle, the normal is always variable, even with the same bitch. She might have several identical whelpings and then catch you completely unawares as she decides that the pattern will change.

Most books will tell you to get your whelping quarters ready a week or so before the puppies are due so that the bitch can get settled in. However, I think this depends upon your bitch's lifestyle and where she is to whelp. When possible, I like the bitch to whelp in the house (for my comfort), as I supervise the complete procedure. In this situation, I have a roomy cage which I cover over with a cloth. This has a small peep-hole so I can keep an eye on progress but leave the bitch undisturbed until she has had her first puppy. In the majority of cases, once a bitch has had her first pup, she will settle down and have the others in the same spot or wherever you have moved her to. So I start the bitch off in the cage, and after the first birth, I move mother and pup to the bed they will have for the next few weeks, and I settle down to monitor the rest of the whelping.

The bedding consists of a deep layer of newspaper with a piece of white flannelette sheet on top. This is ideal, as the sheet is soft, with a bit of grip for bitch and puppies.

THE BIRTH
I like to keep a very careful watch for the moment at which the water breaks. This consists of a clear fluid, which shows up clearly on white bedding. The bitch might appear to be giving birth to a puppy, but this may be the point at which the waters break, which will show up as a damp patch, indicating that the process of the first whelp is well under way. Birth is imminent, and if there is any delay, it is because the bitch is experiencing problems and help will be needed.

The bitch will probably pant and strain, and you should make a note of the timing in between these bursts of activity, as this gives you a guide as to how far the process has proceeded. Once the time interval is very short between the periods of straining, then you should wait no longer than an hour before seeking help if no puppies have been produced. Obviously, an experienced breeder may attempt to solve the problem, and there are many books which offer technical advice. However, I would always advise seeking professional help – no matter how many whelpings you have supervised. In purely economic terms, the bitch and puppies represent a large sum of money; in the case of a much-loved bitch, the value is inestimable.

Fortunately, most Border Collies are very hardy and natural and give birth effortlessly, which is an added reason for taking no chances. The last scan will also have given warning of any difficulties that may arise. I inform my vet of the expected whelping date, and then make contact when she shows signs of going into labour. In fact, I rarely need help – but at least the surgery is prepared. Some bitches whelp so easily that all you see is the bitch investigating under her tail – and the next moment you see a puppy. The birth is so quick that it is difficult to see what is going on. In fact, a dark sac of fluid appears, followed by the first puppy, who usually appears head-first but this is not always the case. The bitch should open the sac quickly to release the puppy, and sever the cord.

If this does not happen, then you may need to assist. You will need a pair of blunt forceps, and you must clamp the cord at the puppy end, and with your nails pull the cord apart. Cutting the cord with scissors seems to make it bleed more. Occasionally you get a very fussy bitch who keeps nibbling at the cord, and so it gets shorter and shorter and a little too close to the puppy's body. In this case, get some Friars Balsam and put a ring of it around the cord on the tummy area, and that will normally stop the bitch interfering. The bitch should lick and massage the puppy into life and it will soon find its way to the teats. If the bitch shows no interest, you will need to help, using an old flannelette sheet and rubbing the pup to get it breathing naturally.

Sometimes puppies follow on very quickly, at other times half-an-hour or even an hour may pass between puppies. This is not a cause for concern, as long as the bitch is relaxed and not straining. If you suspect trouble, call your vet to alert the surgery. I prefer to go to the vet rather than request a home visit, as it saves time if surgery is required, and that could be vital. Put warm bedding in a deep cardboard box, and take any whelps along with the mother – she will be more relaxed if she is not worried about leaving her babies.

If all is progressing smoothly, I take the bitch out between puppies to relieve herself and give her a small drink of warm milk, but apart from that I leave her to it. There is a difference between observing and interfering. You need to observe to ensure that all is well, and I do interfere a little when another puppy is being born. I try to ease the other whelps to the side so that they do not become covered in fluids and suchlike. This gives the bitch less work constantly cleaning the puppies, and the pups remain drier and consequently warmer.

HUMAN INTERACTION

When I first started to breed, all the older and more experienced breeders used to tell me not to mess with the puppies, not to pick them up until they were several days old and many other such things. I could never see the sense in this, for my bitches and I have always been complete partners. No doubt you need to bend according to your bitch's wishes, but certainly all my bitches welcome any person viewing their puppies, right from birth, but they will not permit other dogs anywhere near. This means that the puppies get handled and socialised from the very beginning, which will be very valuable for the future.

For my first litter I bought a fantastically expensive bed with a heater, so that the darling little puppies and mother would be cosy and warm. To my horror, I found the bitch could not stand the heat, and the bed has never been used to this day. Border Collies do not seem to need additional heat, even in the winter. Indeed, one of my bitches has to whelp in the coldest room in the house, otherwise she becomes distressed with the heat. Let nature be your guide. If the puppies are quiet, contented, and lying slightly apart, then they are warm enough. Puppies who are warm and very content tend to lie with comfortable gaps between them and not piled one on top of another.

Nature always tells you what is right and what is wrong – listen to her, she knows best in all things.

If one of the puppies is rather small, then when the puppies are starting to feed, I carefully lift that puppy and put it on the best teat, trying not to disturb the others, so that it gets a head start. Sometimes it does no harm to give nature a helping hand!

The afterbirths, which follow each puppy, are full of nutrients and I always let my bitches eat the majority of them. Some breeders try to restrict the number eaten; it is a matter for you to decide on.

WHELPING AND NURSING PROBLEMS

I find homeopathic treatments invaluable for the breeding bitch, as the remedies are completely natural and cannot possibly harm the mother or the puppies when they are at their most vulnerable. I have used the following treatments with considerable success over the years:

Arnica 3x or 6x: If there is any trauma at all.
Raspberry Leaf and/or Pulsatilla 6x: From six weeks into pregnancy until whelping, to strengthen the system and aid an easier whelping.
Cumicifuga 6x: Given every thirty minutes during labour to activate contractions.
Bryonia 6x: To help a tense bitch to relax.

A contented mother and puppies. The bitch will cater for all the puppies' needs for the first couple of weeks.

Urtica urens 30x: To increase the milk supply if the bitch is failing to produce sufficient.

Urtica urens 6x: To decrease the milk supply when the pups are weaned (do not swap the potencies), or to dry up a bitch producing milk because of a false pregnancy.

Caulophyllum 6x and Secale corriutum 6x: Given alternatively every fifteen minutes if the initial contractions stop.

Sepia 200x: A single dose if the bitch rejects the pups.

CULLING

This is a very emotive subject, and it seems to be an area where every breeder has their own viewpoint. Personally, I prefer to rear four really great puppies than eight smaller ones. There is a limit to the amount of milk a bitch can produce, so she either shares it with four pups or she shares it with eight. To a certain extent, the bitch will produce more milk to feed the larger litter of eight, but this is certainly not double the quantity she would produce for four puppies. I do not believe in breeding for profit, especially in a breed such as the Border Collie, so I lose money; but I feel that I produce a superior puppy – and I live with my own conscience which is not motivated by greed. I accept there is the converse theory, and so every individual must make their own decision.

In the first two or three weeks, there is little difference when you observe a bitch with a small litter and a bitch with a large litter. However, by the time the puppies are four to five weeks old, the bitch is clearly more relaxed. She can enjoy her pups, for she is not being continuously pestered. This has got to be a big plus for the puppies; the more they can have of their mother's time and attention, the better adjusted they will be.

Chapter Nine

REARING THE PUPPIES

THE FIRST TWO WEEKS

For the first couple of weeks you will have very little to do except keep the bitch happy, feed her twice a day, and give plenty of liquid drinks. I find that a bitch benefits from a variety of drinks, and so I give tea, cocoa, ovaltine, and malted milk – which is especially helpful if the bitch is struggling with milk supply. I also find that a bitch is more relaxed and lets her milk down better after a feed, especially as the pups get a little older. When they have reached four weeks old and are not being fed so often, you will notice that the bitch will not settle to feed them so well until she has had her breakfast.

WEANING

Bitches vary greatly as to how long they continue feeding their puppies. I have a bitch who insists on feeding her puppies until they go to their new homes – and for a while after that if she meets up with them. She really enjoys the pups and spends a great deal of time just playing with them for joy and pleasure. When I first encountered a bitch of this extremely devoted type, I became worried because at four weeks the puppies were not moving around much, and I was afraid I would upset the bitch as I attempted to wean the litter. However, there is rarely cause for concern when something completely natural is happening, and at four and a half weeks old the litter suddenly transformed into the type of puppies you would expect for that age, eating normally and playing.

Since then, I have realised that if you allow nature to take its course the puppies will develop at their own rate and will thrive accordingly. Although a bitch may still feed her puppies five times a day, even though they are eight weeks old, they take very little from her in real terms because they are getting all their nourishment from their normal diet. There is no need to worry that the puppies are not 'completely weaned': as soon as they leave their mother and have no access to her milk, they forget all about it, and there is the bonus that the mother has not suffered the trauma of being kept away from her puppies.

With some bitches I will start supplementary feeding at two to two and a half weeks, others maybe a week later, and sometimes even two weeks after that. If the puppies are under three weeks, I start them on a proprietary milk formula. If they are older, I start them on a well-moistened complete-diet puppy feed (or on raw chopped beef), depending on the feeding programme). At this stage, they are still getting plenty of milk from their mother, so I do not offer a milk supplement. To begin with I feed all the puppies together, but when they are feeding easily, I feed them in separate dishes which are raised off the floor. This type of dish aids feeding; it does not over-balance, and the puppy cannot go paddling into the food. The advantage of feeding

A bitch will usually stand to feed her puppies as they grow older.

Young puppies find balance a little difficult to begin with, so it helps if you raise the feeding bowl from the ground.

separately is that you know how much each puppy is eating.

The best guide to correct feeding is to observe the puppies' motions, which should be firm and well-formed. If this is not the case, the food may be too rich, you may be feeding too much, or it may be a combination of the two factors. You will need to reduce rations or the richness of the diet immediately, before you have a problem. I start my puppies with a morning and evening feed for three days. I then add a lunch-time feed, again for three days, then going on to four meals a day for another three days, and then they are ready for the final quantity of five meals a day. Never overload the puppies' stomachs.

ANTIBIOTICS
If the bitch or the puppies have to have antibiotics for any reason, it is advisable to follow this with natural yoghurt. It has been found that the antibiotics also kill off the valuable bacteria in the gut, which are so vital for digesting food, and the yoghurt actually contains the active lactobacilli which have been killed off. In fact, this applies to both humans and dogs, and not just at the

periods of whelping/rearing, but at any age.

NAILS
From about two and a half weeks of age, the puppies' nails will need trimming every week. This is for the sake of the bitch, whose belly would be ripped and sore from numerous scratches if you did not carry out this simple task. It is only the tips of the nails that need to be cut. The new owner should continue to do this until the puppy is getting adequate road work for the claws to be worn down naturally.

WORMING
By four weeks the puppies are ready for their first worming, which is always done with a liquid wormer. The puppy is weighed to ascertain its correct weight, and a disposable syringe (without the needle) is filled to the correct amount, usually 1 ml per lb weight of puppy. The best method is to pick up the puppy, and hold the head slightly upwards and backwards. The syringe can be slipped gently into the back corner of the lips, the plunger is carefully depressed and down goes the liquid wormer.

Worming often upsets the puppies' stomachs, so reduce the food amount for the next twenty-four hours and allow the stomach to settle. I give the worming dose late afternoon, and then beat the bitch to the puppies at the start of the morning so that I can clear up the little worm piles before she does. It is quite normal for the bitch to clean up after her puppies, and, with the exception of this occasion, do not prevent the bitch from carrying out her maternal duties. The bitch herself is always wormed after the puppies have left home.

Worming should be carried out at four weeks, six weeks, eight weeks, twelve weeks, fifteen weeks, and then every six months thereafter. A multi-wormer, which treats a number of the most common worms, is now available. This can be obtained from your vet.

THE BIG 5
This is the term I generally use for the homeopathic nosodes, which can be used as an alternative to providing conventional vaccination (See Chapter Five: Health Care.) The puppies should receive their first dose at four weeks, and then once a month for the next six month, and thereafter, once yearly.

NOISE CONDITIONING
The puppies are handled by friends, visitors and by myself from the moment they are born. From week one, they get a noise conditioning programme on a daily basis. I have recorded several tapes with all sorts of noises, such as thunderstorms, guns, fireworks, weird screeching, etc. Once the pups start feeding, each feed-time is announced by a loud bang, varying daily. In this way, noise becomes a very mundane part of the puppies' lives, and it is so commonplace that it is ignored.

Before they leave home, the puppies will have experienced one hundred or more noises and they certainly see no reason to be worried by such things. Indeed, a loud bang usually means food or some special fussing and attention, so it has a pleasant association. Puppies that are reared in the house, rather than in a kennel environment, will hear the television, the vacuum cleaner and many household noises, and so they will be quite unworried when they go to their new homes.

EXPLORING
Border Collie puppies benefit from the stimulation of exploring the environment. When the pups are about five weeks old, I let them have free exercise in the yard with the older dogs, who are

Puppies relish the opportunity to explore their surroundings.

Bitches vary as to how long they enjoy the company of their pups. Here, Trim, a really devoted mother, allows her puppies to romp all over her.

Bryan Turner

completely safe and wonderfully tolerant with puppies. The pups get used to large dogs around them, and they also learn respect – a valuable lesson for when they leave home. Many items are left around the yard, and the pups learn a vast range of balance, co-ordination and problem-solving attributes. These skills are acquired naturally, learning by example from other dogs or by experimentation.

Even though the puppies spend much of their time outside, they come in daily, and there are plenty of opportunities to meet visitors and to be handled by them. The puppies also learn to come when called. This is so easy to teach at feeding times, and coming for food can soon be developed to coming for a cuddle. So by the time they go to their new owners, all the puppies are sound on the recall.

THE PUPPY PACK
When it is time for the puppies to go to their new homes, each owner is given a pack consisting of:
A pedigree
A diet sheet for up to 18 months
A booklet with training tips and advice on general care
A fortnight's supply of food so that the pup does not get a sudden change in diet
Registration papers.

The owner is encouraged to visit the puppy, if possible, every week from birth, and it is surprising what a bond develops with this system. Before a puppy goes, I stress that I am available – twenty-four hours a day, if necessary – to give help and advice.

TEMPERAMENT TESTING
The puppies actually go away with one more item, their Temperament Test report (TT), which is accompanied by a verbal explanation. This, to me, is *the* most important part of rearing a litter.

Each puppy is tested, an individual report sheet is drawn up, and I discuss the comments with the new owner. The value of this is that it shows up the minor individual differences between the puppies, such as those with a strong chase instinct, those with a weaker retrieve instinct, or those who are a little more dominant than the others. If one has a slightly strong chase instinct and is going to a pet home, then I instruct the new owner to get on top of it very early on, so that the pup can be gently moulded out of the bad habit before it becomes a problem. If a pup does not have a strong retrieve instinct and is going to a working home, then the owner will need to work on plenty of fun games from day one, to encourage the instinct to develop.

My assessment of each puppy starts from the moment of birth. I watch how the pup comes from the sac to the teat: Does the puppy struggle to get there? Is there evidence of disorientation? How quickly does the pup locate the teat? All this gives me vital clues as to how that puppy is going to grow up. Indeed, by the time the litter is three weeks old, I have a ninety-five per cent accurate assessment of all the puppies. I watch them with their mother: Which pup always has the best teat? Which is last to find the teat? Which pushes others off, and so on. Once the puppies are old enough to go outside and play in the yard area with the larger dogs, I watch how they conduct themselves and how they tackle the problems they encounter. All this information is added to the temperament test, so that the new owner knows exactly what they are taking on. This information is not only invaluable for owners, it is also essential for my breeding programme. I can analyse the success of a particular mating, and evaluate the use of new lines introduced.

My set of tests has been selected from a number of researchers and they suit me. The test itself is only useful as a careful interpretation of the information it gives you, so you must assess carefully and accurately.

HOW TO CONDUCT THE TESTS
The tests are carried out as close as possible to the forty-ninth day. They must not be conducted just before a meal or on they day the puppies have been wormed or had their injections. The most accurate results are obtained when the puppies are calm and stable. The tests should be carried out by someone who is not too familiar to the puppies, and in a strange room. Each puppy is tested alone and the rest of the litter must be out of sight.

Following: The tester walks away, encouraging the puppy to follow.

Bryan Turner.

SOCIAL ATTRACTION
The tester calls the puppy, crouching down at the pup's level, and encouraging the puppy to come.
Came readily, tail up, bit hands: 1
Came readily, tail up, pawed, licked at hands: 2
Came readily, tail up: 3
Came readily, tail down: 4
Came hesitantly, tail down: 5
Did not come at all: 6

FOLLOWING
The tester stands up and walks away, encouraging the puppy to follow.
Followed readily, tail up, got underfoot, bit at feet: 1
Followed readily, tail up, but underfoot: 2
Followed readily, tail up: 3
Followed readily, tail down: 4
Followed hesitantly, tail down: 5
Did not follow or went away: 6

*Elevation: The
puppy is held in the
air for thirty
seconds.*

Bryan Turner.

ELEVATION
*The tester picks up the puppy by cradling their hands around the puppy's middle and holding the
pup suspended in the air in front of them for 30 seconds.*
Struggled fiercely, thrashed about, bit: 1
Struggled fiercely, thrashed about: 2
Settled, struggled, settled with some eye contact: 3
Struggled and then settled: 4
No struggle: 5
No struggle, strained to avoid eye contact: 6

SOCIAL DOMINANCE
*The tester sits at the puppy's level, strokes the pup from head to tail and puts their face close to the
puppy until an established behaviour pattern can be seen.*
Jumped, pawed, bit, growled: 1
Jumped, pawed: 2
Cuddled up to tester, tried to lick face: 3
Squirmed, licked hands: 4
Rolled over, licked at hands: 5
Went away, stayed away: 6

*Social dominance:
The tester strokes
the pup from head
to tail and puts
their face close to
the puppy.*

Bryan Turner.

RESTRAINT

The tester gently rolls the pup on to its back and holds it in that position for 30 seconds, using only sufficient restraint as needed to keep the pup in position.

Struggled fiercely, bit, growled: 1
Struggled fiercely: 2
No struggle, relaxed: 3
Struggled, settled, licked: 4
No struggle, licked at hands: 5
No struggle, froze: 6

RETRIEVE

The tester crumples something, like a piece of paper, to attract attention, and then tosses it at eye level about 4ft in front of the puppy.

Chased object, picked up object and ran away: 1
Chased object, stood over object and did not return: 2
Chased object and returned with it to tester: 3
Chased object and returned without object to tester: 4
Started to chase object, lost interest: 5
Did not chase object: 6

LEFT
Restraint: The puppy is gently rolled on to its back and held in that position for thirty seconds.

BELOW
Retrieve: The tester tosses an object about 4ft in front of the puppy and watches the response.

Bryan Turner.

Touch sensitivity: Gentle pressure is applied to the puppy's webbing between the toes. This should be increased while you count to ten.

Bryan Turner.

TOUCH SENSITIVITY

This is the one test which I always do myself, as I feel consistent handling is needed in order to make a valid comparison between litters. To carry out this test, hold the puppy gently. One of the front feet should be supported by one hand, while the other hand is used to apply pressure, with finger and thumb, to the webbing between the toes. The pressure should be gradually increased while you count to ten. Counting is stopped as soon as the puppy shows discomfort.

8-10 before response: 1
6-7 before response: 2
5-6 before response: 3
2-4 before response: 4
1-2 before response: 5

SOUND SENSITIVITY

Using a metal pan and a spoon, the tester raps on the pan a few feet away from the puppy.
Listened, located sound, walked towards it barking: 1
Listened, located sound, barked: 2
Listened, located sound, showed curiosity, walked towards sound: 3
Listened, located the sound: 4
Cringed, backed off, hid: 5
Ignored sound, showed no curiosity: 6

LEFT
An object is tied to a length of picture cord and is jerked in front of the puppy.

BELOW
Stability: A closed umbrella is placed about 4ft away from the puppy. It is slowly opened and the puppy is allowed to investigate.

Bryan Turner.

CHASE
A small towel or similar object is tied to a 6ft length of picture cord, and this is jerked in front of the puppy and across the floor.
Looked, attracted, bit: 1
Looked, tail up, barked: 2
Looked curiously, attempted to investigate: 3
Looked, barked, tail tucked down: 4
Ran away and hid: 5

STABILITY
The puppy is placed in the centre of the test area and a closed umbrella is placed about 4ft away, facing the pup. The umbrella is slowly opened and set down, and the puppy is allowed to investigate.
Not startled, walked forward tail up, may mouth: 1
Slightly startled, walked forward, tail up, may mouth: 2
Slightly startled, walked forward, attempted to investigate: 3
Slightly startled, looked curious, stayed put: 4
Startled, does not recover, retreats, tail down: 5

ANALYSING THE TEMPERAMENT TEST
The problem with the temperament test is that people think that it tells you what the dog will be like as an adult. In fact, the TT is a guide; it tells you the genetic traits that the puppy has been born with, and these will be modified with the environment. A dominant puppy will always be a dominant dog, but knowing this factor when the pup is still young helps the new owner to channel it and modify it. A shy, sensitive puppy will always have these traits, but you can reduce the sensitivity by enriching the environment. If you know your bitch has, from previous matings to different dogs, always produced over-sensitive pups, then you can remove her from your line or ensure that you always mate to a dog known to produce well-balanced puppies. The TT merely gives you a little more insight into your strain. It allows you to guide the new owner and to match puppy with owner. For example, I would not give a very dominant puppy to a very meek person, or vice versa. Remember, the TT is not a means to an end. It is a guide to use *sensibly*.

THE BARRIER TEST
Purpose: Degree of problem-solving ability; degree of learning retention; assessment of personality characteristics.
Method: Set up 'V' barrier with one side against the wall. Pup is set inside centre of 'V' and is encouraged to find way out. Pup is timed from being put down until finding the way out and clearing the end of the barrier. Test is repeated immediately, then repeated one hour later.

PROBLEM SOLVING
Time the test, then do a second test, and if this is under 10 seconds, or faster than the first, it can be considered excellent. If the first test was under 10 seconds, and the second trial takes much longer, discard the results of the first test and score the second test.
    If 25 seconds, and faster than the first : Good
    2nd test 26-45 seconds, and faster than first: Fair
    2nd test 46 seconds or more: Poor
    2nd test longer than first, score next lower rating.

RETENTION

Under 10 seconds is excellent.Wait one hour and test again.

Eleven to 20 seconds is good. Over 20 seconds, or more than 10 seconds longer than the first trial is poor.

The barrier test should be used the same way as the temperament testing: to find out the potential of the puppy and relate that to the potential of the new owner. A puppy scoring 'good' or 'fair' combined with 3/4 on the retrieve test (the degree of willingness) will usually make a reasonable pet or Obedience dog. For sheep-working, I look for a puppy with a medium skull, a score of 3 maximum on the sensitivity and chase (although just slightly stronger is acceptable), a score of 3 on the dominance test, and preferably a 3 on the retrieve and sound sensitivity. This should be added to an 'excellent' on the barrier test and a 3 also on the umbrella test. The sensitivity test is critical. A dog who is too sensitive will get upset too easily; a dog who is too hard on sensitivity will work for itself. This should be evaluated alongside the retrieve, where you want a dog to show a willingness to work with you.

This barrier test gives three different pieces of information about the puppy:
1. Memory retention
2. Problem-solving ability
3. Personal characteristics.

Two to three tests are done. If the puppy on the first test finds the way out immediately, this could be a matter of good luck, so the score on the re-test (an hour later) is carefully analysed. If the score is better the second time round, then the first is scrapped and the difference is taken between the second test and the third, which is an hour from the second.

RETENTION SCORING

Under 10 on the third: Excellent
11-20 second: Good
Over 20 seconds: Poor.
A puppy whose time from the third trial is more than 10 seconds greater than the second one is also rated 'poor'.

PERSONAL CHARACTERISTICS

A puppy who runs about barking in frustration is the one likely to show similar response when stressed or frustrated. A puppy who tries to find a way out, climbs over, digs or chews at the bars, etc. is the one who is likely to be both inventive and active in everyday life.

ANALYSING THE BARRIER TEST

Puppies with an 'excellent' for this test need very careful homes found for them as they are not average pet-owner material. For the average Obedience, Agility, or pet owner, the score of 'good' is often a better dog to train than the one with 'excellent' grading. Dogs with a 'poor' in retention scoring will not learn so quickly and will need more patient handling. This should be explained to the new owner. On the plus side, this type does not have the initiative that can lead to problem behaviour of those scored 'good' or 'excellent'. In the personal assessment, some puppies will merely sit and wait to be rescued. This is not the type of dog for the person who wants a Working Trial dog, or for the farmer who needs a dog to work on their own initiative.

Remember, these results do not make the final product – the owner and the environment can modify all these scores. The benefit of the test is that it indicates the type of environment you need to be working in.

Chapter Ten

THE WORKING SHEEPDOG

I know of no joy to beat the sight of a neatly moving flock of sheep coming on to the horizon. It is only when a sheepdog is working behind the flock that sheep move in this fashion. It is still a sight which thrills me – as much today as the time I first saw it. If any major upset occurs in my life, I tackle it by taking out my favourite bitch, and just letting her work the sheep for the sheer fun of it. The calmness and tranquillity this brings is unsurpassed. On a more practical level, a well-trained dog takes over the workload of many labourers – and does a far better job!

You cannot put a price on the experienced dog who understands the sheep and knows what is required. When I am in my fifteen-acre field, on occasions I have no idea where the sheep are. Out goes my Border Collie, Todd, and before long the flock appears on the horizon. I remember one time when I was at a college, and I was told that twelve students had been trying for two hours to gather a flock of lambs and ewes – without the help of any dogs. In desperation they turned to me and Todd. My old boy had the sheep out of the field, up the road and put into pens within twenty

A tightly bunched flock of sheep with the Border Collie working behind, in complete control.

Black Velvet of Shipelle: Selection depends on whether you want a sheep-only dog or one that will work cattle as well.

minutes – that is what you train a dog for. I can sit in my vehicle, with the window down, and give the dog an odd command while I drive along, and the sheep will be moved any distance required.

The time you spend on the initial work with your trainee sheepdog will be rewarded not merely in full, but one hundred-fold. With a good dog, there is no task which cannot be accomplished. Remember the saying "Rome wasn't built in a day." A good dog is not made in a month, or a year. It takes three to four years to establish a really good working partnership. Dogs, like wine, mature and blossom with time.

For me, the Border Collie is not the eighth wonder of the world – it is the first. I first came into contact with the breed when I was a child and saw Border Collies working in the Pennines, and I am still as much in awe of this most intelligent and versatile of dogs today. Although you might feel that training your dog for sheep does not apply to you, nonetheless, if you understand what is involved, it will give you a better insight into how to train your dog, and there are some techniques which you may find useful.

SELECTION
Before you can start training your dog, you need to obtain a suitable Border Collie – and it is this decision that will have the greatest bearing on future success. If you select the wrong type of dog, training will be difficult if not impossible. It stands to reason that almost as much thought needs to be put into your choice of dog as into your dog's training programme.

Selection starts with accurately assessing your requirements, and your own temperament. There are four main categories to look at:

1. HUMAN TEMPERAMENT
1a. Dominant type
1b. Quiet type

2. SIZE OF FARM
2c. Large-acreage farm
2d. Low-acreage farm

3. TYPE OF FARM
3e Large fields
3f. Small fields

4. SHEEP
4g. Stubborn sheep
4h. Light sheep
4i. Small numbers of sheep
4j. Large numbers of sheep

Different combinations of these factors require different types of dogs, so work through your personal set of factors and find which type of dog best suits you and your farming situation.

TYPE ONE: A dog likely to have a loose eye – 1a 2c 3e 4h – suitable for a dominant owner with a large-acreage farm which has large fields and light sheep.
TYPE TWO: A strong-eyed dog – 1a 2c 3e 4g – suitable for a dominant owner with a large acre-farm, which has large fields and stubborn sheep.
TYPE THREE: A wide-running dog – 2c 4j 4h – suitable for a large-acreage farm with large numbers of light sheep.
TYPE FOUR: Tight-running dog – 2d 3f 4g 4i – suitable for a low-acreage farm with small fields and small numbers of sheep.
TYPE FIVE: Strong and powerful dog – 1a 2c 3e 4g – suitable for a dominant owner with a large-acreage farm which has large fields and stubborn sheep.
TYPE SIX: Quiet, mild dog – 1b 4h – suitable for a quiet owner who has light sheep.
TYPE SEVEN: Dog needing a lot of work – 2c 3e 4i – suitable for a large-acreage farm which has large fields and large numbers of sheep.
TYPE EIGHT: Dog which easily relaxes – 1b 4h – suitable for a quiet owner who has light sheep.
TYPE NINE: Pushy dog – 1a 2c 3e 4g – suitable for a dominant owner with a large-acreage farm which has large fields and stubborn sheep.
TYPE TEN: Quiet, unhurried dog – 1b 2d 3f 4i – suitable for a quiet owner with a low-acreage farm which has small fields and small numbers of sheep.

In addition, you must decide if you want:
1. A dog or a bitch (remember that bitches come in season and need to be kept away from other dogs at this time).
2. A dog to do routine work without supervision, e.g. to go off when asked and bring in the cows.
3. A sheep-only dog, a cow-only dog, or a sheep and cow dog.
4. A good yard dog (one which guards).
5. A dog to work in the pens.
6. A dog without initiative.

If you select the right dog for your individual needs, the job of training is at least halved. A carefully trained dog will work for around ten to eleven years, so it pays dividends to take time over your choice.

GETTING STARTED
Before you start training, read as many books on sheepdog training as possible and try to see some

The instinct to herd is already apparent in this five-week-old puppy.

of the many videos that are now available. There are as many ways to train a dog as there are people training and dogs being trained. Therefore the more you can learn before you s'art on the field work, the smaller the number of mistakes which you are likely to make.

It is impossible to attempt to cover the whole spectrum of training sheepdogs in one chapter – whole books are written on the subject. However, drawing on the experience of many years of working my Border Collies and instructing others in the craft, I would say that all the problems that arise can be attributed to just two training faults – and, in fact, this generally applies to all forms of dog training. The faults are:

1. Slack compliance in the dog's response to commands.
2. Progressing too fast.

If all handlers understood the workings of a dog's mind and eradicated these two faults, all training problems would be solved. Considering the scope of this book, I have decided to concentrate on trying to prevent faults from arising – or attempting to put them right in the very early stages.

Several years ago I would have said that there were four main faults and would have added:

3. Poor stop.
4. Tight out-run.

However, these are really an extension of the two major problems which have been allowed to develop. Every time your Border Collie goes wrong and is not corrected, you are effectively condoning that response to your command. Each successive time the mistake is made, it becomes progressively harder to change the dog to the correct way of doing it.

A well-bred sheepdog cannot be taught anything about sheep; they know more than any human ever will. What the trainer must do is to teach the dog to work sheep in the manner requested – and that is usually different to the dog's concept of working. How often do humans find themselves at cross-purposes with each other, and yet we speak the same language, whereas dogs and humans communicate in a different language, which is yet an added problem.

In this chapter, as in all the others dealing with training, the word 'young' refers to inexperience rather than the actual age of a dog. A dog who has been working or in training since the age of nine months will be far more experienced as a two-year-old than a dog of three years who has just started training.

A well-bred, biddable dog, who has built up a reasonable relationship with the trainer, will rarely disobey a command through 'naughtiness'. It is more likely to be because:

1. The dog has not understood what is required.
2. You have muddled the commands to such an extent that the dog is perplexed.
3. Unbeknown to you, the dog's understanding of your command is different to yours.
4. Some dogs, especially strong-eyed dogs, concentrate so deeply on their sheep that they do not actually hear the command.

If your dog is not carrying out a command, then you should stop and ask yourself: 'What am I doing wrong?'

THE TRAINING LEAD

To me, the training lead is the most important piece of equipment that I ever use, but like any training aid, it has to be used sensitively. In fact, when used correctly, it will rarely ever be in your hands. The lead needs to be held in the very early stages, but no progress can be made until it is left on the ground for the majority of the time. Even when the lead is held in your hand, the hand is only tightened on the lead when you want to stop the dog in the middle of the activity. The rest of the time it should run freely in the open palm, and when restraint is needed, a quick tighten of the fingers, a command to stop the dog, and then immediate relaxation of fingers. You should use the lead like a fishing-line – and as gently as a fishing line. It is there to prevent the repetition of mistakes. The lead should be left trailing on the ground, and if you wish to prevent the dog

The training lead is left trailing on the ground. It is only used as a form of restraint if necessary.

proceeding any further, you just step on it. I find that the dogs soon become so used to the lead that they totally ignore its existence, and then it really begins to be useful. To start with, I might keep the dog on the lead for several months. Then I will begin a training session on lead, and release the dog after a short while. However, if the dog takes liberties and I am not in a position to alter the pattern of behaviour, the lead goes back on for one or more sessions. I never hesitate to put the lead back on. You should never be reluctant to return to basics from time to time, albeit only briefly. If you fail to do this, it will show in the dog's training quality.

The training lead is usually made of rope. It needs to be as light as possible, with a fibrous and hairy twist. A smooth rope is likely to burn your hands if you have to hang on to it in a hurry. Never wash the rope; it gets supple with the mud and dirt which gets into it. When not in use, leave the lead hanging in an airy but dry place.

The less you rely on the lead to correct the dog, the more you use will your voice, and the quicker you will be able to dispense with the lead altogether.

AVOIDING MISTAKES

These methods work, but as with any training method you cannot stop part way through the advice and expect it to work. This applies to whatever branch of training you are active in. I would say that ninety-nine per cent of the training problems arise from trying to progress too quickly. It is no use going on to the next step before the dog really understands and is obeying the exercise you are working on. Training a dog involves teaching parts of the exercise separately, and sometimes it may be difficult to appreciate that an apparently disjointed set of training lessons will finally come together and produce the real finished product. If you do not have patience – and a sense of humour – let someone else train the dog. Many people are so keen to have the dog working that the most important factor gets blown away with the wind – and that is the need for control. The dog must learn to do as you wish – no matter how strong the desire to do something different. Every time you allow the dog to do something wrong, you are reinforcing that action as correct. Every time you ask your dog to stop and the command is ignored, the dog is learning that you do not mind when or if the command is obeyed. A command is one word to be instantly obeyed. For example, the command is "Stand" – not "Stand, stand, stand."

Does your dog really understand the command, or is the exercise being performed correctly by instinct, rather than in response to a command? It is very hard to be certain, and it never ceases to amaze me how often a dog does achieve success by instinct. You can test your dog by standing rock still, eyes closed, hands in pockets, feet together, face emotionless, and then ask the dog to carry out the command. If the command is understood, a biddable dog will obey it. I was having trouble, periodically, with a brilliant bitch of mine, and it was a long time before I realised she was taking eye commands. The problem arose in bright sunlight when my reactor light glasses became dark, and so the bitch could not take her command. The truth sank in twelve to eighteen months later when looking at a photograph, and I grieved at the agony that poor little bitch had gone through trying to carry out my requests.

If you are having problems in training, stop and ask yourself, why? Does the dog usually try to be biddable, or is this an instance of the dog not respecting your wishes? Did you buy the dog partially started? The previous owner may have had slightly different commands or pronunciation, maybe his commands were the reverse of yours, maybe your whistle note is a partial tone different? My best little bitch will refuse a command if I have just got it a hint off-tone, and as she always obeys, I know that probably because of high wind or personal tension, I have got it slightly different. At a Sheepdog Trial, the majority of handlers use the same type of whistle, but it is very rare for any dog to mistake their own handler's commands.

Poised ready to go on the out-run. Do not make the mistake of progressing too fast; this is the cause of most problems that arise in training.

GIVING COMMANDS

Always use the same commands for the same dog. Local traditions may vary. For example, in one area of Britain, the Midlands, the command "Away to me" is used for the anti-clockwise circle, and "Come byc" is for the clockwise circle. However, in the Pennines, where I come from, the commands are the other way round. It does not matter what you use, as long as you keep it the same for the one dog.

A Border Collie working sheep docs so in three ways. The dog may come to a stop, walk straight on the sheep, or move in a circle. The stop and walk-on are easy to keep straight in your mind, it is the circles which cause the problems. If your dog leaves your side facing up the field, and moves to the right side, then this is an anti-clockwise command. However, once the dog has got behind the sheep and is flanking on your right (remember the dog went up the field on your right), the dog is now flanking to its left when moving outward, and therefore needs a clockwise command.

It becomes a little harder when the dog is working a line across the field at right angles to you. You will need to practise, and you need to remember which is the dog's left and right. When my pupils were having trouble with this, I told them to get out the salt and pepper pots and have one as the dog and the other as the sheep, and practise moving the dog as you would when working it and using the right commands. This might seem a mite silly, but far better to practise on salt and pepper pots, rather than confuse the poor dog to such an extent that it has no idea what is required. The problem arises when the dog is dashing about, the sheep are dashing about, and you are all steamed up. Then it is all too easy to get the commands confused, and that makes the dog more perplexed and so adds to the problem.

CONFIDENCE

Many people lose their dog's confidence either in pushing too fast or by over-facing it. Many really good dogs can be three to three and a half years old before they become fully confident. This is a quality that has to be nurtured with careful handling in the earlier stages. Ewes can be really horrible to young dogs, and they are quick to know when a dog is feeling unsure. However, if you help too much, the dog will never learn. Try and read your sheep so that you can allow the dog the scope to perform, but at the crucial moment when you know the ewe is going to beat the dog, give the dog another command and step in to take the pressure off. In this way, the dog does

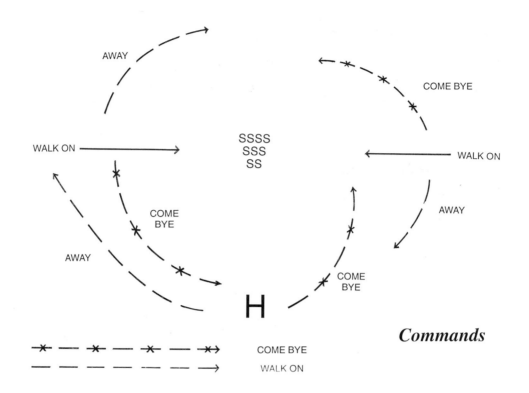

not lose the 'battle' with a resulting loss of confidence, because you gave another command.

This is so easy to do, and it can result in a really powerful dog in maturity, who can apply that extra pressure to the ewe. You can also help out by quietly turning the troublesome ewe. This can be done by adjusting your position, which will result in the rest of the flock moving in front of the ewe. My favourite bitch taught me this trick when a pupil was having trouble with her sheep and her novice dog. Sheep need to be dog-educated, so she asked me if I would come up to her farm and use my dogs and educate her sheep for her. The sheep were Jacobs, with fine horns, and my dogs had never worked this breed before. I decided to try my quiet little bitch who could often move sheep when others failed. She had no trouble whatsoever, and the lady was amazed. She knew all her sheep individually and said that the three troublemakers were always in the middle of the bunch.

I watched carefully, and every time one of the troublemakers came out to confront her, without a single word of command, my bitch would adjust her position and move the other sheep into it, and then carry on working the sheep along. I will never know when or where she learned this, but I have used it to great effect with other dogs. This drives home the truth that you can never teach well-bred dogs anything about sheep – but you can certainly learn a great deal from your dogs about sheep.

Never be reluctant to help a novice dog, but it is equally important not to make the mistake of doing too much. Drawing this fine line is the hardest part in training.

PUNISHMENT
Punishment is negative: it would be far better not to allow the problem to occur in the first place

The dog must have the confidence to exert power over the sheep.

This dog has won the battle for authority, and is now ready to take control and move the sheep.

than to attempt to correct it by punishment. If a problem arises, it is far more effective – and more rewarding – to go back a few stages, working in a smaller area and putting the training lead back on. Dogs appear to dislike being made to repeat an exercise correctly, and so this is far more effective than any form of abuse. Over the years I have never found that physical punishment achieved anything, except to make a dog become more evasive, harder in approach, and less sensitive. It is the handler who gets the most out of physical abuse, i.e. relief from tension and exasperation.

Whatever form of correction you use, it is at its most effective the first time it is applied. The second time it is only half as effective, and on the third occasion it is only a quarter as effective. Unless you can achieve success with the first correction, or at least ninety per cent success so that a second is only minor reinforcement, then the punishment is not going to achieve anything except physical pain, and maybe an intense fear of pain, which is not the type of relationship you are aiming for.

One of the more common problems that arise is the dog who likes to 'pull the wool', i.e. who comes in too close and grabs the sheep. Occasionally, I have had success correcting this by using a high-pitched screech alarm. This must be used as the dog grabs the sheep, but with many dogs it does not work. To be really effective, the dog must respond on the first occasion, and unless you achieve the desired result by the third occasion, you may as well abandon your efforts. You activate the alarm when the dog is a distance from you, and so the dog does not associate the sound with you. To aid this pretence, you must continue with the training session as though you had not heard anything.

If this does not work, you will just have to work much harder at keeping the dog off the sheep and get great obedience in the stop. It also helps if you stop the training at the point the dog grabs the sheep. A bright dog soon realises that this particular misdemeanour results in no more work – and that is sufficient 'punishment' for most Border Collies.

FINISHING WORK

It always helps if you try to see a situation from the dog's viewpoint. For a really keen, enthusiastic dog, who spends considerable stretches of time shut in, working sheep is the high spot of the day. So, when the work is over, would you be keen to leave the sheep when the boss calls you in? In order to counteract potential problems, call your dog in at odd intervals throughout the training, give lots of praise, and then continue the work. This usually solves any problem without the need for compulsion. Always finish the lesson on a good note, if things are going wrong, ask for a very simple exercise and then you can praise the dog and leave it at that. Some dogs give the appearance of not noting praise, but even though it is not always acknowledged, it is always appreciated.

In the early days of training, the dog will be on the training lead. This should be on the ground, and you should be holding it firmly in place with one foot. Call the dog to you – it might help if you put the dog in the down position first. Stand your ground and allow the sheep to drift off, but do not move until the dog obeys the command. Reward a correct response, and then allow the dog back on to the sheep. If you have a trained dog with you, you can use this individual to do the hard work of fetching the sheep back, which is absolutely invaluable.

To begin with I use this method with a novice dog, letting the sheep drift away – the farther the better. I leave the training lead on the ground, and hold on to the end of it with my hand, so lightly that the dog is not aware of it. I then encourage the dog to walk off with me on a slack line, repeating the command "That will do", and giving lots of encouragement. A dog will be totally obedient away from sheep, but a good, keen dog will need training to respond in this way when sheep are in view.

COPING WITH NON-IDEAL SHEEP

The professionals keep a few carefully selected sheep for training young dogs on. In reality you need two different types of sheep: one in the early stages, and a different type later on in the training. Ideal sheep certainly quicken up the training and produce less frustration and fault in the dog. If you have a spare few acres, you can buy in about ten old ewes (slaughterhouse sheep are ideal often), use them for training, and you still have the price back again when you re-sell to the slaughterhouse. You have lost nothing, but you have gained a trained dog. However, it is not always possible to do this, so you have got to be inventive and help your own sheep to behave as you want.

SHEEP WILL NOT MOVE FREELY

Sheep with this fault are ideal for the teaching of out-runs and flanking commands, but they are no use for the other parts of the training. Flex your mind and try to think of ways round this problem. Often the sheep move in one direction better than another and this gives you a few options to try:

1. Place a few free sheep on the other side of the fence so they pull the sheep towards them.

2. Fasten one of the group to a stake, and a rope from the sheep to the stake. This will encourage the sheep to pull towards the individual.

3. Place a few sheep nuts on the ground in the direction the sheep do not want to move, so they want to get back to have a quick feed. Do not be too generous or the sheep will tire of the nuts.

4. Contact someone who has slightly better sheep to give your dog a chance to work effectively.

HEDGE/FENCE

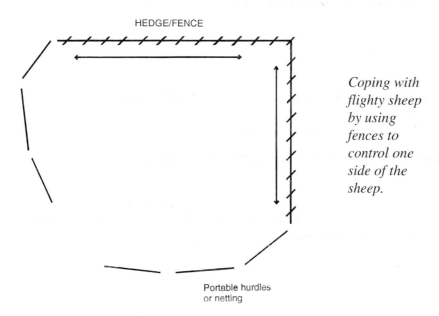

Coping with flighty sheep by using fences to control one side of the sheep.

Portable hurdles
or netting

FLIGHTY SHEEP

These can be just as big a problem as the 'will not move type'. The tethered sheep can be of use to slow them down, as can the feed nuts. However, in most cases you are better off making use of the field fencing – a great deal of early, basic training can be achieved along the boundary fencing. Make use of the corner of the field where you have two fences at right angles. The fences help to control one side of the sheep, leaving you with only one side of sheep to control. The corner acts as a stop to the sheep so, in the main, the sheep will not run past the corner – especially if you block the side that you are in charge of. You can extend the distances by working gradually further and further up the barrier away from the corner.

With a right-angled corner, in one direction you are on an anti-clockwise circle and the other direction you are on a clockwise circle. By this method, all your basics can be taught; out-runs, driving along the fence, flanking commands, pace, stopping, etc. Gradually move further and further out from the corner into the middle of the field. In this way, your dog gets used to working alongside a fence and working into a corner to turn sheep – a job that many well-trained sheepdogs

Using a fence to help the novice dog.

cannot do. A few portable hurdles or netting can also help to slow the sheep down and keep them into the corner area.

WORKING A DOG INTO A CORNER

In the early stages of training, the youngster will need help to move sheep out of the corner. Sheep have a great understanding of the advantage a corner gives them, but a dog who can manipulate sheep in this position will be an asset in numerous situations. Start off by walking into the corner yourself, with the dog on the training lead, positioned slightly behind your knee.

Encourage the dog to walk on to the sheep, although it is actually your presence that is forcing the sheep out of the corner. At this stage your roles are reversed: you are where the dog should be, and the dog is where you should be. Gradually (never allowing the sheep to stand on the dog), the dog will be able to take over the leading role. Moving sheep out of a corner will rarely be achieved by brute force; slow, relentless steady pressure is the way to get them to move, and you can instil this method into the dog right from the very start.

Helping the novice dog to work sheep out of a corner.

THE FLIGHT DISTANCE

We are able to work dogs on sheep because both obey the ancient laws of prey and predator. All prey has what is called a 'flight distance', which is variable in different species, and there can even be slight variations within the same species. This needs to be fully understood, as it makes the handling of sheep a much easier proposition.

You need to work out the flight distance for each training session, as it can vary slightly from day to day, and you must keep the dog just on the outside edge of that distance. If the dog oversteps it, the sheep will become awkward and they might stand up to the dog. They will certainly give more trouble than if the dog stays a mere inch behind the flight distance line. Sheep-wise dogs learn about this 'line' and, with experience, will work to it, adjusting their pace accordingly.

Sheep will almost always respond more readily to the quiet, relentless approach than to the dog who is all fired up and dashes in with gusto. So try to keep the dog working quietly, at the right distance, and without giving any ground to the sheep. In this way you will be able to get the sheep where you need them – and with less upset to the sheep.

THE TROUBLEMAKER

If I need to help a young dog, I move, forcing the sheep to move their position, and as the sheep move round in relation to my movements, they envelop the troublemaker and take her out of the action for a short time. The troublemaker will frequently manoeuvre herself into a key position again, so either you keep applying this method, or you get rid of her.

PROBLEMS WITH THE DOG'S WORK

A pupil came to me for a refresher lesson after several months break, and a number of problems had developed. Before you can find out what the real problem is, the dog must do a little work in front of you. I asked the handler if his dog could fetch my group of sheep, although I expected him to say they were too far away. However, he replied that this was no problem. The dog had not got very many yards before I knew where the trouble lay. It was the same old problem that everyone makes: too fast a progress and non-insistence with unobeyed commands.

There is no use in asking a dog to do a 100 yard out-run unless you have total success with a 50 yard or a 75 yard out-run. Extending the out-run before it is perfect will result in severe problems. In this case, my advice was that the handler had to go right back to short out-runs. I also observed that the dog only obeyed the commands it wanted to, and had no natural respect for the handler. The handler did not use his voice to help the dog, and gave little praise when the dog did achieve success.

BREAKING THE STAY

Before you can start to improve the situation, you must have the dog carrying out the instant stop and the perfect stay in the back yard. Until your dog is totally reliable in this situation, you cannot expect instant response when the dog is working sheep. You need a perfect stay so that you can help the dog to get the out-run pattern right. You could use a helper, but if the dog is disobedient with the stay command, you are likely to have additional problems. If I have a strong-minded dog, I do some obedience training near the sheep before allowing the dog to work. The dog is thoroughly disgusted at having to do simple heelwork, stop, sit, recall and stay, with the sheep close by, but unless you have that control, how can you expect to get it on the sheep?

The training lead can be a help with the dog who breaks the stay. Tie the end of the training lead to the fence, ask the dog to wait, and walk towards the sheep. If the dog breaks, the training lead acts as a restraint. I then walk back to the dog and growl a reprimand. You can repeat this as often as is necessary. I do not allow the dog to work until I can walk at least twice to the sheep and back to the waiting dog without the stay being broken. Remember to give lots of praise when the dog responds correctly. It is important to tie the lead low down on the fence and to leave it trailing loose on the ground. The dog must be sitting close to the fence so that there is no awareness of restraint. You can fix the training lead in position before you take the dog out to the sheep. Then take the dog out on a lead, and as you unclip the lead you simultaneously fasten on the waiting training lead. In this way, the dog is unaware of the restraint, which is a useful aid when teaching the lesson.

CORRECTING THE OUT-RUN

If problems arise with the out-run, you will need to start back at the beginning, and this requires quite a bit of effort on your part, especially if you have allowed a fault to develop. Give the down command, making sure the dog is facing the intended direction for the out-run. Command the dog to stay, and start walking the out-run yourself (see diagram), and at about three-quarters of the way up, ask the dog to lift sheep. The dog must carry out this action on the outside of you. Carry on with your circle, and when the dog has arrived at the lift position, give the stop command.

Again, think like the dog. If the dog is always asked to lift sheep once behind them, the dog will assume it has a right to do this, and there is no need to stop, in the full knowledge that the next command will be to get up and move the sheep on. You can stop this from happening if you only ask the dog to lift the sheep once in every five out-runs.

Setting a dog up for the out-run.

Directing the dog for a wider out-run.

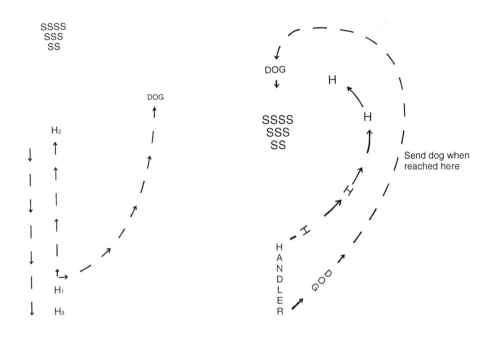

Helping to extend the out-run.   *Widening the out-run.*

If your sheep are free-moving, they will probably move off down the field from where you have just come, which is ideal. You can then repeat the out-run, once the sheep have got far enough away, thus repeating the full sequence. If the sheep are very obliging (free-moving sheep often are), you can repeat this with the minimum of human effort. If you are lucky to have a trained dog to help you and the sheep are not free moving, the trained dog can move them for you. This will teach both the out-run and the stop in one action. Once the dog really understands what it is you want, you can reduce the distance you move up the field and allow the dog to do more on its own. However, if there is any hint of moving in, then you must go back to walking further up.

In between sessions of out-run training, practise square flanking – a method popularised by Glyn Jones (Bodfari, Wales, GB). Here, you make the dog work the sides of a square on flanking commands (see diagram). You must not allow the dog to cut in. Square flanking, correct out-run teaching and instant obedience to the stop will result in a dog who will do little wrong. It is up to you to ensure you take the dog thoroughly and slowly through each stage. If you do not have the patience for such techniques, then you should not be training. In reality, a badly-trained dog wastes far more of your time over the years, and you will save all that with more effort in the early stages.

A word of warning about dogs becoming one-sided. Most dogs, like humans, favour one side more than the other. So it is up to you, the trainer, to ensure that the dog gets a great deal of practice on the unfavoured side. It is also worth asking yourself how a dog knows when it is going well or badly. There is little problem with knowing when things are not going well as the handler will make this clear. But it is equally important to be enthusiastic in praise when the dog is doing right – the dog needs to know.

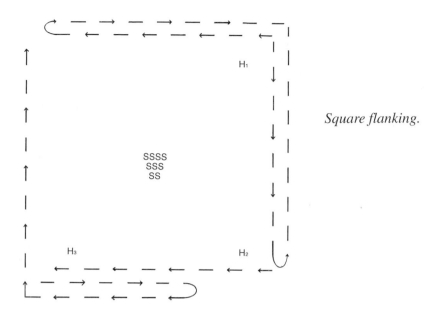

Square flanking.

Dogs which have a strong eye will free up with plenty of work, a dog with little eye will benefit from less work, as eye tends to intensify without work.

DOWN OR STAND
A dog who will stop in the stand produces a more fluid run, but the beginner will find it easier to teach the down for the stop, and then hope that with time the stand position will develop.

Remember, a working dog reflects the effort which the handler has put into its training – you are the key to a good dog – no-one else.

THE DISINTERESTED DOG
On quite a few occasions I have had to re-activate a dog who has lost the natural instinct to work. For example, the pup who was stopped from working the hens and horses in the yard, and then at fifteen months old was expected to do flock work. Or the person who wanted a disinterested dog to go hill-walking with, and then decided, when the dog was five years old, they wanted the dog to work sheep. In this situation, commonsense should tell the owner to get a new youngster and start from scratch, but sometimes, loyalty and lack of space for another dog plays a role.

The way ahead is generally hard, frustrating, full of early despondency, and few rewards. Generally, the greater the rapport between owner and dog, the greater the chance of success. You will also need to work with someone else who has a good working dog, who can control sheep easily and with calmness and authority. Like all training, lessons must be based on rewarding the right behaviour, and until the dog begins to show even the slightest thought of chasing sheep, nothing can be achieved. The handler has to put one hundred per cent enthusiasm into the job, and a great deal of encouragement via the voice. Your tone of voice should be exciting and provocative, and at the very first hint of wanting or even thinking about starting to chase, you must show great enthusiasm and encouragement. It will usually take in the region of five to seven

Getting a disinterested dog going. The sheep are controlled by one person while the handler concentrates on the dog.

sessions before the first sign is shown – hence the early despondency.

These dogs are often so 'safe' with sheep that you cannot start them free, as they will veer away from the flock, so a light training lead is needed to keep the dog behind the sheep all the time. I then place the sheep alongside a fence or a hedge, so that the one side is controlled, and the trained dog walks along quietly on the outside, with minimal commands. The handler, with the disinterested dog on a training lead, walks directly behind the sheep, encouraging the dog to walk on with plenty of praise. Timing must be balanced so that you give sufficient stimulation but do not bore the dog. The session must finish with great praise and enjoyment, whether the dog has responded or not.

Gradually you may notice that the dog gives a quick, direct look as if it would like to chase (although you may go several sessions with no sign): stop and praise greatly, and then continue, and so this is repeated. Once the dog is enthusiastic, then with the help of the trained dog to keep sheep up to the dog, the trainee is allowed to learn to follow and actually move the sheep. This should continue until the dog is confident that this is the correct response. At this stage, very insidiously, control is commenced. In the main, this type of dog is under very good control, so it is a matter of getting the dog to relax enough to move the sheep. From here, it is a slow and steady progression, as with any other trainee dog.

Sometimes it helps to fasten the dog up for a few days when working your other dogs, so that the dog can watch what is happening. While the dog is fastened, I get my work dog to work the sheep directly in front of the dog in a tantalising manner. Both these activities can spark off some reaction.

Chapter Eleven

TRIALING IN NORTH AMERICA

Since the Border Collie first arrived in North America, trials have been as diverse as their participants. Vast distances, varied terrain and unique local cultures have resulted in the creation of assorted courses, judging systems and championships. In recent years, Border Collie trials have become more standardised, largely through the efforts of the United States Border Collie Handlers Association.

TRIAL HISTORY

According to an article written by Arthur Allen for the *American Sheepdog Journal* in 1975, the first trial held in the US was in Philadelphia in 1880. The first US National Championship was held in Staunton, Virginia in 1941. Prior to that, the trials, held at Buck and Doe Run Valley Farm in Pennsylvania for five years, were considered to be 'national' trials. Unfortunately, there are scanty details about trialing during these early years.

An extremely popular trial that was run from 1959 through to 1982 was the Bluegrass Trial, held at Walnut Hall Farm in Lexington, Kentucky. While some local trials drew only a dozen or fewer entries, the Bluegrass was considered one of the "big three" (the other two being in Ohio and Canada). It is a tribute to this trial to note that during the 1970s there were usually over seventy dogs running. The Bluegrass course was a typical 'national' style course. In early years, there were deviations from the typical scale of points. In 1977 the point scale used was:

Gather: 10
Lift: 5
Fetch: 10
Drive: 15
Pen: 15
Shed: 5
TOTAL: 60 points.

One long-time handler I talked with felt the Bluegrass Trial was far more prestigious than the Supreme Championship trials held in the US during those years. The first Supreme Championship in America was held in 1954 at Olney, Illinois. In 1979 the United States Border Collie Handlers Association held its first USBCHA National Finals. This Trial enjoys a similar prestige in America to that of the International in the British Isles. The influence and impact of the USBCHA on Border Collie trials has been remarkable. During the years of the earlier Supreme Championship trials the number of competing dogs was low, sometimes as few as a dozen entries. A total of seventy-seven dogs were entered in the 1993 USBCHA National Finals competition.

Local area trials have increased in numbers almost exponentially. Once there were only a dozen or so trials during the year. Now handlers are often forced to choose which one of several to attend in a single weekend. The majority of trials are held from April through November. However, states in areas of the country that are not hard hit during the winter months, such as California, Texas and Arizona, continue to hold trials year-round.

THE NATIONAL FINALS

The Association has experimented with schemes to determine eligibility for running in the National Finals. Initially, members of the USBCHA could qualify dogs by placing in the top ten per cent of any Trial. More recently, qualifying trials must be sanctioned by the Association well in advance of the trial date. This has helped to standardise the trials throughout the country. Beginning with the 1994 Trial season, dogs placing in the top twenty per cent become qualified to

*ABOVE: Patrick Shannahan
sending his dog off on the drive.*

*BELOW: Lewis Pulfer at the pen
with his dog, Mirk.*

ABOVE: Ralph Pulfer, USBCHA Finals winner in 1988, and Nap, showing winning style at the pen.

RIGHT: Harry Holmes celebrating a successful pen.

run in the Finals. The USBCHA Finals is run over several days, usually starting on a Thursday and ending on Sunday. Scores from two qualifying runs are accumulated to determine which dogs compete in the final run. Last year, the top twenty dogs proceeded to the Championship run. Scoring was begun anew for this run. In past years, the scores from the qualifying and Championship runs were accumulated to decide the winner. The trial committee is again proposing changes to the Finals and so more changes may be introduced.

JUDGING SYSTEMS

Different judging systems developed during the history of trialing in the United States. In the seventies and early eighties quite a few point system trials were held and, in some areas, these trials are still being held. John Shropshire, in a June 1978 issue of *Border Collies Magazine* discussed the reasoning behind the point system for judging a Sheepdog Trial. Comparing the ISDS rules to his ideas of measuring the worth of a dog, Mr. Shropshire wrote:

"This didn't make much sense to me, especially after I had run several trials and was having trouble getting qualified judges. As a practical sheep man, it was even less appealing. If the dog didn't bring the sheep home or put them through the gate I didn't give a damn about style.

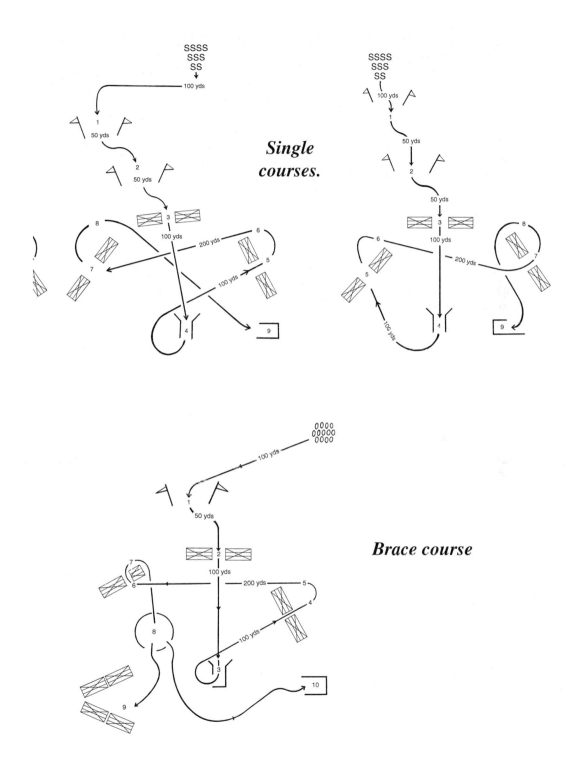

Single courses.

Brace course

*Ted Johnson,
USBCHA Finals
winner in 1985,
demonstrating
the art of
shedding.*

*Pearl, trained by
Chuck O'Reilly,
completes a
successful pen.*

"What would be a more practical way to measure a dog's ability than by awarding points for the number of sheep put through a gate or into a pen? The quality of the dog's work was deemed important – style, command and eye – but could these be bad if a dog accomplished what he was set to do?"

Mr. Shropshire questioned the judging system used by the ISDS and actively promoted "point system" trials. Shedding was dropped, because: "Although American and British systems give 16 per cent and 20 per cent respectively for shedding, Australia and New Zealand have dropped shedding. In point of fact it is not done very often at a lot of American and British trials. It is time-consuming, difficult to judge, hard on sheep and dogs. It was dropped from our trial."

A trial called the World Championship Trial, held in 1973 and 1975, was promoted by Mr. Shropshire. Handlers from South Africa, Australia, New Zealand and Great Britain were invited to compete. The trials were judged as point system trials, and Raymond MacPherson won on both occasions. According to Mr Shropshire, adequate time was allowed to complete without making it a race to win the competition. Retries were allowable to successfully negotiate obstacles. Off-set fetch gates, a blind race and a bridge were developed at his trial. In case of a tied score, time was the deciding element.

Since the mid-eighties, point system trials were seldom held, as popular opinion swung to the side of judged Trials. We are currently seeing a slight resurgence of point trials (sometimes called timed Tials). Many of these are Trials held in arenas with large audiences. One popular trial in the West is held in a rodeo arena. The sheep are manoeuvred through a clover-leaf pattern around barrels and penned. Each obstacle must be successfully negotiated before proceeding to the next. The spectators become enthusiastically involved with each run as they compare a large time clock, suspended over the arena, with each dog's progress. The timed trial appeals to many American spectators who are from urban areas and are not educated in the nuances of sheepdog work. It is obvious that the winner is the dog who completes all the tasks in the best time!

CLASS DIVISIONS
Competitors at trials in the United States and Canada have the opportunity to compete on several different levels. Novice, Pro-Novice, Ranch, Open Ranch, Open or Nursery classes may be offered at a trial.

NOVICE: Novice classes vary from one part of the country to another, depending upon the local association's rules. In some areas, entries are confined to novice handlers with novice dogs. In another area there may be an age limit (often 18 or 24 months) for the dog to compete. The dogs are often required to only gather and pen.

The Ontario Border Collie Club in Canada added a 'wear' to their Novice classes, where, once the sheep are brought to the handler's feet, they are taken through or around an obstacle and then penned. The handler often precedes the stock, with the dog 'wearing' the stock toward the handler. Some associations in the United States have recently added the 'wear' to their Novice class. It gives the competitor more time on the field as well as being able to maintain control of a young dog.

PRO-NOVICE, RANCH, OPEN RANCH: These classes may simply differ in title, depending upon what part of the country the trial is held. With the advent of the USBCHA, however, these classes have become more standardised. The Ranch class may be synonymous with the Novice class, and the Pro-Novice may be synonymous with Open Ranch. Often the Pro-Novice class will consist of a gather, one drive leg, and a pen. Open Ranch will be a full course, without a shed.

NURSERY: This also consists of a full course without a shed, but there is an age limit. (The USBCHA rule reads: "30 months or younger on or before December 31st of the year previous to the Nursery Finals.") Dogs placing in the top twenty per cent of a USBCHA Nursery class can go on to compete at the Nursery Finals held in the fall of the year.

Most local associations have a method for determining when a handler is required to move his dog up to the next level of competition.

OPEN: The Open class is a full course, usually complete with a shed or single. There are variations in the exercises in Open at some trials. One popular variation is to replace the single with a Maltese cross. For the most part, the Open class at a trial venue will be run on Saturday and Sunday. Some trials are billed as two one-day trials, where each day is a new beginning for the competitors. Other trials accumulate scores over both days to decide the winning dogs. Another variation at some of the larger trials is to have one or more qualifying runs from which the top fifteen to twenty-five dogs compete in a final run for the prizes.

TRIAL ARENAS

Another source of variety in our trials is the size of the field on which the course is set. Most of the USBCHA-sanctioned trials will have an outrun of 150 to 300 yards, with an average drive of approximately 300 to 450 yards. These figures may vary, depending on the terrain and workability of the field being used. Arenas, which are generally used for equine events at local fairs, range from quite small (e.g. 75ft by 100ft) to what is considered good-sized (e.g. 100ft by 300ft).

The trial committee may need to be inventive in setting up a course in the smaller arenas. At first glance, these smaller areas may seem far too easy to present much of a competitive challenge. However, it should be considered that even the tiniest over-flank leaves little room to repair the line before the next panel is reached. Spectators just feet away from a drive panel may distract the sheep, and some dogs are not keen to work in noisy, crowded areas. The handler must react quickly to any untoward situation that may occur.

REGIONAL DIFFERENCES

There are many local associations in the United States which have their own rules regarding trials, and some states have more than one of these clubs. In areas where there are fewer members available, an association may encompass several states. Because local associations are autonomous they do not answer to an overseeing organisation. This is one reason why there is so much variation in trials in the US. Perhaps some day the USBCHA will act as a parent association with local chapters throughout the country, enabling further standardisation of the trials.

Americans in different regions are unique and their outlook on sheep dog competition can vary greatly. There are groups of handlers who are all fairly new to the sport, and they are feeling their way slowly into the field of competition. These handlers will tend toward holding classes and trials which are less demanding, thus enabling them to achieve personal success. In other areas, especially on the eastern and western coasts, trials have been held for many years, and so competitors are more accomplished and trials are highly-developed with keen, tough competition.

The differences found from one region to another generally will be in minor variations of the rules. The courses and rules at most trials run by established associations will closely parallel those of trials found in Britain. Local trials often reflect the main interests of their entrants. In areas where cattle production is high, quite a few "cattle dog" trials are held. The courses set for these events may vary widely. Sometimes the cattle are worked on a typical sheep course in a pasture and judged accordingly. In other trials, the cattle are fetched across a pasture, moved directly into a working area, and then driven through panels and chutes and into a pen or trailer. The cattle may be worked in an arena.

The manner in which the trials are judged varies widely. Although many cattle trials are "judged" trials, there are also some which are point and time trials, or a combination of judging lines and workmanship as well as time. Generally, cattle trials are held to promote use of the dogs in working cattle. Cattlemen like to see tasks performed which are similar to those they do on the ranch, such as working in a chute or loading a trailer. Because of exposure to the dogs at the trials, more cattlemen are taking an active interest in using Border Collies for cattle work.

LEFT: The 1990 USBCHA Futurity Champion Tweed, with his owner-handler, Hubert Bailey.

BELOW: Jack Knox, a USBCHA Finals winner in 1979 and 1980, with his dogs.

THE COMPETITION TRAIL

Keen competitors often travel great distances to get to favourite trials. It is not unusual for a handler to drive over twelve hours to attend a trial. Some states, such as Virginia, Texas and California, have a great number of trials, thus minimising travel for local participants. In many of the Midwest states – Missouri, Kansas and Iowa, for example – local trials are scarce. This means a handler must "hit the road" to compete. There are also some handlers who are retired or who train and handle dogs for their living. These handlers spend most of their year away from home, going from one trial to another.

Trial circuits have developed in a few parts of the country to allow handlers to attend more trials in a short period of time. One especially popular circuit is the Virginia Triple Crown, held in May of each year. The first trial is held on a weekend, the second trial in the middle of the week, with the third trial on the following weekend. Handlers from all over the country drive or fly to Virginia to compete. Those attending from California and Washington State may be well over 2,000 miles from home. Handlers for whom trialing is a hobby will spend their vacations attending a circuit of trials.

A number of women are now making their mark on the competition trail. Kathy Knox (above) is working her dog, Jess.

LEFT: Maxine Netherway of Ontario working with her Border Collies.
     Rainer Leipscher.

When attending trials far from home, handlers either make arrangements to stay at hotels or motels, or carry their home-away-from-home with them. It is easy to spot a trial field, as there will be the customary collection of dog trailers, vans, trucks with campers, motorhomes and even tents. Some campers and motorhomes are quite elaborate, enabling the handlers to have all the comforts of home, including television. At the very least, most will have refrigeration and cooking facilities and a comfortable bed. For many, trials are social events to be savoured. The temporary city of trialers at the trial field allows for camaraderie between friends with a much-loved common interest.

Trial competition in North America has left its mark on both the Border Collies and their handlers. Breeding has become more selective, ensuring our Border Collies will continue to be chosen for farm and ranch work as well as the trial field. Handling and training have improved and

Line-up at the 1993 USBCHA Finals (left to right): Bill Berhow and Nick, Ralph Pulfer, Gordon Rogerson and Bud Boucheau and Patches.

The famous Nick, aged nine years old, in winning form at the 1993 USBCHA Finals.

progressed as competition has become keener. The variety offered by our trials enables handlers with an assortment of interests and abilities to be part of this exciting and rewarding competition.

USBCHA NATIONAL FINALS WINNERS

1979: Jack Knox and Jed
1980: Jack Knox and Jed
1981: Etroy McCaslin and Max
1982: John Bauserman and Bess
1983: Ted Johnson and Craig
1984: Bob Childress and Fy
1985: Ted Johnson and Jan

1986: Bruce Fogt and Hope
1988: Ralph Pulfer and Dan
1989: Bill Berhow and Nick
1990: Bill Berhow and Nick
1991: Dorrance Eikamp and Rex
1992: Bruce Fogt and Molly
1993: Bill Berhow and Nick.

Chapter Twelve

COMPETITIVE OBEDIENCE TRAINING

There are many Border Collie owners who become interested in Obedience training. Some go on to competitive Obedience, and others simply enjoy the challenge of working with their dog and overcoming problems in training that may arise. As far as the Border Collie is concerned, this is an excellent form of stimulation and it develops the relationship between dog and owner.

In the scope of this book, I cannot go into detail of training for competitive Obedience, but there are a few exercises which are worth highlighting, focusing on the most common problems that arise.

THE STAY

I have never had a dog who has a real problem, although I have had some sensitive dogs who have found it difficult to stay in the position commanded, i.e. Sit, Stand or Down. This type of dog may become worried by the hustle and bustle around, and may go from Sit to Down, or from Stand to Sit, but the dog will not move from the place allocated – and that is a significant difference.

The dog needs to learn that "Stay" does not just mean stay on that allocated area of ground, but also in the position that has been stipulated. To a slightly worried dog, the Stand and Sit positions are rather more vulnerable than a lower one, and so the dog may go down a notch in order to appear less noticeable. My dog, Trapper, had this problem in a particular hall, but only there. If I returned to put her (albeit it very gently) into the stipulated position, she became even worse.

I stopped to ask myself why she was going wrong, as she is a submissive little bitch and always tries to get it right for me. I tried her in less prominent positions, first up on the stage above the others, then in a corner, and there was no problem. On the stage, the other dogs were close, but she was above them and felt safe. In the corner, she presented only her front to the others and so felt much safer. It was merely a case of building confidence slowly and gently.

Other reasons for not staying are:

1. The dog does not understand what is required.
2. The dog is not really bothered about obeying you.
3. The dog is somewhat dominant and you are not totally accepted as Alpha Leader.
4. The other dogs are more interesting than the owner.

There is always the dog who will discover a new reason for failing in the Stay, which is what stops dog training from becoming boring. However, the solutions to the most common causes are obvious. The fundamental problem is that the dog does not accept you as Alpha Leader, and so you need to establish your position by means of control and correction exercises (see Chapter

Three: Problems in Training). There is also the problem that the dog does not understand what is required – and, in my experience, this difficulty crops up on a very regular basis.

I watched a lady (who should have known better) come into the training club, tie up her three dogs to a rail, put them in the Down, saying "Stay" and walk off to take the class. Naturally, the dogs got a little restless; they inched about, and as other dogs walked close by, they had a quick sniff. Doubtless they got a bit stiff lying in one position for a long time on a hard floor, and so they moved to be more comfortable. The result of this scenario was that the owner had reinforced to the dogs that Stay did not really mean remaining in the stipulated position. No wonder there are Stay problems.

There is another classic mistake which I see so often, and I have even seen trainers teaching it. The sequence goes as follows:

1. Get your dog ready for a recall.
2. Command the dog to Stay.
3. Leave the dog.
4. Call the dog to you.

The next time the dog is put in the Stay, the dog, thinking the owner has forgotten the command to come, runs up, only to be greeted by a fierce reprimand. The answer is to always use separate commands (see Chapter Two: Early Education). My dogs know that "Stay" means stay put until I return, whereas "Wait" means another instruction will follow within moments.

There is another body signal that your dog may misread. If your dog is in the Stay and looks unsteady, you give a reinforcing "Stay" command. However, you must ensure your body is in a completely upright posture; do not lean towards the dog at all. Think of your body posture when you call your dog, it is usually a lean forward as an encouragement signal. So do not say "Stay" with your voice while your body language says "Come".

Another common mistake is that the handler gives a reinforcement command once the dog has shown daylight: that is too late. You need to reassure with "Stay" before daylight occurs. There is no harm in the occasional reassurance command, especially in the early days of training, and even in the experienced dog, it helps to ease the tension. If you are being really attentive to your dog, then you should have advance notice that the dog is about to move. Maybe the dog takes its gaze from you, looks at another dog, drops its head, fidgets, or from a relaxed position goes rigid. You know your dog and you will know the sign. Once the sign has been given, act immediately, not with force but with reassurance.

Do not hype the dog up just before the Stays, and do not have a difference of opinion just before the Stays. Go to the Stay position with a quiet, calm, confident and relaxed attitude and you are part-way there. Build up both distance and time separately, and in a very small steady progression. Do not take a huge leap ahead even if the dog appears to be learning quickly and well. This could be the result of a lucky chance rather than the dog really understanding what is required.

HEELWORK

More marks are lost in this exercise than anywhere else. If you are doing a Stay, the dog either stays or it does not, but Heel work it is a graded action. Competition Heelwork is covered in many specialist books and videos, and in order to reach a reasonable standard you will have to enrol with a club that specialises in competitive Obedience. In this context, I will focus on the most common problems that arise with this exercise.

Border Collies are notorious pullers on the lead, and so the first mistake usually occurs when the

HEELWORK
W.T. Ch. Wicklow Lad and his owner, Gary Atkins,
demonstrating the correct heel position.

owner tries to stop the dog pulling on the lead – and does so by pulling back on the lead, which actually reinforces to the dog that this action is correct. I have often been asked for help with this problem, and the most typical situation is a lady with a strong, young dog. In most cases, I have broken the back of the problem within half an hour, and then it is up to the owner to continue the work.

The solution is quite simple: you only move forward when the dog is at the correct place at heel. Immediately the dog pulls forward, the lead is allowed to go slack and you stand still. There is no verbal contact for the moment. If the dog does not return to position, the correct command is used, "Heel" or "Close", and the dog is encouraged back into place. Once there, forward movement may commence. Each time the dog goes ahead, the same procedure is followed. In the first lesson you may not advance beyond a few yards, but this does not matter.

It does not take the average, bright dog long to realise that the walk goes nowhere unless the right position is maintained. There is no need to pull back, to use force, or to make an issue of it. All you need to do is quietly assert your requirements. Naturally, rewarding with a tidbit and praise once in the correct position will allow the dog to be very sure that the Heelwork position is what you require.

We teach our dogs to work wide by a variety of situations, e.g. walking crookedly into the dog, flapping clothing at dog's head height, being rough so the dog keeps clear of you, swinging into the dog when you turn. Ask someone to video you and your dog working, and when you play it back you will be quite amazed at what you see. A useful tip is to teach your dog to walk backwards at an early age. This action can often be made use of on about-turns, left turns and one or two other positions. Distant control is another exercise where the going back can be utilised. It also teaches the dog to use the body with more flexibility. A slightly forward Sit can also be corrected with this command.

Never forget to give a tidbit or a toy reward. There seems to be a small percentage of people who regard the giving of tidbits as a bribe; they want the dog to work for them, not for a tidbit. It takes somewhere in the region of two years to build up a working partnership. Tidbits help this bond to develop more deeply, they are an extra tool in the language barrier, and they reassure the unsure dog. Any dog who respects you, will, given time to understand and develop a bond, work quite happily just for your praise. However, many dogs work only through fear, and this is small satisfaction to the owner. The bond between you and your dog should be continually growing and developing. In human partnerships, an occasional gift adds a little cream to the relationship, and the same applies when you reward your dog with tidbits.

THE CAN-DO METHOD

I have said earlier that it is not within the scope of this book to teach the competitive exercises, but I make one exception with my method of Heelwork. This was taught to me by Jean and Arlene Haines of Can Do, Winnipeg, with whom I have had many wonderfully instructive holidays. I have never seen this method used elsewhere; I find it excellent as it is based on positive teaching and the dogs really enjoy it. With very little effort, I can get a dog to quite a good standard in a very short space of time, and unlike so many methods, it is not boring.

The programme can start off in the smallest area of the house and then extend into the garden.

STEP ONE: Start with the dog sitting in the Wait position, approximately two feet behind you. With your back to the dog, step back with your left foot into the Heel position. Reach your hand down to the dog's collar, use the dog's name and the Heel command, and guide your dog forward with your left leg to one pace in front of your right foot, placing the dog into a straight Sit. Practise this without the dog first and get the flow of movement right. Do this a couple of times a session, and do it two or three times a day. Continue with this daily until the dog is working with you. The amount of time this takes depends upon the dog; some pick it up extremely quickly. Once the dog can do it, practise for one extra day – a good maxim in all training.

STEP TWO: Leave the dog in the Wait, two feet behind you, and with your back towards the dog. Without physical assistance, command the dog to heel position, to the straight Sit, and reward. Once the dog is doing this well, then carry on for two or three days before going on to the next step.

STEP THREE: Stop a moment. Do not hurry your training, this causes so many problems.

Leave your dog in the Wait and make a quarter turn away from the dog, still approximately two feet away and in line with the dog's hindquarters. Use the dog's name and command to Heel. Ensure you have a straight Sit and then reward. Note that we are still not moving from the spot. The aim is to teach the dog the correct Heel position, without allowing any scope for failure.

STEP FOUR: Leave your dog in the Wait, and this time make a half turn. The dog will now be facing one direction and the handler in another. Again, give the Heel command, and reward your dog once in a straight Sit. In each step, the dog must have practised the previous one until you are confident it is fully understood – and then practise for two or three days before moving up a step.

There is a chance that the dog, as dogs are prone to do, will anticipate the Wait position. In order to prevent this, every three or four times you carry out this procedure, do not follow the action through, but go back and reward the Wait, and then finish the session for that one training period.

STEP FIVE: With the dog sitting in the Heel position, use the dog's name and the Heel command. Then step off with the left foot for three steps, starting and stopping on the left foot. Ensure the dog sits straight and reward. Do this at three steps for two days and then go back to Step One for a couple of days. Work your way back up to Step Five, a couple of days at a time. This back-to-basics training is necessary from time to time as it reinforces all that you are asking the dog to do and prevents sloppiness setting in.

You now need several days of walking to Heel for five steps and then several days at seven steps. Return for a quick revision of basics before progressing to nine steps. It sounds like a lot of fuss but it is amazingly easy and effortless, and the dog really becomes automatic in position. Distance is only built up in an odd number of steps.

STEP SIX: This has a double action. Regardless of where the dog has been placed, it teaches that, on the Heel command, the dog must achieve the desired Heel position. It is also teaches ninety per cent of the Advanced Recall without the dog knowingly being taught anything different, or more importantly, becoming mixed up.

The set-up is just the same. You place yourself at all odd angles in the room and ask the dog to come to Heel. If the dog is coming into a moving Heel position, then you must stop and reward as soon as the dog makes the right position. This is all done on the lead. Develop the work in numerous places before starting on Heel-free, and then it is back to basics again to learn Heel-free.

This programme can be started quite early in the youngster's training, for there is no stress, and no chance of the dog not achieving (unless you are in the wrong). It is positive learning, and it is, therefore, relaxed and easily assimilated. I used this method on my bitch to qualify for her Versatility Award, and although she has not competed in Obedience since, she really adores being asked to demonstrate it. She retained the lesson far better than any other dog taught by conventional methods. Like all things to do with dogs and dog training, you "pays your price and picks your tune". There are as many different ways of training dogs as there are trainers and dogs. Select the one which suits you and your dog best.

ADVANCED RECALL
This seems a good time to discuss a problem which can arise with this exercise as we have already discussed one way of teaching it. Many handlers, when teaching it, uses the command "Come". Ask yourself where you usually require the dog to be positioned in response to this command (in front of you), and where do you want the dog to be positioned for an Advanced Recall (in the Heel position) – there is no wonder the dog gets confused. The command for coming to Heel must always be "Heel".

As in all training, including sheep working, do not go on and on, nagging at the dog: it is far better do ten minutes in the morning and ten in the evening – and always end with a play session. You want your training to be done professionally, but not so seriously that it excludes all feelings.

DISTANT CONTROL
Teach the dog to do all the three exercises – Sit, Stand and Down – independently of each other, and only join them as a sequence when the dog is totally happy with obeying them quickly, easily, and in a relaxed manner. This stops repeated commands and movement. Most dogs have a problem

The Stand: The left hand is held out to the side.

The Sit: The right hand is touching the forehead.

The Down: The right hand is held forward at an angle of forty-five degrees.

with the Stand, and as, by now, tidbits are only given occasionally, do not give a reward from the Sit to the Down, but reward for the Stand. Obviously, if your dog has a problem with one of the other positions rather than the Stand, you reward for the 'problem' position.

Again, many problems with this exercise are due to progressing too quickly. I start with the dog at my side until perfect on the commands, progressing to just in front of me, then two foot away, then a couple of yards, using no barrier. I then use the top stair to practise on, graduating slowly down the stairs until the dog cannot see the hand signals. I then use a natural barrier, such as a ditch, and I stand on one side with the dog on the other side. Commands need to be distinct from each other so that the dog cannot get them mixed up. Spoken commands must be said distinctly; poor commands often cause confusion for the dog. In all training, always revert to an occasional tidbit, it takes away tension, reassures the dog that the exercise is being performed correctly, and it builds up confidence.

SCENT DISCRIMINATION

This exercise seems to be a problem for some people. First, ask yourself what you are trying to teach the dog. It certainly is not scenting, for the dog has forgotten more about this than any human will ever know. Your aim is to teach the dog to select an article from a number with one hundred per cent accuracy. Notice how many totally untrained dogs can always find the branch or stone they have been playing with, no matter how many branches or stones are in the same area. So why does the trained dog get confused when asked to perform a similar task? I will list some of the possibilities in a show set-up that cause a dog to seemingly fail.

1. The steward or the judge had stood on that spot, and so there is a stronger scent just under yours.
2. Draughts have a habit of wafting across the arena indiscriminately, and this could have masked the scent on the chosen object.
3. Outdoor scents can clog up the dog's nose and affect the scenting ability temporarily.
4. The dog's concentration is broken by something outside the ring.
5. The dog may be a little below par, so little that you have not noticed, but sufficiently to affect the dog.
6. Strong scents on other humans, such as perfumes, deodorants, cigars, cigarettes and other such scents.
7. The 'Greyhound syndrome' (see Chapter Five: Health Care) has a drastic effect on many bitches during the twelve weeks of a seasonal cycle. Indeed, a friend of mine had to plan her Working Trials around her bitch's seasons.
8. The dog is not given sufficient experience and is only used to the same article. The dog does not understand what it is you actually want.
9. A male may have caught the scent of a bitch in or nearly in season.
10. The dog may be air scenting instead of ground scenting. This happens quite frequently, and it is the fault of the handler for not making it clear that ground scenting is required.

With Scent Discrimination, it is essential to remember that the dog has *not* got it wrong. Either you have not taught the dog what is required, or else the scent available to the dog is not what *you* think it is.

RETRIEVE

The major problem with this exercise is the handler boring the dog to the limit by being too serious. I have seen many really nicely retrieving dogs being put off because of the handler's 'nit-picking'. There really is no need to keep practising a formal Retrieve over and over again. It is far

THE RETRIEVE

LEFT: When teaching the Retrieve, work at the formal Sit in front as a separate exercise before trying to put the whole sequence together.

ABOVE: The Retrieve should be fun – this dog is clearly enjoying the exercise.

BOTTOM LEFT: A nice straight sit in front, presenting the dumb-bell.

BELOW: The dumb-bell should be removed by slipping a finger into the dog's mouth behind the dumb-bell and gently easing it out.

better to do one or, at the most, two a week. Practise the formal Sit in front and Sit at heel on separate occasions in their own entity. If you really want to do other retrieves, then, when the dog returns, bend down into a crouched position and make a fun thing of calling the dog in and giving a tidbit.

In the early days, and occasionally even when experienced, set the dog up, throw the dumb-bell, leave the dog sitting and pick it up yourself. The dog should realise that a thrown dumb-bell does not mean a right to retrieve it. If you have a dog who is constantly anticipating, then out of every five throws the dog should only be allowed a single retrieve – the others must all be collected by the handler.

I had a very sensitive little bitch who would dash out to retrieve with gusto, but got puzzled when asked to wait first. I placed the dumb-bell on a small stool and asked her to fetch it from there, and she had no problems with that. I next set her up for the Retrieve and left her sitting in place while I put the dumb-bell on the stool, returned, waited a fraction and then sent her. There was no problem. I soon built up the Wait and dropped the stool down lower until she was retrieving the dumb-bell placed on the floor.

The next stage was to get a friend to throw the dumb-bell from behind me. It did not take very long, and I ended up with a dog who won enthusiastic comments from judges about her tremendous enthusiasm for the Retrieve, but with one hundred per cent control. If I had made an issue about it, I would have had severe trouble and probably would never have had a reliable Retrieve. This was a sensitive bitch who always did her best to please me, and when she had problems I knew she needed my help, not a stream of abuse. This is true for very many dogs, but they are totally misunderstood by their owners and are exposed to abuse and correction when they do not even know what they have done wrong.

For some dogs, the Retrieve means chasing not retrieving, and so when the Wait is put into the exercise it is no longer a chase game – in the dog's eyes, it is no longer the same exercise. This is a common problem with Border Collies because their chase instinct is so strong. I often throw the dumb-bell for fun, for my dog knows whether it is fun or serious. However, if you are worried that your dog is becoming mixed up, then on every non-competitive occasion when the dog brings back the dumb-bell, throw a toy at the end of the exercise so that you keep an element of fun in work.

PROGRESSING TOO FAST
The classic mistake with a reluctant retriever, once the dog is just starting to get interested, is to move on too quickly. This is fatal. If I have a reluctant retriever, I spend at least three-quarters of the training session playing. In this way, interest turns to keenness and eventually the dog develops a craving for the article. I then casually drop the dumb-bell and let the dog pick it up, and endeavour to let the dog hold it while I give lavish praise.

These fun games will continue for as long as six months, with distances increasing so gradually that the dog does not realise that we are doing a Retrieve. I continue tantalising the dog by playing with the dumb-bell – and sometimes I do not let the dog have it at all. Sometimes you can excite the dog by holding on to the collar as you throw the article and then getting the dog excited just before you give the command to Fetch. All too often, I see this slow progress being hurried, and I see the dire results. It is three times as hard if you lose what you have just gained, so, *do not be in a hurry!*

CHOICE OF ARTICLE
The choice of article can have a major effect on a dog's willingness to retrieve. Put a bone-handled

knife into your mouth and hold it by your teeth. Is that comfortable? The same applies to the dog who is asked to hold a hard, plastic article, or to the gentle little soul who is asked to pick up a wooden article. Never, never start Retrieve training with a dumb-bell. Use something soft, like a rolled up soft leather glove, a duster, or a similar item. Once the dog adores this soft item, it can easily be fastened round the dumb-bell and the dog will usually have no problems retrieving it. The 'mouthy', gripper type of dog will not mind what the article is, but many smaller, gentle dogs need to have exactly the right-sized dumb-bell; one too large, even by half an inch, can be quite hard for them to balance.

SENDAWAYS

This exercise is not included in Obedience competitions in North America, and in Britain, it is a different exercise for competitive Obedience people and for Working Trials. In Obedience, the exercise is shorter and more precise, with markers indicating the spot the dog must go to. In Working Trials the Sendaway is long, and, often, there is no visible marker for the dog.

I had problems teaching this exercise to my dog Bracken, until I decided to give her a reason for going away – and then she would go with great enthusiasm. She had one article she really craved for – my leather wallet – so once we had reached her position, I would throw this for her. She then decided that Sendaways were the prelude to retrieving my wallet. Since then, all my dogs have had a special 'Sendaway only' toy, and they all go out with great enthusiasm.

I always do a Sendaway to a barrier, such as a fence, a hedge, or a wall, and I build up a distance by working back from the barrier. This stops the desire to look back for the Down command, for the dog knows that this will not come until the barrier has been reached. I never start to teach the Sendaway until the dog will do an instant drop anywhere on command. You must have this first, otherwise you are teaching two lessons at the same time – and you cannot get a smart Sendaway without an instant drop.

Setting a dog up for the Sendaway.

The dog has reached the correct spot and has dropped as requested.

Some Border Collies have a strong out-run instinct. In order to overcome this desire to run out in a curve, use a large, heavy ball and roll it to your barrier, so that the dog follows the line of the ball. This will need to be done for quite a while so that a straight line is put into the dog's 'computer system' instead of a wide curve.

JUMPS AND JUMPING

Major problems arise with this exercise because the dog does not truly understand what the word 'Over' means. In fact, it is amazing how many dogs manage to comply with what the handler wants without truly understanding it. The other problem is the handler's desire to practise, practise, practise, until the dog gets thoroughly bored with the whole exercise. Both situations can easily be prevented.

When first training the dog to jump, start with a straight pole, positioned low, and as the dog becomes more accomplished, this can be raised gradually. There will come a stage when the dog will be able to walk underneath the pole. This is the moment when the dog begins to understand that the requirement is to jump upwards and *over* the pole.

Right from the very start, even when the dog can only manage very low heights, find as many different natural obstacles as possible for the dog to jump. Do not attempt any formality, just let the dog have fun, and it helps if *you* get into the spirit of it, as the dog will become infected with your enthusiasm. Play ball at the same time, and ensure you give one pleasantly spoken command and one action. In the early stages attach a light training lead so that you can guide the dog and ensure success. Border Collies are natural and enthusiastic jumpers, and a dog who is encouraged to jump for fun will never fail you.

With this type of training, a dog needs very little practice on the scale. Over the years I have proved this point on several occasions. I have taken a dog (sheep-trained only, except for jumping for fun and to get into the sheep field), and given the command to jump a 5ft 6ins scale. On each of the three occasions I attempted this, the dog had never seen the obstacle before, and each of the three dogs did it without hesitation. As far as my dogs are concerned, jumping is fun – it is never regarded as a chore.

Dogs fail a scale for one of three reasons:

1. The dog has not learned to enjoy jumping.
2. The dog has become despondent because of their unsympathetic human partner.
2. A bitch with a false pregnancy fails to perform because of the effects of her seasonal cycle.

The first two problems are easy to deal with. It is a matter of going back to basics and introducing fun into the exercise. The third problem can only be solved by waiting for the bitch to come through her hormonal upset. This normally lasts for twelve weeks from onset of the season, unless you treat for false pregnancy and then carry on as before. Bitches in this hormonal cycle are unlikely to be able to jump. I have no explanation for this, but experience has shown me it is so. Sometimes the bitch fails on only one of the three types of jump, but it could be on two types or on all three.

I know of quite a few competitors, myself included, who have to plan their schedule round their bitch's heat period. There is no point in nagging at your bitch at this time, as she cannot help it. It is better to give her some time off for fun and relaxation. She will be back on form within a couple of weeks.

Everybody has to work for something. Humans may be motivated by the need to earn a living, or simply because they enjoy the work. Which of these two groups produces the best quality work

Start off by letting your dog enjoy natural jumps.

and will put in extra time without extra pay? Relate this to your dog. If your dog normally jumps well and then becomes hesitant, do not employ force. Stop and ask yourself why? We have a language barrier, and your dog is telling you all is not well. There could be many reasons for this: a strained muscle, a stomach ache – it might be all sorts of things. A dog who is normally obliging will never refuse unless something is wrong. It is up to you to find out what the problem is, or at least bide your time until it ceases to be a problem. The dog will soon tell you when this is the case – it is all a matter of getting in tune with your dog.

Chapter Thirteen

THE VERSATILE BORDER COLLIE

The Border Collie is bred to work sheep, but if you have no plans to use your dog for this work, it is advisable to take up another discipline which will provide interest and stimulation. A dog that is bred to work will soon become bored and restless, and it is no time before this turns into deviant behaviour. However, a Border Collie with a purpose in life will thrive and will prove to be the most rewarding of canine companions. The type of activity you choose will depend upon your own inclination, and your dog's capabilities. If you are of a competitive nature, you may aspire to the highest honours in your chosen discipline. There is nothing wrong with that – but remember, working with your Border Collie should always be fun. If you lose sight of this in pursuit of your own ambitions, you will be the loser. To achieve at the highest level you need a happy dog who loves being with you, and is always eager to please.

SHEEPDOG TRIALS

Sheepdog Trials are supposed to represent actual farm work, and it is more likely that a good, hard-working farm dog, who has had a little 'polish' added to general work, will make a better and more reliable trial dog than the 'hobby trialist's' dog. The content of Sheepdog Trials varies from one country to another, often based partially on the type of work the dog does in that country, but

Sheepdog Trials are a hugely popular form of competition; they are devised to resemble real sheep work a closely as possible.

LEFT: The shepherd's crook comes in many shapes and sizes.

BELOW: Precision is all-important when competing at the highest level.

much of the trial is the same whatever country you are in.

Most require an Outrun, a Lift, a Fetch, some form of Drive, and some form of Penning, whether it be into a trailer, over a bridge, or into a box made up of hurdles. The trial run is judged on a marks system based on perfectly straight lines, with marks being taken off for any slight bend or fault. The dog with the highest number of points is the winner.

Farm work varies from one part of the country to another, and there are even differences from one farm to the next. Some dogs are always running the hills, other dogs would not know what a hill was. Generally, the dogs are required to fetch the sheep and/or cattle. Sometimes they are both sheep and cattle dogs; sometimes they will only work one type of animal. Invariably, the dogs need to take the sheep back, driving them across fields, and they have to put them through gateways, into sheds, barns or pens. The dog will also need to cut one out, or a few out, depending on what the shepherd requires.

When times are hard and the sheep are desperate to get at the feed troughs, the shepherd cannot get the feed into the troughs because of all the pushing. It is the little dog who will hold the flock away, giving the shepherd time to put the feed into the troughs. In bad snow, the sheepdog is invaluable for locating buried sheep. On the hills, the good hill dogs know where all their sheep can be found and where the individuals lie up. British hill sheep live as any truly wild animal. Each ewe has her own little piece and this is handed down from ewe to lamb. Consequently, when a section of hill land comes up for sale, the sheep are also sold with the land.

In Britain, the majority of Sheepdog Trialists will be actually involved with sheep farming, although there is an increasing number of hobby trialists. Naturally, all the sheep-working Border Collies come from British stock. Donald McCraig, a well-known author and Sheepdog Trailist, sums up the trial scene stating: "Because sheep are not helpless and people sometimes are, nature gave us the Border Collie. The Sheepdog Trial? We brought that on ourselves!"

He tells me that in the USA back in 1981 the vast majority of competing Border Collies were imported, whereas today, at least two-thirds are American-bred and trained. He estimates that two-thirds of competitors are hobby trialists and of those, at least fifty per cent are women. In Britain, there are still very few women trialists, although the number does seem to be increasing yearly.

WORKING TRIALS

This activity is much better suited to the Border Collie than Obedience, for the dog's mind is more occupied and stretched. There is less emphasis on precision and it utilises the dog's natural skills. With the exception of the lowest grade, all the grades require the dog to complete a track of increasing skills as it moves up through the grades. The nose work requires access to extensive grounds, and the scale is constructed of a high, rigid jump. You need to be quite a handyman to construct a safe scale, but there are ways around this for the enthusiast. The need for extensive grounds for nose-work is one of the reasons why there are a limited number of clubs that specialise in Working Trials. It is difficult finding enough ground for one dog – to find enough ground for a

Val Jones with Bluealloy Nutmeg tracking. This is one of the elements required in Working Trials.

ABOVE: The 6ft long-jump presents a challenge for some of the smaller dogs.

RIGHT: The 6ft scale presents no problems to this Border Collie.

group is a major headache. The tests in Working Trials are of a practical nature, with the emphasis on achieving an all-round working partnership. Unlike Obedience, where failure in the Stays is marked on a graded point system, in Working Trials the slightest move loses all points and so prevents qualification, for each section requires a minimum mark to qualify. Even if only one section of the complete test lacks a qualifying score, the dog cannot qualify on that occasion.

In the more advanced tests, gunfire is used. The dogs in the lower grades may well hear the gunfire for the upper grades, so you need a dog who is not noise/gun shy. On one occasion my bitch was doing a ten minute Stay out of sight, and in the adjoining field they were doing the gun tests for another grade. My bitch was alright, but several dogs broke their Stays. The dog who is noise-shy can be affected even when not working an exercise, and that is usually enough to upset the dog for the rest of the day.

Working trials is one of the few canine disciplines which is not dominated by the Border Collie. Any dog has a chance to succeed, whatever the breed. In fact, Border Collies are not easy to read when they are tracking as they tend to carry their heads and tails low, and do not lift them as so many other breeds do. Some handlers find this aspect a little difficult, but, with experience, most find that a sensitive-nosed Border Collie is hard to beat.

LEFT: Agility is clearly enjoyed by both dogs and handlers. This dog is being taught to negotiate the weave poles.

BELOW: Altricia Wide Awake, with handler Roy Wilce, showing winning form at Agility. This discipline requires great stamina on the part of the handler as well as the dog!

Bill Bunce.

AGILITY

This is an exciting sport for competitors and spectators alike. However, it can be misleading to the uninitiated, as the competitors at the highest level make it look so easy. If only that was the case! The majority of Border Collies adore jumping and do so effortlessly. It comes as naturally as working sheep does to sheep-bred Border Collies. However, there is a vast difference between a dog clearing obstacles in a natural environment and a dog working through an Agility round in competition. Indeed, there is no comparison.

The average Agility course consists of an A-frame, a scale-jump, a narrow, raised walk-way, a tunnel, a tyre, weaving poles, plus a variety of other jumps. The dog is timed on each round, and penalties are imposed for failure to clear obstacles, deviating from the course, missing the 'touch points' which are painted on some of the obstacles, and for exceeding the time limit.

The Border Collie is designed to be agile and athletic. I used to marvel at my dog, Bracken, who would stand by the 6ft high scale-jump, and with one leap she would land on the top, making it look so easy. Border Collies are designed also for speed, and it is this combination, with the added bonus of their intelligent, biddable nature that makes the Border Collie virtually unbeatable in Agility, Obedience, and increasingly in Flyball.

At competition level, some problems can occur which are directly related to the very nature of the breed. Border Collies are fast, often so fast that their handlers cannot keep pace with them, and

Bluealloy Tarn (ISDS 177177) 'Glen': A Gold Utility Award holder. Owned by Adrienne Mcleavy.

Bryan Turner.

TOP LEFT: Altricia Wide Awake going through the tyre.
Bill Bunce.

ABOVE: The successful Agility competitor needs control as well as speed to negotiate the different obstacles.
Bill Bunce.

LEFT: Eunice Morgan's Tuxedo coming down the A frame.

so faults creep in. Agility is the only other sport which excites the Collie in the same way as working sheep, and the handler can easily lose control of a dog who has become over-excited. Faults and penalties can also occur with the dog who finds it so easy and effortless that carelessness starts to creep in. The Border Collie is so quick to learn, and it may be that the handler teaches an exercise the wrong way – due to lack of knowledge or understanding – and it sure takes a while to eradicate these 'faults' from the dog's mind. These are the drawbacks, but we should not lose sight of the fact that Agility is a wonderful sport which can really be enjoyed by both dog and owner.

Many of the clubs do both competition agility and pet agility, which provides an ideal opportunity for pet owners to enjoy the sport without getting involved at the highest level. I would not allow a dog to attempt Agility training before fifteen months of age. This is because the bone structure must be given the chance to develop before stressing the young growth. I also believe that a young dog should not be exposed to too much intensive training, and, it is also essential to ensure that your dog is fully under control before attempting this discipline. Lack of control, on the part of the handler, is often sadly neglected in the sport.

While you are waiting to start formal Agility training, you can do much in the way of foundation work at home, getting your dog used to responding to you quickly and positively. You can even make one or two simple bits of equipment. The weaving poles can be garden canes or broom handles pointed to go into the lawn. You can use a scrap cycle tyre from a bicycle repair shop for the tyre, and use an old oil drum with a plank placed over it for the see-saw. Buy some cheap plastic hoops (children's) and cut about a third off. Stick these in the ground and place an old sheet over them, and you have a tunnel. This is all easy to do, and you can make considerable progress without needing more sophisticated equipment.

However, the most important lesson to teach is that you have control, and the dog is only allowed to attempt an obstacle when you say so. Build this into the structure from the very start and you will have a sound foundation for the future. Control can be achieved in a simple, quiet way. For the non-sheep-working Border Collie, this discipline is the perfect antidote for coping with the working instinct, for the dog is both mentally and physically challenged.

For the majority of dogs and their owners, Agility is a fun sport, with perhaps the occasional competition between clubs. For those handlers who compete at the very highest level, it is a discipline which requires hard work and dedication, not only in training the dog, but in keeping both the dog and themselves at the peak of physical fitness.

FLYBALL

I was first introduced to Flyball on a trip to North America a few years ago. I had never seen or heard of the sport before, but I had a crazy, ball-retrieving bitch, so I decided to bring a box home as a present. That was quite a journey, coping with the box on the plane!

When I first saw Flyball in action, I was extremely impressed with the way the sport was taught – both in the initial training of the dog and also in instructing the team for competition work. Basically, the sport involves the dog running out, clearing four hurdles (approx 16ins/40.6cms in height), reaching the Flyball box, operating the pedal, releasing the ball, catching it, and then making the return journey. The sport is conducted on a relay system, and each team is marked as a group.

On a subsequent visit to the United States I had the bonus of a trip to Minneapolis to one of the big Flyball tournaments. I was thrilled to see the big hall, the club team colours, and the dogs competing with such skill and enthusiasm. In Britain, the sport is now becoming increasingly popular, although it is not so advanced as the American equivalent. Their events are run on the

This young dog, Nellie, is being taught to compete in Flyball.

lines of a big athletics meeting, and over the years the boxes have become increasingly sophisticated.

However, the British have learnt a great deal from the Americans, and we now have some top-quality Flyball competitors. This is particularly true of the record times. The current record for Canada, held by the McCann Team, is 17.37; the British record, held by the Tornadoes, stands at 18.25. There have been numerous exchange visits between the two continents, which has all helped to promote good relations.

It is more expensive to compete in Flyball in North America than in Britain, and the British also have the advantage of having far shorter distances to travel. Britain has adopted the North American system and the various levels are selected on team times:

Division 1: Less than 20 seconds
Division 2: 20 to 21.99 seconds
Division 3: 22 to 23.99 seconds
Division 4: More than 24 seconds

In Britain there are Flyball leagues, but this is not applicable in North America. To become a Flyball Champion in North America a dog must accumulate a certain number of points. Dogs running in less than 24 seconds gain 25 points, 24-28 seconds wins 5 points, and from 28-32 seconds wins 1 point. Qualification FD requires 20 points, FDX requires 100 points and FD Ch. requires a score of 500 points.

Flyball is great fun for spectators and competitors alike, and the dogs clearly enjoy themselves. It is becoming increasingly popular, but I do hope that it remains a fun sport rather than becoming too fiercely competitive.

SCENT HURDLE RACING

Scent Hurdle Racing is only run as an organised event in North America. It is similar to Flyball, in that it is a team event. The dogs have to jump a line of four hurdles. However, instead of retrieving the ball from the box, the dogs are required to collect their own dumb-bell from the four assembled. The first Scent Hurdling Champion was a dog from Brandon in Manitoba; the second was a Canadian dog, also from Manitoba, who was produced by a bitch called Flora, who was taken out to Canada in whelp to my own dog, Bluealloy Lad.

OBEDIENCE

This is a discipline which has a huge following both here in Britain and in North America. It is an activity which requires relatively little in the way of equipment and so it is an inexpensive sport for participators. In the hands of a skilled trainer, the Border Collie takes a great deal of beating, but there is a percentage of people who think that the dogs train themselves – not a belief shared by those competing in top-level Obedience competitions. The Border Collie is an extremely quick learner, but the problem lies in the fact that the majority of people are extremely poor in communicating to the dog what they are trying to teach, and so these very quick acting and quick learning dogs learn the 'wrong' response – meaning a response not intended by the trainer.

Today, the emphasis is very much on precision in footwork, with regard to both the handler and the dog. In Britain classes are large (now limited to sixty entries), and, with only one first prize, many find this form of competition frustrating. To my mind, the North American system, where dogs may qualify upwards on a percentage and gain titles for each grade, is much more rewarding. In Britain, Border Collies and the Working Sheepdogs dominate the Obedience scene, whereas in North America the qualification system gives other breeds more of a chance. Amerian Obedience qualifications start at CD, graduating to Open CDX, and then third grade Utility UD. The dog requires three different qualifications in Utility to become an Obedience Champion.

In the early fifties German Shepherd Dogs virtually dominated Obedience. I was one of the first to break this chain in Britain, but not with a Border Collie. At this time, Border Collies were still regarded as exclusively sheep-working dogs. I remember one of the earliest – and greatest – Border Collies to make an impact on the scene. It was a rough-coated, black-and-white ISDS No.12273, registered under the name of Megan, and owned by Muriel Pearce. Megan (KC registered as Megan of Monksmead) became an Obedience Champion and from her came a long line of very successful Obedience working Border Collies. Megan came from top sheep stock. Her

Bluealloy High Hope, owned in Canada by Arlene Haines, a prolific winner, with CD, CDX, HIC, FDX and TT awards.

Ob.Ch. Sh.Ch. Whenway Mist of Wizaland: Britain's only Obedience and Show Champion. Owned and trained by Sue Large.

Russell Fine Art.

sire, Mindrum Moss, was from one of the best sheep-working strains. (Megan's details can be found Volume 10 of the ISDS Stud Book.) All the early dogs were ISDS registered, and dogs such as Ob. Ch. Pantanne (No.14511), Ob. Ch. Danny of Huntsview (No.65793), and Ob. Ch. Mirk of Monksmead (No.23822) are remembered among the greats. Obedience dogs were a major source of income for the shepherds, but gradually from the Monksmead line, came a strain of Obedience-bred dogs. Nowadays, competition dogs come from pure sheep stock or pure Obedience stock, or a combination of the two, with most trainers having strong views as to which is best.

There is something a bit special about being the first to achieve anything, and I am sure that Pat Kaiser still feels that little thrill when thinking of her Pallisons Passion, who gained the accolade of being the first USA Obedience Champion – a great feat. This was followed by Dot Wellbourne with her Brightmorors Lisa, and the third title went to Mary Somerville's Scherry Star Sussie. Joint fourth were Karl Nussbaum's Dreamalot Ben amd Max Parris' Wondereye Val.

Although North American and British Obedience are very different from each other, the basics remain the same. Both require Heelwork on and off the lead, Recalls to the handler, Stays in various positions, Retrieves and Scent Discrimination. In Britain there is a Sendaway exercise, but no directional jumping, which is part of the syllabus in North America. The British Sendaway is directional, and directional commands are given at a distance in the three positions. In North America and in Britain you can make your dog up into a Champion. The differences are not vast, and with a few weeks training, a dog from either country would be able to make the switchover – although quarantine laws do not permit this.

I believe that the main difference between Obedience in North America and Britain lies in the handling of the dogs. I have observed that the North American handlers have a much more professional manner than their British counterparts and take the sport far more seriously. North American handlers seem to rely much more on hand communication, whereas in Britain both hand and word commands are used, with a bias on verbal commands. In Britain the scoring and award system benefits the Border Collie/Working Sheepdog, and so the vast majority of Obedience Champions are made up from this breed. In North America all breeds get a much fairer chance, and so there are not so many Border Collies made up or worked as in their homeland.

Certainly, many of the British Obedience handlers would favour the North American system of grading by winning titles, and those who do not like the emphasis on precision work would be happier if they had the British Working Trial system of awards (which is like the North American Obedience system). I would also favour directional jumping, which is perfectly suited to Border Collies – although *most* dogs enjoy jumping.

In North America there is a special Tracking Dog Qualification and title. In Britain, tracking comes under the jurisdiction of the Working Trials, and all but the lowest grade require the dog to track. Likewise, jumping is restricted to Working Trials, where a Border Collie would be required to clear a 3ft high jump, a 9ft long jump, and to scale a 6ft foot high wooden wall, returning back over the wall.

GUIDE DOGS
There have been a number of Border Collies who have qualified as Guide Dogs for the Blind (Seeing Eye Dogs), but the breed is not favoured for two reasons – their size and their brains. They are a little too small for the average blind person, and their intelligence means that they will take short cuts or modify routes. In Britain there has been a more recent experiment using bloodlines imported from New Zealand, and one from this litter qualified as a Guide Dog. It is still early days in this field and it will be interesting to watch future developments.

THERAPY DOGS
In the present climate where the public in increasingly 'anti-dog', it is important that those involved with dogs should put something back into the community in an attempt to promote better relations. This may be a matter of visiting schools and other youth groups and just giving youngsters a chance to meet a well-trained, well-behaved dog. There are also dogs and owners who visit hospitals, homes for the elderly and other institutions to give the residents a chance to stroke a dog, and to benefit from that very special relationship with a living creature.

GUNDOGS
As a breed, Border Collies seem to be divided between those who are very noise-sensitive (therefore gun-shy) and those which are not. If you intend to use your dog to the gun, you will need to choose from a good line of dogs which are not over-sensitive to noise, and you will need to test that your puppy is not noise-shy. Quite a number of dogs from my line have become extremely good working gundogs, and Trim, the first Platinum winner, has 'wiped the eye' of

Border Collies are used as guide dogs for the blind, but their extreme intelligence and relatively small stature can be a disadvantage.

Guide Dogs for the Blind Association

many a good working Labrador Retriever in the shooting field. There are a few Border Collies who work with gamekeepers, and cross-breeding on to Spaniels has proved successful. I reckon the finest gundog is a Border Collie/Springer Spaniel cross. The Border Collie has a great desire to work for the handler, it has an extremely sharp marking ability, and those gifted with a keen nose and natural ability to use scent (not all are) are definitely second to none. They have the Border Collie dedication to stick to the job without distraction and they maintain a high level of concentration while working.

SNIFFER DOGS
A few years ago the Border Collie was not considered as a contender for the armed services, drugs or police work, but I now hear of them in increasing numbers especially where nose-work is required. As a patrol dog, a Border Collie does not have the bulk to instigate fear in the criminal, but a nose-orientated worker is a wonder to see. There is no way that we humans can ever measure a dog's powers in this role. I have seen feats of detection I would never have considered possible, and I now wonder why we are so bold as to say that we *teach* the dog scent discrimination.

Each type of work requires a slightly different technique, but on the whole, the same basic characteristics are required from the dog. The really good sniffer dogs have a very singled-minded approach to following a scent, and this is to such a degree that nothing can distract them. This is exactly the same instinct coming to the fore as with the really good sheepdog working sheep.

I notice with my own dogs that some seem to have a much better sense of smell than others, and this can be within the same litter. The differences show up at a very early stage, and the scenting attribute often goes with a dog/pup who is slightly more independent, amuses itself, and is very inventive. This is a useful set of traits for a working sheepdog, who often has to be inventive and make decisions when out of sight and handling a flock of sheep. Some of my sheepdogs will wind-scent their sheep naturally rather than look for them, which is most valuable when the sheep cannot be seen. It is these very basic sheep-working instincts, which, when channelled, make the Border Collie so good as a sniffer dog.

MOUNTAIN RESCUE

In Britain there is not the same need for Avalanche dogs as there is in parts of North America and Europe. Originally, this was the domain of the German Shepherd Dog, but Border Collies are making themselves much better known in this work. In fact the Border Collie is ideally suited to Mountain Rescue work. They have a natural genetic ability to work in close liaison with their handlers, they cope easily with difficult terrain and harsh conditions, they are agile, they have great stamina – both in mind and physique; their dark coats makes them less susceptible to snow blindness, they have excellent noses and high levels of concentration, and they will always give one hundred per cent. Again, all these qualities are required when working sheep.

Clarin Maton, whose dog will shortly be an overseas Silver Award winner, is a regular competitor in Breed, Obedience, and Agility, works sheep daily, and has gained her Certificate in Mountain Rescue. During the course the dogs and handlers have to learn how to search for people under snow, and so good team work has to be established between handler and dog. Great importance is placed on obedience and on playing with a dog. (I have found that the dogs which will play best, work best, and I always encourage owners to develop games with their dogs.)

After each session in the field, discussion takes place, and some of the theoretical knowledge is taught in lectures. During these lectures, subjects include: method of instruction, how to 'read' the dog, knowledge of snow and avalanche, using a probe and electronic search devices, plus learning about salvage, search and hunting techniques.

Generally dogs and handlers go out twice each day to work in the snow, for there is no substitute for experience. Not only must the handler be protected from the cold and snow, the dog also needs to be protected, and handlers learn how to build a bivouac especially for the dog. Handlers need to experience extreme conditions, and so they learn about the effects of being buried in varying depths of snow, and they also learn how to build a snow hole.

Dogs have to be taught not to follow their handlers at the heel position, because by doing so they use up vast amounts of energy having to continually break trail for themselves. They must therefore learn to walk in the steps of their handler. The dogs are taught to search for people hidden under the surface of the ground, and they become capable of indicating such presence, working independently. They also learn how to track buried people by the use of electronic search devices and probes.

SLEDDING

Border Collies have long been used by some serious sled dog breeders to introduce certain desirable traits into their lines of sled dogs. Most serious dog sled racers run a cross-bred dog that is made up of generations of careful cross-breeding and selection. Many of these dogs' markings and coloration bear testimony to their Border Collie heritage.

During the nineties dog sledding and to a lesser degree dog sled racing started to become popular with some of the sheepdog handlers in the Northeastern United States. The phenomenon began in Maine with the efforts of a competitive sheepdog handler to keep her dogs in top physical condition for summer trials. The sport's appeal led to its spreading among dog handlers in the

Beverly Lambert, Mike Canaday and Pat Canaday competing in a sledding competition in Center Conway, New Hampshire.

Northeast and, more recently, into Canada.

Border Collies make very good sled dogs. The 40-50 pound dog is an ideal weight for sledding. The Border Collie's enthusiasm, stamina and excellent physical condition and health (especially among working dogs) ensures their easy adaptation to a new form of exercise. In selecting dogs for a team it is best to start with young dogs, not yet a year old. These dogs seem to more readily enter into the spirit of the sport than do older, more sedentary animals. For sledding, three dogs are a good starting place and up to twenty are possible, depending upon the courage of the driver and the size of kennel. The rule of thumb is to assume that each dog can pull his own weight. For short trips the dogs can pull considerably more, but too heavy a load will take much of the fun out of the sport for dogs and driver alike.

To begin sledding, it is necessary to have harnesses for each dog. These are inexpensive cloth affairs, designed to spread the load across the dog's body without interfering with movement. Each dog must then be harnessed to what needs to be pulled. When pulling a sled, a central rope 'gangline' is used, with each dog snapped into place in the team. It is also possible to use the dogs for ski-joring. This can be done with cross-country skis and a rope, with one end of the rope attached to the dog's harness and the other end held by the skier. One or two dogs pulling a cross-country skier certainly increases the pace of skiing!

In the United States there are three main types of sled dog races: sprints, mid-distance and marathons. The Northeast is home to some excellent sprint and mid-distance races. Border Collies have participated in a number of each. Mid-distance races are generally run through largely unpopulated, wilderness areas. The scenery is beautiful but rugged, and it can be dangerous for the unprepared. Each team (the dogs and driver are referred to as a team) is required to carry winter survival gear and be able to use it.

The longest one-day, mid-distance race completed by a Border Collie team was the Sandwich North 60. This is a sixty-mile race through the mountains of central New Hampshire for teams of up to six dogs. Teams leave the starting line at two-minute intervals, starting at 10:00 in the morning. The race makes a sixty-mile loop through the wilds of central New Hampshire. Drivers are required to sign in at three checkpoints during the course of the race so that their progress can be monitored. Teams take anywhere from five and a half hours to fifteen hours to complete the race. Beverly Lambert finished this race in 31st place out of 50 teams in 1990 with a team of Border Collies. Her team was made up entirely of working dogs who successfully competed in Sheepdog Trials during the summer.

Border Collies have also done respectably in sprint races in the Northeast. Sprint races consist of four-mile races for four-dog teams, six-mile races for six-dog teams, and ten-mile races for larger teams, with two heats run on consecutive days. Sprints tend to be much more exciting than the mid-distance races, and large crowds frequently turn out to cheer at these events. These races are much less demanding on the drivers, and they are run at a much faster pace than the longer endurance events.

Border Collies are good, but not great, sled dogs. The dogs pull eagerly and never quit. They are well-mannered and under good control at all times, making sledding with Border Collies a much safer sport then sledding with 'real' sled dogs. However, the Border Collie is bred to be able to accelerate and stop quickly and turn sharply. This creates a short, choppy stride that is less than desirable in a top sledding dog. Most Border Collies tend to be quite a bit shorter-legged than the cross-bred dogs specifically bred for dog sledding. The result is that the Collies can run and perform respectably in races, but they are not physically built to win dog sled races any more than they can expect to win Greyhound races. But, as with everything else done with Border Collies, they are always competitive and give their driver one hundred per cent when asked for it.

The best part of dog sledding with Border Collies or any other breed of dog is hooking up a team of eager dogs, and going out with several friends and their teams of dogs to explore snow-covered trails. This aspect of dog sledding has proven alluring to many sheepdog handlers, and provides yet another demonstration of the incredible abilities of the Border Collie.

Chapter Fourteen

STATUS AND DEVELOPMENT

There is always a debate as to where a breed first originated, and each breed has its own specialist historians. In order to trace the history of the Border Collie, I shall start from the early documentation which shows a dog working in the accepted fashion of the modern Border Collie.

I am a keen rider of Arab horses, and it is hard to say which grew first, the love of the Arab horse or the love of the Border Collie, for I find they share many attributes. They are both spirited, extremely tenacious, unbelievably intelligent, and a challenge to their owner. They have both developed out of their lifestyle and, as such, cannot be replaced in their working role. The Border Collie should never be considered purely as a pet, for it is a very specialised animal, bred specifically to work as a sheepdog, and it is more single-minded than any other breed of dog. Before taking on the responsibility of owning a Border Collie you must understand that the dog has very specific needs. You cannot destroy the working instinct, and so must find a way to channel it that is acceptable to both dog and owner.

EARLY RECORDS

No one knows for certain when the breed originated and, like very many breeds, it probably developed over a vast number of years incorporating breeds such as the Bearded Collies, Harlequins, bob-tailed sheepdogs, and very likely a sprinkling of the early gundogs. Many of the early dogs were owned by drovers who were out on the roads for weeks on end. Their dogs had to be multi-disciplined, handling the stock, acting as guards and helping the 'boss' get his food along the route.

The earliest written record I have found which refers to the Border Collie, as we know it today, is in Dr John Caius's *Treatise on Englishe Dogges*, written in 1570. He refers to the "Shepherd's Dogge" as being a dog of medium size which answered to his master's will, shaking of fist or shrill hissing and would bring the sheep to the place of his master's will. Based on this description, Dr Caius would probably find little difference in the modern Border Collie. He goes on to say that the English method of using sheepdogs was very different from that used in other countries. Unfortunately, he does not mention colour or what the dogs looked like. We have to wait for this until 1790 in a work entitled *The General History of Quadrupeds* by Bewick, who devotes a whole chapter to "the Shepherd's dogs" and illustrates his writings with a rough-coated Collie. This provides written proof that this type of dog was in existence from the mid 1700s – and probably long before that.

The name 'Collie' seems to be in the English language by the year 1617, but before that a Bishop of Aberdeen who died in 1617 was nicknamed "Collie" due to his mode of life, which was akin to the following and sponging habit of the Collie dogs. In 1721 a poet named Allan Ramsay, who was a Scotsman, mentions the Collie dog. The power of the eye seems to have its first reference in the writings of James Hogg, the Ettrick Herd. Both James and his father seem to have taken this characteristic for granted, and so it was obviously a trait of shepherding dogs from the 1700s. It is interesting to note that all these references to this early Border Collie are of Scottish origin.

THE FIRST SHEEPDOG TRIALS

Sheepdog trialing did not start in Scotland, as might be expected, but in the delightfully named Bala, in Wales, 1873. Sheep trialing is very different from everyday work and it has developed a style of its own. The first documented example of this seems to be at the Hawick Trials, which were held in Scotland in 1883. The well-known William Wallace amazed spectators and other handlers alike with his apparently revolutionary technique of very quiet communication, close to a mere hiss, and using a quiet whistle when the dog was working at a distance. This is the mark of a brilliant handler/trainer, and more than one hundred years later trialists still try to copy this method – often with mixed results.

THE INTERNATIONAL SHEEP DOG SOCIETY (ISDS)

A meeting in Scotland, in July 1906, resulted in one of the most important of all breed registering societies in the world. This is well-documented in Eric Halsall's book, *British Sheepdog: A History of the ISDS.*

The first two-day Sheepdog Trial, which was an International, was held in Lanark in 1919. In 1926 ISDS members decided to host a really major event, and this has become one of the great international canine events, now running over three days. The trials were originally held in England, Scotland and Wales on a rotation basis, but in 1993 it was agreed to include Ireland in the cycle. James Reed was the ISDS secretary from 1906 until 1946. The current secretary, Philip Hendry, took office in 1977, and he has taken the Society to its established and highly respected position of today.

PROBLEMS IN THE BREED

By 1965 it was very apparent that there was a problem in the breed with the inherited eye condition, Progressive Retinal Atrophy (PRA), and all leading Collies were eye-tested by a specially qualified vet. This was obviously helping with the selection of breeding stock, for by 1968 there was a noticeable decrease in the number of puppies being registered from blind parents. The ISDS has devised a three-tier registration system to cope with the problems of PRA.

Dogs were eye-tested for this condition at the age of two years, and puppies registered from eye-tested stock over two years old had a much cheaper registration fee than puppies registered from parents who were too young to have been tested. However, the highest fee was reserved for puppies from parents who were over three years old and had not been eye-tested. Naturally, puppies from parents who failed the eye test were refused registration. This system meant that even if breeders were not interested in eye-testing for the future well-being of the breed, there was a sound financial reason for adopting the policy. By 1975 there were only two per cent of dogs failing the eye test.

However, there was still a very small nucleus of breeders who did not eye-test, and so in 1993 a new ruling was introduced, refusing registration to puppies from parents who were three years or older and had not been eye-tested. In the early 1980s Collie Eye Anomaly (CEA) became a new problem in the breed, and so in 1988 similar registration action was instituted for eye-testing to include CEA as well as PRA. This method has been so simple and yet so effective – and it has prevented a major problem of blindness in the breed. It is a pity that the English Kennel Club has not adopted a similar policy.

THE ISDS STUD BOOK
The International Sheepdog Society (ISDS) produce an annual Stud Book which lists the names of the breeder, parents, owners, date of birth, colour and coat type of every puppy registered with them for the preceding year. Originally it was only the bitch's owner who had to be a member of the ISDS in order to register puppies, but from 1985 the stud dog owner also has had to be a member in order for the puppies to be registered. The Stud Book also contains the details of the International and Nationals, a list of dogs who have failed the eye test, plus a cross-checking system for the dogs registered, so you can look them up under their owner or by their registered number. This means that by using the number only, any ISDS registered Border Collie can have its parentage traced and written in pedigree form. It is possible to go back to the 1800s using this system.

Names are traditional, representing the sex of the puppy, and they must be a short, single-word (unless the breeder has a prefix), and this precedes the short name. Obviously names are duplicated, but as each dog has its own registered number there is no cause for confusion. However, you should always include registration numbers when writing out a pedigree.

REGISTRATION
In Britain, the Border Collie is the only breed of dog which has a dual registration system with the Kennel Club. An ISDS registered puppy may be registered with the KC on production of its ISDS card, or by giving details of the registration of both sire and dam. A puppy may be KC registered with proof that both parents are KC registered.

The KC has another registration system for dogs who do not have documented paperwork but may be registered on the Obedience and Working Trials Register. This means they are allowed to enter in Agility, Obedience and Working Trials, but they are not allowed to compete in conformation classes. These dogs are known as Working Collies or Working Sheepdogs; they can be cross-breeds and of unknown parentage.

MODERN SHEEPDOG TRIALS
In Britain, the BBC television service produced a series of programmes called *One Man and His Dog* (although there are some lady competitors), featuring Sheepdog Trials. Competitors were drawn on a regional basis, and competed for a trophy in the final. The first series was screened in 1975 and televised in the Lake District, and it caught the public's imagination. The programme has gone from strength to strength, and has encouraged many people to take up Sheepdog Trialing. Conversely, it has also attracted many pet owners to the breed, and this has not always been to either the dog's or the owner's advantage.

As well as the national ISDS trials, World Championship Sheepdog Trials are also staged. Handlers from the UK have won on several occasions, but quarantine laws are a major handicap. There are a vast number of trials held all over the UK every week of the year. They fit into one of several categories:

1. Nursery for the very inexperienced dogs.
2. Novice.
3. Open.
4. South Wales Type (includes a cross instead of drive).

Supreme International Champion Turk in action.   *B. Carpenter.*

5. Doubles/Brace.
6. Devon Cross (similar to South Wales).
There are a few other individual types with regional variations.

INFLUENTIAL WORKING DOGS

Probably the most well-known ancestor of the modern Border Collie is Old Hemp. In 1894, Adam Telfer mated his unregistered dog, Roy, to his unregistered bitch, Meg, and from this liaison was produced what is classed as the Father of Border Collies – Hemp, usually referred to as Old Hemp. Hemp was given the number 9 in the ISDS Stud Book and all the International Champions are descended from him.

Many great dogs followed. However it is worth mentioning several very notable Border Collies. Herdman's Tommy (No.16) was a grandson of Old Hemp on his maternal side and a great grandson on the paternal side. When Tommy was mated to Ancrum Jed, he produced Herman's Tyne (No.145) and Wallace's Moss, who, in turn, produced Gilhome's Lille (No.26). This bitch was the dam of two other noteworthy dogs, Loos I and Robert's Int. Ch Jaff (No.379).

Herdman's Tyne (No.145) produced Craig (No.1048), Loos II (No.435), Fly (No.824) and Roy (No.1665) – all Championship winners. Tommy (No.16), bred to Nell (No.205), produced Spot (No.308) and Glen (No.698) – all Championship winners. Tommy (No.16), bred to Old Maid (No.1), produced Batty's Corby (No.338), Brown's Lass (No.19), Fenwick Jed (No.33) and Armstrong's Trim (No.37). Trim (No.37) produced Don (No.17), winner of the 1911 and 1914 Championships. Trim (No.37) and her son, Armstrong's Sweep (No.21), produced four lines of International Champions.

Brown's Old Nell (No.205) was another very famous early bitch. She was a wonderful worker who produced in excess of eighty puppies and so gave some early sound stock for the breed.

Another great early bitch was Fingland Loos (No.435), who won the International Farmers Champions Cup at the Criccieth International in 1925. She was known as the Mother of Champions. McKnight's Gael (No.14463) will still be seen on the end of some pedigrees today. She was a stylish worker with a great temperament, fairly strong-eyed, and said to be very easy to train, showing natural ability.

Kirk's Nell (No.3514) was a well-known dog in the late thirties who produced some extremely sound stock. She was grandmother to the famous Whitehope Nap. The Huddleston family produced many dogs which are the forerunners of many of the blue dogs who crop up today, but they were also known for their true, sound, working dogs. They had quite a line of Maddies – Maddie (No.4338) won many awards in the early forties, and was said to make working stock look easy.

One of the most famous males is Cap (No.3036), if only through Wiston Cap (No.31154), but Cap (No.3036) was the major stud dog during the War years. It was very lucky for the breed that he was such a sound dog with few natural faults. Cap never a got chance to prove himself on the trial field, but then the true worth of a dog comes through the stock produced from that dog. He was a dog with a natural outrun, great control and power.

Gilchrist's Scot. Nat. Ch. Spot (No.24981) was another dog who had a great impact on the breed. He was also a grand worker with great control, and he worked more upstanding than many. His half-white face came through from his grandmother, Ann (No.4545), and many dogs of today who have a white or partial white stripe over their hindquarters usually stem back to Spot, who had a very distinctive white stripe going right across his quarters from one side to the other. Indeed, I, along with many others, say that it proves the pedigree.

International Champion Bosworth Coon (No.34186) and Wiston Cap (No.31154) were both dogs of the mid-sixties. Coon was a strong dog and he put much power back into the breed. However, he had a stubbornness, which is extremely valuable in small doses, but is difficult to cope with if too much of his blood runs through the veins. Brocken Robbie (No.24636) was not used as much at stud as some, but even in limited use, he produced some wonderful workers who achieved great honours. He is one of the dogs I like to see in a pedigree. He was a powerful but sensitive dog, who came from really sound, solid, proved workers and he seemed to throw this quality. Another for the list – which could go on and fill a whole book – was a bitch called Mindrum Nell (No.11106), who was a powerful dog, extremely good-natured and easy to train. The Mindrum line was the forerunner of the early Obedience strain of Border Collies.

The only dual activity Champion (work and breed) in the show world is Sue Large's Obedience Champion and Show Champion Whenway Mist of Wizaland, who really does deserve a mention. All credit must go to her owner/trainer, Sue. Two reasonably modern dogs that I rate extremely highly are John Wilson's late Res. Sup. Int. Ch. Peg (No.125220) (who twice came second to the Sup. Int. Ch. and it was thought by many, including myself, that she deserved to win it on one occasion) and her son, Dual Int. Sup. Ch. Spot (161819). Peg was so beautiful to watch in action, so stylish, but in such complete control, and she obviously produces this in her offspring. Her son, Spot, is very similar. He is dog of power, natural outrun, and is very biddable. He also reproduces these very desirable qualities. As a bonus, his offspring are extremely handsome – you could not ask for more.

To the best of my knowledge, the only triple Champion in the breed is Kathryn Gillard's Sealight Harty of Zullmarg, who is an English Obedience Champion, an Irish Obedience Champion and WT Champion. He was bred by Bing Bellamy from Sealight, the renowned stable of Obedience and Working Trial dogs. He was Kathryn's first Border Collie and was acquired at eight months of age. Known as 'Baida', he worked sheep and cattle as well as picking up regularly on a shoot (i.e.

working as a gundog). He also won many Agility awards, qualified CDex, UDex, WDex, and TDex in England, and would surely have become a quadruple Champion had he not had to be retired due to a hock injury. He was a good specimen, conformation-wise – a truly great dog.

THE 'PEDIGREE' BORDER COLLIE

In the eyes of the show world, the Border Collie was never thought of as a 'pedigree' breed, although in reality their authenticated breeding went back much further than many accepted pedigree dogs. The movement to give the breed official status started first from the Obedience fraternity and was then developed by people wanting full recognition for their dogs instead of being confined to the Kennel Club's Obedience and Working Trial Register. In 1960 there were several meetings between Captain Whittaker, then Chairman of the ISDS, and KC officials, but Captain Whittaker's death left the matter in temporary abeyance.

However, the Obedience fraternity started campaigning again and the various parties came to an agreement in 1964. The KC agreed to register only those dogs who were already registered in the ISDS Stud Book. This is how the unique registration system came into being and it is still operational today. For ISDS registration both parents must be ISDS registered. However, for KC registration one of three situations is acceptable:

1. The puppy is ISDS registered.
2. Both parents are ISDS registered.
3. One parent ISDS registered and the other is KC registered.

Sadly, not many show/dual breeders have dogs with dual registration. It is something to be proud of and once lost would be virtually impossible to regain.

The inaugural meeting of the Border Collie Club of Great Britain was held on Tuesday, 6th August 1973, with Marion Leigh (now Hopkinson) as the first secretary. However, it was not until 1st August 1976 that the Border Collie was upgraded to a breed in its own right. At this point there was no official Breed standard, and it was quite some time before classes were scheduled for them at shows. Until 1989 all the show stock was quite closely related to the farm working Border Collies. Then Bruce and Sheena Kilsby imported their New Zealand dog, Sh. Ch. Clan-Abby Blue Aberdoone, into Britain. This most unusual liaison does allow for fresh blood to be introduced and may one day be a very necessary and valuable asset.

The first Breed Standard which was brought into service was the one formulated by the Australians. In July 1979 the KC published an Interim Standard which remained in force until 1981. The Breed Recording Scheme was put into action in 1980, with Dr Malcolm Willis, the world-famous geneticist, commissioned to record and monitor the breed's hereditary progress. Shortly after this, Dr Peter Bedford took over the responsibility for recording all the data on the eye diseases.

CHAMPIONSHIP STATUS IS GRANTED

In April 1981 the British dog papers published news that the Kennel Club had agreed to award Challenge Certificate to the breed. Eight sets would be given in 1982, a further eight in 1983, after which the breed's situation would be reviewed.

Many people in the breed had mixed views about this development, and this has become more evident as the breed has progressed in the show ring. Many breeders seem to be moving further away from the conformation that is needed to carry out the job of work for which the breed was evolved. It is acknowledged by the majority that coats have become heavier and bones are stronger, which is detrimental to the working dog. However, this is justified by others on the grounds that the Border Collie is now a show breed.

The first major honour for the pedigree Border Collie was when Tilehouse Cassius of Beagold qualified for invitation to the Challenge of Champions in 1981. Handled to perfection by Felix Cosme, he looked a wonderful sight as he was put through his paces, the beautiful black and white dog contrasting with the red carpet at the Cunard International Hotel in London, where the event was staged. Cassius, along with Tracelyn Gal, were the first joint CC winners, and Cassius, with Muriend Border Dream, became joint first Show Champions a year later. Muriend Border Dream was the first Border Collie to gain a junior warrant.

The majority of the breed clubs support the dual roles of the Border Collie, some putting much more effort into providing their members with events than others. In May 1982 the first sheep test for the members of the Border Collie Club of Great Britain was organised by the Midland branch. This consisted of a modified Sheep Trial course consisting of an outrun, lift, fetch and pen. A total of seventeen dogs competed in the two stakes, one for very inexperienced dogs and the other for the more advanced. The first non-club trial to be arranged for show-type Border Collies was at Pastors Hill Farm near Lydney, Gloucestershire and was organised by Barbara Carpenter. It was a smaller class within the main trial with nine competitors from Border Collie clubs.

FULL CHAMPIONSHIP STATUS
By 21st April 1982 there were two British breed clubs, the Border Collie Club of Great Britain and the Southern Border Collie Club. Three members from each of these two clubs, along with Philip Hendry from the ISDS met at the Kennel Club to finalise a Working Test which any Border Collie had to pass in order to become a full Champion, rather than just a Show Champion. It was agreed that it should be judged by two ISDS qualified judges in the presence of a KC representative. The qualification for entry was any Border Collie who had gained a KC Stud Book number.

The test has been slightly altered over the years, but the main content is still the same. The test is limited to only three attempts with a maximum of two in any single year. The minimum pass mark is set at sixty per cent and the time is set at fifteen minutes. The dog has to carry out the following exercises:-

The outrun (200yds)
Lift, fetch, short drive (100yds)
A pen in to a 12ft pen.

The test is judged by trial judges under trial conditions. The dogs who have passed to date have all run in trials and so are experienced in this type of test. The test is biased against a show dog becoming a full Champion, and this is what makes it so disheartening for those eager to gain the full title. To date, only six dogs have qualified in the ISDS/KC Test and none of these has actually become a Champion – so there is still no full Champion in Britain. The six dogs are:

Ann Leigh's Fordrought Fen
Hazel Monk's Viber Red Baron at Monkfield
Philip Russell-Davies's Joamp Black Jack
Fiona Russell-Davies's Barrow-ness Bronte of Blaeneinon
Bruce and Sheena Kilsby's Ma Biche of Whenway
Heather Turnes's Locheil Look North.

RIGHT: Fordrought Fen, trained by Ann Leigh: The first winner of the ISDS/KC Sheep Test, and a notable Sheepdog Trial winner.

BELOW: Viber Red Baron at Monkfield: Winner of the ISDS/KC Sheep Test; a red and white CC winner.

MULTI-DISCIPLINE AWARDS

The Midland branch of the Border Collie Club of Great Britain decided that as the breed excelled in many spheres, there should be encouragement for people to compete in more disciplines. A certificate was devised, with seven sections, which could be achieved in stages. The parent club then took the certificate over. The sections were:

1. Breed
2. Obedience
3. Working Trials
4. Reliability
5. Agility
6. Working sheep

Bruce and Sheena Kilsby's Ma Biche of Whenway: Winner of the ISDS/KC Sheep Test.

7. Heredity (dogs passed as normal for the major eye problems and a hip score of less than 20).

Dogs had to qualify in five sections to gain the Bronze award, six sections for the Silver, and all sections for the Gold. The first dog to achieve silver was Julie Mockford's Sh. Ch. Snowmere Tweed; this was quickly followed by my Bracken of Bluealloy CDEX, and Bracken was later to become the very first dog to qualify for Gold.

The Midlands Border Collie Club (formerly Midlands Branch BCC of GB) produced the Utility Certificate, which consists of ten sections. There were the original six sections, excluding Heredity, and adding Flyball, gundog work, searching back for a lost article, and the KC Good Citizen Test. A Platinum award is given to those who achieved all ten sections. By mid-1994 two dogs had qualified for the Platinum award. They were Little Fern of Jetril and Bluealloy Trim, who is a granddaughter of the very first gold winner.

NEW BLOODLINES

The importation of Clan-Abby Blue Aberdoone by Bruce and Sheena Kilsby is now recognised as another milestone in the breed's history, and the full influence of introducing new bloodlines into the breed has yet to be fully evaluated. Blue came to England as a New Zealand Champion,

*Bluealloy Bracken:
The first Gold
Award winner.*

*Bluealloy Trim:
Joint first Platinum
Award winner.*

arriving in 1989. He came out of quarantine in September 1989 and entered North West BCC Champion show, where he gained his first English CC and also went Best of Breed. The other two certificates came quite quickly, and so he became a British Show Champion.

Blue has now produced stock which is winning in all spheres. A mating to Altricia Zoe was undertaken by the Guide Dogs for the Blind Association, and from the resulting litter one dog became a fully-fledged Guide Dog, two others went to Holland to work sheep, and a third became a top Agility dog. Obviously there are a great many dogs in the breed ring sired by Blue. One of his most famous daughters is Ma Biche of Whenway (Polly), who is not only a winner in the breed ring but also the winner of two top open novice trials and the sheep working test.

Further imports followed from New Zealand, and many have found immediate success in the show ring. I have now seen some very nice one-quarter New Zealand-bred–three-quarters UK-bred Border Collies, and it would seem that it is best to use the bloodlines in this diluted form. In

NZ.Ch. Sh.Ch. Clan-Abby Blue Aberdoone: Imported from New Zealand by Bruce and Sheena Kilsby.

1994 all expectations were surpassed when Blue's daughter, Sh. Champion Dykebar Future Glory, achieved the accolade of being Reserve Supreme Champion at Crufts. Many breeds of much longer standing in the show ring have never achieved this honour. This bitch, owned by Lorraine and John Ritchie, is out of Altricia Pandora at Dykebar.

Of course, the New Zealand stock originates from UK breeding which was exported to Australia and New Zealand in the first place. The tables have certainly turned from that period in the twenties and thirties when the UK was responsible for exporting the breed worldwide.

BREEDING PROGRAMMES
Many of the shepherds in Britain who work Border Collies on sheep have little thought for appearance. They may try to avoid smooth-coated dogs or wall-eyed dogs, but working qualities are always given priority. However, you do need to consider conformation in a working programme: good shoulders, a well-set tail, sound hindquarters, correct length of coupling and correct width of skull are all vital in order that the Border collie can carry out its work. Both show and working breeders must ensure that the Border Collies they produce are sound, healthy, and capable of working, if required.

THE BORDER COLLIE IN NORTH AMERICA
Alex Reid (Alberta), Sam Stoddart (N.Hampshire), Luke Pascoe (Chicago) and several others first imported the Border Collie from Britain to North America in the thirties, and since then the breed has gone from strength to strength. Enthusiasts in all spheres of canine activity have recognised the versatility of the breed, and the Border Collie has won honours in Obedience, Working Tests, Agility, Flyball, Sheepdog Trials and Herding Tests.

The title of Obedience Trial Champion is fairly new to the American Kennel Club, and the first Championship points were awarded in July 1977. In order to become an Obedience Trial Champion, a dog must have a Utility Degree and earn a total of one hundred points, including a first and second placing in Open B and Utility classes. The dog must also have won places under three different judges with a first in both Open B and Utility classes. The number of points awarded is based on the number of dogs entered. The current top dog in the USA is OT Ch. Birdwood Tess TD, and she has earned an all-time record of 1,235 points. Tess is owned and trained by Sharon Hobbs of Regina Sask.

The McCann team hold the world's Flyball record. Marty and Debbie McCann watched Allison McIntosh work OT Ch. LJR's Katie (1984) and this sparked off their interest in Obedience. Marty started to train a dog called Yankie, a grandson of Kylie, and he became the first dog to hold the title in both Canada and the USA. The first two Champions won their titles in 1984. They were OT Ch. LJR's Katie and OT Ch. Degears Final Edition. The third Champion, OT Ch. Nibs, gained his title the following year.

REGISTRIES

Currently, there are three main Border Collie registries in the US – the North American Sheep Dog Society (NASDS) in McLeansboro, Illinois, the American International Border Collie Association (AIBC) is Des Moines, Iowa, and the American Border Collie Association Inc. (ABCA) in Perkinston, Mississippi.

The oldest of the three, the North American Sheep Dog Society, was founded about 1941 with the help of James A. Reid (former secretary-treasurer of the ISDS). In 1942 the NASDS started registering American-bred dogs. NASDS's secretary-treasurer, Dr Don Bell of Ohio, with the help of Mr Reid, drafted the first set of official trial rules to be used in America. NASDS embraced a certification program, which enabled owners to have their dog 'certified' as to working ability. If the dog met the work requirements defined by the NASDS, the owner would be given a certificate of Recognition of Proven Working Ability, and the dog would be officially recognised by NASDS for "reproduction of progeny eligible to Registration in the Stud Book". Society directors felt this program would be a guarantee of a dog's working ability and trainability, to be used as a guideline in selection of breeding stock.

In 1952 the Iowa Border Collie Association was incorporated. By 1953 the directors decided: "members of the Iowa Border Collie Association Inc. may register Border Collies in the American International Border Collie Stud Book upon proof furnished of a four-generation pedigree. The Iowa Border Collie Association shall conduct the 'American International Border Collie Stud Book Registry'". Initially, only Iowa dogs were allowed to register. It was not long before owners from other states requested to register their dogs, and the book was opened to dogs outside Iowa. By the late 1950s 'Iowa Border Collie association' was dropped from the name. The registry has registered over 200,000 dogs and continues to be active. All pedigrees are produced manually.

In 1982 there was a major upheaval in the NASDS, which caused a number of members to switch their allegiance to the AIBC. Others, in hopes of forming a democratic, progressive registry, founded the ABCA in February of 1983. ABCA's founders felt that there was a need for an organisation wherein the membership had a voice and a vote, and which would be a non-profit registry that would provide a five-generation pedigree at a reasonable cost. Initially all pedigrees were done manually, but it was not long before a computer system was put into place. This has enabled the registry to provide litter registrations and transfers of ownership with very little time delay.

More recently ABCA has adopted a voluntary certification program on hip dysplasia so that pedigrees can be marked, indicating those dogs that have been X-rayed and certified free of this disease. From its inception, this registry has refused to register dogs or progeny of dogs known to be positive for progressive retinal atrophy (PRA). The registry has also decided to indicate dogs on pedigrees which have won the United States Border Collie Handlers Association National Finals (which is similar to the ISDS International Supreme). All three registries operate much the same. Those wishing to register dogs must be members (paying either an annual due or one lifetime fee). Only two registries, NASDS and AIBC, will register dogs on merit. Generally, this is accomplished by supplying as much information as possible along with either a statement of the dog's abilities by a well-known Border Collie breeder/trainer; a video of the dog working, and, if the dog has been trialled, its record of wins. ABCA will only take a registered-on-merit dog if it has been registered by one of the other registries. All three registries will register dogs if they have been registered by one of the others, or, in the case of an import, by the ISDS. They all use ISDS stud books to verify and provide pedigree information.

WINNING TRIAL DOGS

The first dog that comes to mind is Bill Berhow's Nick. Not only has Nick won the United States Border Collie Handlers Association Finals an unprecedented three times (1989, 1990, 1993), he has won nearly every major trial in the US at one time or another during his eleven years. Nick has been a two-time winner of the prestigious Purina Award for the Outstanding Field Trial Herding Dog, in 1990 and 1991. Nick won the 1985 Futurity when less than a year old. He was the USBCHA Reserve Champion in 1986.

Ralph Pulfer bred Nick from his imported Nan (A.J. Campbell's Hemp 72301 – G. Davidson's Beat 87115) by his imported Shep (A.T. Ainslie's Moss 883837 – A.T. Ainslie's Fly 86251). Nan and Shep are two more dogs that are remembered as top-winning trial dogs. Shep won numerous trials, was fourth at the 1983 USBCHA Finals and Reserve in 1985. A prepotent stud dog, he produced many top working dogs. In 1993 two of his progeny, Berhow's Nick and Bud Bourdreau's Patches were Champion and Reserve Champion respectively in the USBCHA Finals. His line is carried on through his sons (two well-known offspring being Berhow's Nick and Charles O'Reilly's Shep), who have produced many sons and daughters currently placing 'in the money' at trials throughout the US.

Tommy Wilson's imported Roy ISDS 157864 (J.J. Templeton's Moss 103923 – D. Baker's Pat 153441) has been outstanding as both a trial winner and a sire. In 1989 he was the Purina award winner, having earned that award by being a consistently winning dog at 'Purina Point' trials held throughout the country. Roy's son, Cap (Roy – S. Demewolf's Speed ISDS 80395) won the 1992 USBCHA Nursery Finals, and his daughter, Hope (Jil Gil NASDS 366881, who is by D. Lamb's Roy 108945 out of F. Moffet's Dot 118274) won the 1993 USBCHA Nursery Finals. Hope was Reserve in the 1994 Nursery Finals. Both dogs were trained and handled by Tommy. Bruce Fogt's Molly (the same breeding as Wilson's Hope) was the 1992 USBCHA Finals winner. Under Bruce's able hand, Molly has placed well at most trials.

Few bitches make their names as consistent trial winners, but there are two that many US handlers think highly of – Bruce Fogt's Hope and Dodie Green's Soot. Both bitches go back to similar breeding. Hope is a daughter of Lewis Pulfer's Dell, who was imported by Lewis from John Brownlie in Scotland. Dell's sire was McConnell's Moss 77473, her dam was Brownlie's Fly 74537. Dell was bred to Craig (a Fortune Glen son) prior to being sent out to the US. Hope was from this mating. Not only was Hope a winner at many trials throughout her competitive years, she won the USBCHA Finals in 1987 and also the Purina Award.

Dodie Green's Soot won her share of trials in the southwestern states. In 1993 Dodie decided to pursue the Purina Award, which meant travelling throughout the trial season, criss-crossing the country several times in order to compete in the various Purina Point trials. Soot placed well during the year, winning many of the trials, to achieve the coveted award. American-bred Soot is a paternal granddaughter of Pulfer's Dell. Brownlie's Fly 74537 (Dell's dam) also appears as a maternal great-great-granddam.

When considering American trial winners, it is important to keep in mind the vast size of the country. There are many dogs, both imported and American-bred, who are top winning dogs in their own geographical areas. Unfortunately, they do not achieve national recognition simply because their handlers are unable to compete at many trials each year due to the cost and time required for travelling long distances. In each small group of states there are exceptional dogs winning and producing top-notch workers.

HERDING INSTINCT TEST

In the USA a test has been organised for herding dogs with the aim of seeing the dog has the basic instincts to work stock. Dogs can also work for the title Herding Dog Champion, through the grades HTO, HIDX and so to HTCh.

Many in Britain would prefer the North American system of the Herding Instinct Test. This is a more flexible test, not requiring the dog to work stock with great expertise, but demonstrating in a much more relaxed manner that the dog has inherited ability, and would very likely be able to train for stock work. Certainly, when I see a dog work or approach sheep, even if it is the first time (I actually prefer it to be the first time), I can give a confident assessment of the dog's potential with training. In those first few moments with sheep you can see the dog's inherited qualities in the purest form, without any modification imposed by training.

The Herding Instinct Test in North America is carried out in favourable conditions, with easily-handled livestock, in a non-competitive manner. The testor is an experienced person in stock dog training, and the test can be taken on sheep, cattle, ducks and goats – although it is usually taken on sheep or ducks. A minimum of three animals are used and the dog has fifteen minutes to prove its natural instinct. The dog does not necessarily have to start immediately, for often a short time is needed to activate the latent instinct. The testor can take the dog from the owner and use their experience to get the dog started.

In order to pass, the dog will have to show sustained interest in the herding of livestock either by circling or attempting to gather, but a dog which follows and tries to drive will also pass. Dogs can be loose-eyed or they can show eye. Various approaches and styles are acceptable, even a dog who barks or gives a slight nip (so long as there is no threat to the livestock) is accepted as showing instinct. However, if after fifteen minutes the dog fails to show sustained interest, tries to leave the working area or does not demonstrate a definite style, the test is failed. Any threat to the safety of

The American Herding Instinct Test can be carried out on cattle, sheep, goats or poultry.

the livestock also calls for an automatic fail. However, dogs who have failed can retake the test on another occasion.

CONTROVERSY OVER 'PEDIGREE' STATUS

In 1993 the USA and Canada took a vote on whether the Border Collie should be allowed to compete in conformation and other KC activities. A campaign to defeat the motion was organised by Donald McCraig and Ethel Conrad, and they had vast fighting funds, totalling over 8,000 dollars. This is an issue where feelings run very high, and working enthusiasts feel there is a very real need to protect the working Border Collie. It will be interesting to see what happens in the near future.

There are currently new moves afoot for the AKC to register the Border Collie, but the working fraternity remain deeply opposed, as they were in Britain when KC recognition came about in the seventies. However, there should be no need for working stock to be changed even if the breed did achieve show status. Work fashioned the Border Collie, and it should only be the changing demands of work that necessitates any variation in breeding programmes.

The present status of the Border Collie in Canada is that any dog registered with their Kennel Club prior to December 31st 1993 may continue to compete in all activities except conformation for the rest of their life. This was decided by a poll taken by the Ministry of Agriculture in August 1993, and it means that the only activities available for other Border Collies will be Flyball and Agility. Prior to 1994, dating back to 1971, Border Collies had been eligible to compete in all events other than conformation.

I have been sent a copy of the Breed Standard for the American Border Collie Alliance (ABCA), and while there are some parts I would like to see included into the British Breed Standard, there are other aspects which could result in a great rift between the show Border Collie and those able to work. The Border Collie is an athletic breed, and the ABCA Standard states that it is a breed that can change speed suddenly; endurance is its trademark, and it can move with great stealth, strength and stamina.

If this is the case, I fail to see how it is compatible with a height as low as eighteen inches and a well-boned forelegs. This appears to be an invitation to breed heavy, solid dogs. The British Breed Stand uses the word 'solid', and this has led to an increase in the bone-size of show dogs. The original British Standard which called for 'medium bone' was a far more accurate portrayal.

Conformation is all-important to the working dog, and in order to assess this it is a useful guide to measure the body length and divide this into the height at the withers. If this ratio is wrong, then a real working dog will have back problems and a very short working life. I took the following measurements from a selection of the correct and true types in several spheres: show, work and multi purpose. The results were:

Sh. Ch. Snowmere Tweed: 1 to 0.81
Sh. Ch. Fieldbank Professional: 1 to 0.85
Caristan Forever Amber: 1 to 0.84
Bluealloy Trim: 1 to 0.84
Sup. Int. Ch. Reed's Turk: 1 to 0.82

I measured several dogs who had a very incorrect balance between these two factors, and they came out with measurements around 1 to 0.65. A dog with a height of only eighteen inches would find great difficulty in working all day, let alone running up a hillside or round a thirty-acre field to collect a flock of sheep. On paper there does not seem to be much difference between 0.84 and

0.65, but it makes a vast difference to a working dog. In the years I have been giving out Challenge Certificates in the breed, I can truly say that my top winners have conformed closely to the 1 to 0.84 ratio, and in some cases, they have been really good working Sheepdogs.

As far as the show Border Collie is concerned, it can be argued that it does not matter if a dog cannot run the hills all day. Indeed, with such a capability a dog would be very frustrated if confined to the show ring. However, show breeders have a great responsibility to preserve the overall soundness of the breed. Hopefully, in North America, the same situation will emerge as in Britain where there are a number of pure-bred show dogs, but there are a good percentage of sound, multi-purpose Border Collies who can perform in several disciplines.

The American Kennel Club has now formally recognised the Border Collie, with the first registrations being made in February 1995. The British Breed Standard has been adopted.

Chapter Fifteen

THE BORDER COLLIE WORLDWIDE

The Border Collie has now travelled outside its British home, and is now becoming firmly established in many countries worldwide. To date, the breed has not become widely accepted in the show ring, but it is highly valued as being the most versatile dog in the world, one which can undertake a wide variety of occupations.

AUSTRALIA AND NEW ZEALAND

It is amazing how things in life have a habit of going full circle. British Border Collies were exported to Australia in the 1800s, and now in the late 20th Century they are being exported from their adopted home to their country of origin. There is a feeling among many British breed enthusiasts that this is a means of importing back pure stock which has come from earlier exports. However, this not really the case as there is quite a sprinkling of Kelpie blood in the ancestors of the present-day imports. Bantry Girl is a classic example of this: of the eight dogs that make up the third generation, four are Kelpies. Bantry Girl herself features very considerably in the early Border Collie pedigrees.

King and McLeod were prolific breeders of Border Collie/Kelpie crosses, stemming from the need to breed a working dog suitable for conditions in Australia and New Zealand. In all fairness, any country would do the same with an imported breed. The leading strains in Australia and New Zealand have a very definite type as they are heavily in-bred, much more so than the British Border Collie.

In the early part of the 20th Century some extremely good British dogs were exported to this part of the world. They included dogs such as Supreme International Champions: Moss (No.22) – whose name was changed to Border Bess, Lad (No.19), Don (No.17), and the illustrious Ben (No.891). Other outstanding dogs included: Fenwick Jed (No.33), Yarrow (No. 23), Bagshaw's Lad (No. 639), Armstrong's Sweep (No.21), Trim (No.37), Glen (No.698), Jaf II (No.2199) and Kep (No.31), to mention just a few. In the first eight years of running the International, no less than six of the Supreme International Champions went across the water to Australia/New Zealand.

Other influential imports were: Roy (No.978), Moss (No.454), Hindhope Jed, H.T. Little's Maudie, Foozle (No.350), Kep (No.535) and Old Kep (No.13). Some dogs, such as Ancrum Jed, were not registered; others had their names changed, like Roy (No.978) who became Robbie Burns, and Old Kep who became Ancrum Jed. During this era Australia and New Zealand took the cream of the British dogs, but not before they had left their mark with sizeable numbers of their progeny. Many were sold for very low prices. Hindhope Jed was bought by A.E. McLeod for £25, and he was probably the first dog of note to go to Australia. James Lilico imported a considerable number of British Border Collies, and Tom White, Arthur Collins, James Moore, Bill Marshall, and Dr Kelley of the Boveagh fame, all made influential imports at this time.

So with stock like this, and a dash of Kelpie blood, the Australian/New Zealand Border Collie show Border Collie was evolved. Although it would seem that the current imports to Britain are coming from three distinct lines, they are, in truth, very closely related. As such, British breeders would do better to incorporate British breeding, rather than breeding between these imported strains. I have seen some lovely 1/4 New Zealand – 3/4 British-bred stock, and there is the up-and-coming stud dog by Sup. Int. Ch. Spot, who when mated to British stock will contribute 1/8th of New Zealand breeding. His progeny will be watched with interest.

INFLUENTIAL DOGS
The following dogs are all very prominent in the New Zealand dogs that are currently in Britain, as well as in other countries that have imported stock from this part of the world. The Kelpie lines are: Epson Tinker Belle, Epson Shep, Epson Thunder, Bonnie Laddie and Rockbank Lad.
EPSOM THUNDER: Goes back through Epson Shep and Epson Bint.
EPSON SHEP: Very prolific; goes back through Epson Tinker Belle, Bonnie Laddie and Clivus Twist.
EPSON TINKER BELLE: Goes back through Bonnie Laddie, Epson Bint, Clivus Twist and Rockbank Lad.
BONNIE LADDIE: Goes back through Rockbank Lad, Clivus Twist and back through The Gaffer, who stems from the imported Moss of Ancrum and Kep (No.13).
ROCKBANK LAD: Encompasses the older dogs with lines through Nell (No.205), Old Maid, Brown's Nell, double dose to Renwick's Don, Spot (No.308), Fenwick Jed (No.33), Hemp (No.153) via Renwick's Don to Old Maid. The bitch Wattle Grange Blue Lady is quite common via Ben (No.454), Spot (No.308), Fly (No.165) and Don (No.17). On the dam's side is Bantry Maid, who is a daughter of Bantry Girl.
CLIVUS TWIST: Goes back through Epson Bint, Loos (No 459), Lille (No.26), Loos II (No.435), Roy (No.1665), Hemp (No.153) and the imported Sprig (No.2881).

BREEDING OF MODERN IMPORTS
ABERDEEN BOY: Sarasota Saretta, Epson Thunder, Rullion Joy.
THUNDERBOY: Epson Thunder.
LORNA'S LOVE: Lorna Doone, Thunderboy, Epson Thunder, Gay Lord.
FRANCESA: Sarasota Saretta. Lorna Doone, Thunderline, Epson Thunder.
MERRYBROOKE LAURA: Aberdeen Boy, Thunderboy, Sarasota Saretta, Epson Thunder.
WIZALAND NEWZ SENSATION: Casanora, Thunderline, Thunderboy.
CASANORA TOO: Thunderline, Thunderboy, Epson Thunder.
BLUE: Thunderboy, Sarasota Saretta.
PHANTOM LOVE: Casanora, Lorna Doone, Thunderboy, Thunderline.
LOVE STORY: Sarasota Saretta, Thunderboy, Lorna Doone.
RULLION JOY: Sarasota Saretta, Epson Thunder.
LORNA'S BRAE: Thunderboy, Sarasota Saretta, Lorna Doone.
SILVER LEGEND: Aberdeen Boy, Lorna Doone, Rullion, Sarasota Saretta, Thunderboy, Epson Thunder.
ABERDOONE: Rullion, Thunderboy, Sarasota Saretta, Epson Thunder.

SOUTH AFRICA
The main working authority is the SASDA, which, in 1977, established a register of dogs. It runs a

magazine called *Shepherds' Pie*, which gives trial results, reports on seminars as well as featuring many other interesting articles. South Africa is a very large country and Border Collie activity is limited to a few areas, but no doubt it will become more extensive.

One of the finest books on how to train your dog to sheep work, *Training Sheepdogs*, comes from South Africa, written by the much respected Ron Philps.

ZIMBABWE

Zimbabwe has a very thriving and active Border Collie community, and activities include Obedience, Working Trials, Breed, Agility, and working sheep. Karen and Steve Peel, of the Fragglerock prefix, have led the way with SA Champion Beagold New Venture. They also have Zim. Ch. SA Ch. Clan-Abby Silver Fern at Beagold. Steve and Karen are involved in a variety of activities with their Border Collies. The three major exporting kennels in the UK are Altricia, Beagold and Fenacre.

Alan and Jenni Gray recently had a wonderful week with their three dogs. Altricia Krafty gained her title, Altricia No Nonsense won his second CC, and Altricia Blue Mac, a blue merle puppy, then nine months old, gained a CC, BOB and BP. Mac is an extremely talented sheepdog with trial potential.

FINLAND

During the nineties, Finland started importing quite a number of dogs from the UK. Since 1977 around seven hundred Border Collies have been registered with the Finnish Kennel Club. The British imports seem to have the same difference of type as in Britain, some buyers wanting stock which is from New Zealand lines and others who want only British breeding.

As in the UK and elsewhere, there is a big division of opinion between the working fraternity and the Kennel Club fraternity, also between the two governing bodies – neither accepting the other. As in many other European countries, a Working Certificate is required by the Kennel Club. However, this working certification is in Obedience, or is an adult temperament test, similar to our puppy assessment but done only when the dog is adult. It seems a little detrimental to a sheep-working breed that a sheep qualification is not acceptable

This leads to a situation where, for example, Anu Kajan's Kamu Finnish KC No.SF-09051/92U is pedigree, comes from registered working stock, and is a good representative of the breed, but may only compete in Agility and Obedience. The 'U' at the end of the registration means that these are the only acceptable activities. Flyball is a new activity which is just beginning to catch on, and it will, no doubt, become a very popular sport.

SWEDEN AND NORWAY

An increasing number of Border Collies are being imported from Britain, as people discover the tremendous versatility of the breed, combined with its good looks and sound physical make-up.

Norway gave the Border Collie Championship status for Agility in 1989, with Sweden following in 1993. To be able to compete in conformation classes, the dogs must have been proved in herding dogs tests. They can also gain Champion status in sheep trials, Obedience tests, Conformation and Working Trials. In order to become a Norwegian Champion, a dog must gain a first prize in conformation, which necessitates a first prize in a sheepdog competition before being allowed to enter conformation. However, a way has been found round this, with dogs gaining their conformation prize in Sweden. Incidentally, 332 Border Collies passed their sheep trial test in 1993, which is an excellent result.

As in many countries, the movement of dogs is being relaxed so that Norway and Sweden can

NACH Ludwig of Norway, owned by Magne and Marianne Akvag.

now interact more widely, rather than being restricted to their own two countries. Since May 1994 they may travel to all EF and EFTA countries.

The Border Collie is now the sixth top dog in the league table. Recent registration figures for Norway are:

1989: 686
1990: 807
1992: 728
1993: 678, ninety-five per cent being Norwegian-bred.

Agility has a big following in Norway and Sweden, and the contests between these countries take place yearly. This has now been enlarged to include Denmark and Finland as well. Leading lights in the Norwegian team are the husband and wife team of Magne and Marianne Akvag with their dogs Zico and Ludwig. Zico has been in the 'winning team' on the three occasions, coming seventh in 1989, fourth in 1990, and second in 1992. Ludwig has twice been in the team, gaining first in 1991 and third in 1992 – not a bad track record for one family!

BELGIUM

I exported my first dog to Belgium in 1981. Numbers are now increasing and the friendly Belgium contingent at Crufts are always a popular addition. As in other countries, it is the breed's versatility which is the major attraction, and like other countries, the Belgians are interested in Agility, Obedience, Flyball and Conformation, as well as the breed's real use, working sheep.

There are about seven Border Collie breeders, as well as a few private individuals who raise the occasional litter. There are two clubs for the Border Collie in Belgium, The Belgium Border Collie Club and the British Sheep Dog Club, and both clubs encourage multi-use and inter-club competition.

In Obedience there are four classes: Puppy Class A, Class B and Class C. Dogs who pass the exam at Class C may enter Class D, and when the dog achieves scores between 90-100, it may move up to Class D2. In Agility, dogs must be qualified to work in Class C before being allowed to compete in Agility. I heartily approve of this, as lack of control is a major fault among many British Agility dogs.

SPAIN

The Border Collie is not a popular breed in Spain, with approximately thirty representatives of the breed, mainly around Barcelona. They are mostly of British breeding, with a few from New Zealand lines. Francisco Soro imported a pair of Border Collies from Great Britain into Spain in 1982, and he made up the first Spanish Champion, Kirkfield Kaley, who later became World Champion in 1983.

Dogs can be shown from five months old, and four National CACs are needed under four different judges to become a Champion. Three CACIBs from three different countries are needed for a dog to become an International Champion. Border Collies require a working qualification, but they do not have to work sheep.

One of the top dogs in the country is Spanish Champion and Gib. Champion Hattersdown Cedar, winner of the World Cup 1992, with a total of twenty-seven Best of Breeds, twenty National CACs and seventeen CACIBs. He is of British breeding and was born in the last litter sired by Sh. Champion Tilehouse Cassius of Beagold, who was the very first British Champion. 'Tops', as he is called, had to beat fifty-two other dogs in the group to achieve this award. He is now working to gain his working trial to become an International Champion.

HOLLAND

World, Sp., Gib. Ch. Hattersdown Cedar: Winner of the World Cup in 1992.

Janjays Zealanna, owned in Holland by C. Maton. This is a real multi-purpose Border Collie who works sheep, competes in Flyball, Agility and Obedience, and is also trained in avalanche rescue.

There are roughly 3,500 Border Collies registered with the Kennel Club, and a number of them are British-bred. They are not yet very popular in the breed ring, with a total entry of ten being shown at the Amsterdam Show including ones from Germany and Belgium; at Rotterdam 1993 there were five shown, and at Arnhem International Show only four competed. No working qualification is needed for a dog to become a Champion.

Maramin Betty, owned by Joe and Betty Kat, was the first Border Collie to become a Champion. Shortly afterwards, she became an International Champion. Joe Kat was a frequent visitor and judge in the UK, and many of the longer-serving members of the breed will remember him well. He last judged the breed in 1986 in Amsterdam, but, sadly, he died shortly after this. He was one of the first people on the BCC of Great Britain's 'A' judging list.

In Holland Border Collies participate in the full range of activities – Obedience, Flyball, Agility, Conformation, and working sheep. Rosehurst Kiri, owned by Hans and Joke Smit, has made a name for herself, winning the youth title 1992 and 1993, and becoming a Dutch and Luxembourg Champion. The top dog is Fieldbank Independence, who is a British Show Champion and a Dutch Champion, owned by B. Hinzinga. Wizaland Newz Talk, owned by Marine Hageraats, gained Champion status in record time.

GERMANY

In the main, Border Collies entered Germany in the seventies, but registration did not take place until 1981 when, as in Britain, ISDS dogs were accepted for registration. Werner Kupka, who was originally a farmer in Wales, imported some Border Collies into Germany in the seventies. In 1981 when the stud book was opened up, his black-and-white home-bred bitch was given No.1. There are now about seven hundred Border Collies registered in Germany. Entries in the breed ring vary from ten to thirty, but it is Agility where they have reached new heights of popularity. As in most countries, there are the three divisions – British show stock, New Zealand lines, and ISDS dogs.

There are two national titles. Dogs need four CACs under three different judges, and between

Kliff aus dem Hause Kriese (Kliff): A CACIB winner and Agility competitor who works sheep every day of his life.

Bundesjugendsieger Indianheart vom Weideland: Competes in Breed and Agility, and is a very promising sheep-worker.

the first and last CAC there is a minimum time-gap of a year. In order to enter one of the classes, the dog must be at least fifteen months old. No ISDS dog is allowed to compete. To become a German Champion, the dog has to pass a sheep test – and yet, to date, no such test exists! One particular dog who is affected by this is the very brilliant Kliff aus dem Hause Kriese (Kliff), who has got sufficient CACIBs and works sheep everyday, as his owner, Christel Killer, is a part-time shepherdess. Kliff is also a highly successful Agility competitor. Christel has also worked her bitch, Gael, demonstrating working geese with a dog, in the main ring at the World Show at Dortmund. Another extremely noteworthy Border Collie is Petra Konig's Tansterne Fun VB Sc11 H11 FH, who qualified to represent his country in tracking.

APPENDIX

USEFUL ADDRESSES

KENNEL CLUBS
American Kennel Club: 51 Madison Avenue, New York, NY 10010. Tel: 212 696 8200.
English Kennel Club: 1 Clarges Street, London W1 8AB. Tel: 0171 493 6651.
Canadian Kennel Club: 89 Skyway Avenue, Etobicoke, Ontario M9W 6R4. Tel 416 675 5511.

ANGLO-AMERICAN ASSOCIATION
Roy Hunter, Abelard, Dyers End, Stambourne, Essex CO9 4NE.

AMERICAN INTERNATIONAL B.C. REGISTRY INC.
J. Dean Kaster, Runnels, IA 50237.

AMERICAN B.C. ASSOCIATION
Gerry West, Rt. 1, Red Banks, Mississippi 38661.

RANCH DOG TRAINER
Rt. 2, Box 333, West Palins, MO 65775.

HOMEOPATHIC MANUFACTURER/SUPPLIER
Weleda Inc., 841 South Main Street, Spring Valley, New York 10977.